BRIT GUIDE

Disneyland Paris

AND PARIS ATTRACTIONS

2010/11

Simon & Susan Veness

foulsham
LONDON • NEW YORK • TORONTO • SYDNEY

foulsham

The Oriel, Thames Valley Court, 183–187 Bath Road,
Slough, Berkshire, SL1 4AA, England

Foulsham books can be found in all good bookshops and direct from
www.foulsham.com

ISBN: 978-0-572-03566-2

Text copyright © 2010 Simon and Susan Veness – Veness Travel Media Inc
Series, format, logo and layout design copyright © 2010 W. Foulsham & Co. Ltd

Dedication
To Anthony, Mark and Ben – our perfect research team!
Special thanks to research assistant Andy de Maertelaere for all his hard work.

Look out for the latest editions in this series:
Brit Guide to Orlando and Walt Disney World, Simon and Susan Veness
Brit Guide to New York, Amanda Statham
Brit Guide to Las Vegas, Karen Marchbank with Jane Anderson

While every effort has been made to ensure the accuracy of all the information
contained within this book, neither the author nor the publisher can be liable for any
errors. In particular, since prices, times and any holiday or hotel details change on a
regular basis, it is vital that each individual checks relevant information for
themselves.

Printed in Dubai

CONTENTS

Brit Tips

Got a red-hot Brit Tip to pass on; the latest info on how to beat the queues or the best new restaurant? We want to hear from YOU to keep improving the guide each year. Drop us a line at: Brit Guides (Disneyland Paris), W. Foulsham & Co. Ltd, The Oriel, Thames Valley Court, 183–187 Bath Road, Slough, Berkshire SL1 4AA. Or email us at **britsguide@yahoo.com**. You can also see more of Simon and Susan's work at **venesstravelmedia.com**.

A close-up of Sleeping Beauty Castle

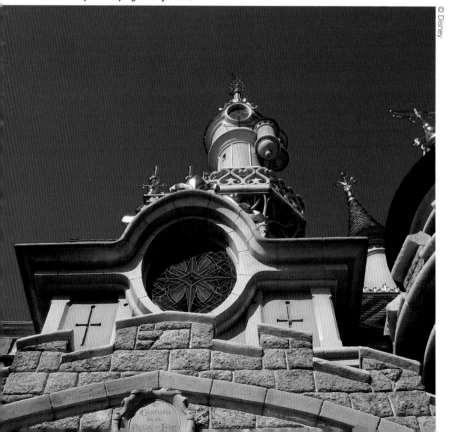

© Disney

FOREWORD

Simon says …A hearty *Brit Guide* 'Welcome!' to the 5th edition of the brightest and most up-to-date guide to Europe's No 1 tourist attraction, as compiled by Britain's leading Disney experts (that would be us!). Susan and I have clocked up hundreds of visits to the House of Mouse in the past 30-odd years (in both America and France) and never tire of exploring, researching and detailing our experiences. We have a deep and lasting understanding of the excitement and thrills the Disney theme parks generate and are keen for every visitor to get the best experience possible, whether it is their first trip or their 101st. The great thing about *Disneyland Resort Paris* is that it continues to change and develop, adding new rides and attractions all the time, and there is a LOT in store for 2010 and beyond, especially at *Walt Disney Studios Park*. Therefore you need a good book to help you prepare for and enjoy your holiday – and that's where we come in. This is a realm of fantasy and adventure, but it's also detailed and demanding, especially in summer, so it is vital you have all the necessary info to tackle it. We can ensure you get it right, from the moment you start planning, to your journey there, how to enjoy it all and the many extra things to appreciate in the area. It is a remarkable and astounding place – just remember to take us with you!

Susan says … Daily life has become increasingly demanding for many of us, making our holiday time more precious then ever. The desire to get the most value for money, the best experience for the lowest cost, and million-pound memories on a moderate budget makes doing a bit of homework a crucial part of your pre-holiday requirements. Challenges to the bank account don't have to mean less enjoyment, though, when there are still plenty of wallet-friendly options in and out of the parks. With diligent preparation, your holiday can be truly magical without breaking the bank, and knowing what's on offer and how to work it to your best advantage is the first big step in the process. With your *Brit Guide* in hand, you're well on your way to a thrilling adventure, with all the information needed to make it a relaxed, revitalising experience as well. And now … on with the planning!

Simon and Susan in Frontierland

Introduction

There is one simple reason why Disney's theme parks are the world's most-visited attractions, be they in America, Japan or, in this case, France. They are simply the best family entertainment you will find anywhere.

And the fun is not restricted to families either, as, while children find the allure of Mickey and Co almost irresistible, there is something for *everyone* in a Disney park – young or old, singles, couples or with Uncle Tom Cobley and all in tow. In fact, we reckon there is more all-round entertainment value here than anywhere else we've seen.

It is a great short-break destination, perfect for a week (or even longer, given the additional attractions of the Paris region) and is easy to reach; it is ideal for families (especially those with young children), yet also attracts honeymooners and other couples; and its appeal is timeless, harking back to a nostalgic yesteryear but remaining contemporary in so many ways.

Pixie dust

A holiday at *Disneyland Paris* is a beguiling prospect and is also one that is sure to bring out the child in everyone. If you can envisage grown-ups rushing to hug Mickey or Minnie, then you can imagine the effect Disney's 'Pixie dust' has on just about everyone who walks through the gates.

Indeed, Roy Disney, nephew of the great Walt himself, opened the Paris park with words his uncle first used for *Disneyland California* in 1955. He said: 'To all who come to this happy place, welcome! This is your land. Here age relives fond memories of the past and here youth may savour the challenge and promise of the future. We hope it will be a source of joy and inspiration to the world.' It certainly shapes up that way.

Welcome to the Park

© Disney

But, if that's the broad outline, let us fill in the detail and provide you with a good understanding of how it all works – because this is a complicated business and you must keep your wits about you at all times. Holidaying the Disney way is immense fun but it can be confusing and tiring. When the crowds flock to the parks, it is a challenge to keep up with the ebb and flow of it all. When the queues for many rides top an hour, you need a strategy and the basic tool of all park-goers: a Plan!

In fact, planning is an essential component of your holiday. At quieter times you might just get away with a free-wheeling, make-it-up-as-you-go-along approach. But there are plenty of pitfalls that await the unwary and unprepared even at only moderately busy times. This is not like a trip to Alton Towers or Thorpe Park, where a day is usually enough to 'do it all'.

With two fully fledged parks in the *Disneyland Paris* experience, there is always an element of choice. Behind that lies a matter of scale that is hard to convey in advance and that includes an attention to detail both breathtaking and a little bewildering. It is easy to get side-tracked by some of the clever scenery, shops and other frippery, so that's why planning is so important.

Shopping at Constellations

Monsters Inc Scream Academy

The very name *Disneyland Paris* should convey the fact that this is a resort experience *par excellence*, and that means a multi-dimensional approach in all things: from the attractions to the hotels, the restaurants and even the shops. There is fun almost everywhere you turn and a host of options at any one time. Therefore, you *must* do your homework in advance.

Chequered history

The *Disneyland Paris* story began in the mid-1980s when Michael Eisner, then the new Chief Executive Officer of the Walt Disney Company, came to Europe in search of a new outlet for its theme park creativity. Both France and Spain were firmly in the frame, and the former was chosen for a variety of reasons, not least the strong French connection in many Disney films (*Cinderella, Sleeping Beauty, Hunchback of Notre Dame*) and the wonderful central location offered by the Paris region.

As far back as December 1985, Mr Eisner signed a letter of intent with France to build a park in Marne-la-Vallée, 32km/20mls east of Paris. That agreement was formalised with Jacques Chirac in March 1987 and what was then about 1,900ha/4,700

Who owns the Disneyland Resort Paris?

The Walt Disney Company actually owns only 39.8% of the *Disneyland Resort Paris*, but runs 100% of the management. The other 60.2% is owned by private investors, including 10% by Prince Al-Waleed of Saudi Arabia.

acres of beet fields became the planning ground for a great adventure in architecture and engineering, or Imagineering, as the Walt Disney Company likes to call it.

The first earth-moving equipment moved in on 2 August 1988, and a 4-year construction period began. Despite some challenges from Mother Nature, the *Euro Disney Park* (as it was then known – the name soon changed to *Euro Disneyland*) opened on time on 12 April 1992 to a blaze of publicity. However, despite the glittering launch, a sceptical press, some French hostility (going back to the project's announcement) – aimed at the supposed 'Americanisation' of their culture – and over-optimistic attendance forecasts all contributed to a painful initiation for the new park.

The media focused on the negatives: long queues for meals and longer ones for some rides, high prices, rumours of empty hotels and staff unhappiness – and the combination of problems, both real and perceived, almost brought the resort to its knees. The whole development – parks, hotels, shops and restaurants grouped around a 'village' core, then called *Festival Disney* – had gone way over budget. The lack of immediate profits to pay off the short-term debt, coupled with a Europe-wide recession, meant there was a real possibility it might close down, despite 10.8m visitors in the first 12 months.

Major financial restructuring was necessary in 1994, at which time it became *Disneyland Paris*, and, from there, the story has been one of recovery, although battles with that initial debt continue. Attendance grew through the late 1990s and more development began to spring up around Marne-la-Vallée, both commercial and residential.

BRITTIP

Disneyland Paris is just 2 hours from Ashford in Kent on the direct Eurostar service and only 2 hours 35 minutes from the new London St Pancras terminal. For the great convenience the train provides, it's definitely worth considering.

The success of Disney's on-site hotels (6 of them, plus the camping ground of *Disney's Davy Crockett Ranch* a short drive away) encouraged a mini proliferation of hotels in the vicinity, while the development extended to a new town centre at neighbouring **Val d'Europe**, a combination of businesses, shopping and housing, which adds even more to the picture locally. Here, the immaculate shopping mall is part of an excellent centre that includes the outlet shopping of **La Vallée**, the **Sea Life Centre** and some enticing restaurants.

At the same time, a Disney-run **golf complex**, with 3 9-hole courses, was developed just 10 minutes' drive from the resort itself, offering yet another diversion for people wanting to enhance their theme park experience.

La Vallée

The second park

The original plans for the resort included a sister park along the lines of *Disney's Hollywood Studios* in *Walt Disney World Resort* in Florida. This was scheduled to open 3 years after the first park, but the financial woes of 1994 meant the concept went into storage until 1998. Construction began in earnest shortly afterwards. The eagerly awaited Walt Disney Studios opened on 16 March 2002 with another burst of publicity – and a new name, *Disneyland Resort Paris* (new CEO Philippe Gas once again removed the 'Resort' part of the name in 2009).

Here, finally, was the true resort expansion as originally envisaged by Eisner and his Imagineers, completing a well-rounded picture of accommodation, shopping, restaurants and theme parks, and providing a multi-day experience, even out of busy periods. Festival Disney, now known more appropriately as *Disney Village*, has grown to encompass 9 restaurants, 3 bars, a multi-screen cinema (including an IMAX screen theatre), an adjoining dinner show (the family-

Stars 'n' Cars at Walt Disney Studios

friendly Buffalo Bill's Wild West Show … with Mickey and Friends!), a big nightclub and a choice of 8 shops. There is also the wonderful Panoramagique tethered balloon ride and a host of other games and activities (see Chapter 8).

With the Marne-la-Vallée railway station at the heart of the whole development linking the resort with central Paris, Charles de Gaulle Airport and, more importantly, London via Eurostar, it is a wonderfully convenient location. It is easy for arrival and well organised to allow access either straight to the theme parks, the hotels (using an efficient bus service) or directly to *Disney Village*.

Anyone familiar with the Orlando resort set-up – 12,173ha/30,080 acres of 4 parks, 2 water parks, 20 hotels and a mini-town area called *Downtown Disney* – will almost certainly be impressed by the comparative ease with which you can move around this resort. Everything is within a 20-minute walk at most. The scale is big enough to be exciting, yet manageable enough not to be daunting. Indeed, it is a triumph of the designers' art in making this hugely complex development one of very human dimensions, a riot of visual stimulation and yet easy to negotiate. Yes, there is a lot going on here, but it is easy to enjoy it all.

Disney Village

Facts and figures

- The whole site of *Disneyland Paris* covers 1,943 hectares/4,800 acres, or one-fifth the area of Paris.
- Groundbreaking began in August 1988.
- 51km/32mls of roads were built and 120,000,000m³/157,000,000yd³ of earth moved.
- Around 450,000 trees and shrubs were planted.
- It employs an average of 12,000 people every year.
- All Disney employees are known as Cast Members, to signify they are part of 'the show'.
- The *Disneyland Park* covers 51 hectares/126 acres.
- The *Walt Disney Studios Park* stands on 25 hectares/62 acres.
- The 7 themed hotels have a total of 5,800 rooms.
- There are 68 counter and full-service restaurants throughout the resort.
- In all, there are 54 different shops and boutiques.
- More than 180 million people have visited since it opened.
- Around 42% of visitors are French, 21% British, 8% German, 8% Belgian, 8% Dutch, 8% Spanish and Italian, with 5% from other nations.

Disney Village

Offering a positive riot of sights and sounds, both by day and at night (when the contrast is quite startling, from the peaceful Lake Disney in early morning to the near-disco proportions of the late-evening hubbub), *Disney Village* acts as a conduit between the parks and hotels. It is an exit for weary park-goers (and you can be pretty tired by park closing!) and offers a new source of fun for all those who enjoy their nightlife. It is a heady cocktail but also requires a good deal of forethought, especially if you have the family in tow, to ensure you get the most out of it (whether for a meal, shopping or the games and other activities) before heading back to your hotel.

Of course, *Disney Village* is not reserved purely for Disney's on-site guests; it also attracts a good number of locals (especially on Fridays and Saturdays). Its large car park makes it easily accessible for guests at nearby hotels, while the RER service (the main local commuter train) runs until after midnight.

The European touch

Disneyland Paris is a wonderfully impressive set-up and is easily the equal of any of Disney's other resorts around the world. In fact, we believe the clever 'Europeanisation' of the traditional Disney style gives it extra appeal. There is more than a hint of

Sleeping Beauty Castle

© Disney

French flair, Italian chic, Spanish partying, German organisation and Dutch friendliness about the resort, which come together best in the Village. Yes, there are some drawbacks – the price of the Euro against the pound can make things seem distinctly expensive – and the mixture of cultures occasionally causes some awkwardness. The toilets could be kept cleaner in many instances (for some reason, this seems a bit of a blind spot in all public areas) and there is occasionally a bit of push and shove (which you don't usually find at the American parks), notably in the scrimmage for character autographs, getting in position for the parades or trying to board a hotel bus at the end of the evening.

It won't be a restful holiday, unless you go out of season in winter and are lucky enough to be blessed by mild, dry weather, and it can make a serious dent in your bank balance. But, all in all, it offers great value and richly rewards those who go with an open mind and the willingness to try those few words of school French they can dredge from memory.

More importantly, it is guaranteed to put a smile on the faces of young and old alike, and reaffirm simple family values. When Walt built Disneyland in California back in 1955, his most famous statement (now etched on the bronze Walt 'n' Mickey statue in front of Sleeping Beauty Castle) was: 'I think most of all what I want Disneyland to be is a happy place … where parents and children can have fun together.'

Pirates of the Caribbean

© Disney

Our top 10 family attractions

1	Pirates of the Caribbean
2	CinéMagique
3	'it's a small world'
4	Disney's *Once Upon A Dream Parade*
5	Peter Pan's Flight
6	Art of Disney Animation
7	Buzz Lightyear's Laser Blast
8	Phantom Manor
9	Animagique
10	Cars Quatre Roues Rallye (Cars Race Rally)

So, don't forget to take time out to enjoy that aspect during your visit; watch your children's faces at the parades, on the Dumbo ride or as they meet the characters (or just look at the reaction of other children); and ensure you do things together, however silly they may be! There is artistry all around you, in the rides, the architecture and the Cast Members, but the most meaningful feeling you can invoke is the bond with your loved ones – and nowhere brings that to the fore quite like a Disney park, whether it be for kids of 6 or 60.

However, perhaps the question most seasoned Disney-goers will want to ask is: 'If I have already been to *Walt Disney World* in Florida, do I need to go to *Disneyland Paris*? We would say unequivocally 'Yes'. Apart from the obvious advantage of this being a closer and more convenient short-visit destination (no 9-hour flights and long queues at Immigration to deal with), we believe the more luxurious theming of the *Disneyland Park*, the updated versions of classic rides like Space Mountain, Haunted Mansion (or Phantom Manor as it is here) and Big Thunder Mountain, and the all-new thrills of most of the *Walt Disney Studios* make it an absolute must to visit. For some, it is also a

Our top 10 thrill attractions

1	Rock 'n' Roller Coaster starring Aerosmith
2	The Twilight Zone™ Tower of Terror
3	Space Mountain: Mission 2
4	Indiana Jones™ and the Temple of Peril
5	Big Thunder Mountain
6	Star Tours
7	Armageddon: Les Effets Spéciaux (Special Effects)
8	Panoramagique
9	Crush's Coaster
10	Driving in central Paris!

See the city

Another big bonus of the location is the lure of nearby Paris. You certainly do not need to have a car to get to the city (in fact, driving into the city is not advisable). The reliability of the RER service and local buses means you can easily enjoy an evening along the Champs-Elysées or the Bastille district and get the train back to the resort.

BRITTIP

Need to find your way around Paris public transport? Options are the Métro (the underground), RER train service (regional rail, part underground), Transilien SNCF (suburban rail – not strictly relevant to *Disneyland Paris*), bus and tram. Visit **ratp.fr** for more info.

handy 'refresher' of Disney Magic in between visits to Orlando (and, of course, it is cheaper to spend a few days in Paris than 2 weeks in America). Anyone familiar with the vast Florida resort will also appreciate the convenience of being able to walk everywhere!

BRITTIP

All web addresses given in this book are preceded by www.

A highly recommended night out for couples is the *Lido de Paris* show in the Champs-Elysées, while a really handy option is the **Cityrama** bus tour of the city, picking up at *Disney's Hotel New York* every day. The latter provides an excellent whistle-stop tour of all the main features of this fabulous city, with the great convenience of staying outside the crowds and hubbub. It is only about 40 minutes on the RER train into

Big Thunder Mountain Railroad

© Disney

central Paris, however, and it is then easy to negotiate either on foot or by the Métro and bus. It is a truly magnificent city with a wealth of history, architecture, art and amazing monuments, plus a dazzling array of fine restaurants and shops. If you are planning a 4-day Disney visit, you should definitely think about spending at least half a day and an evening in Paris itself.

Those who bring the car can benefit from exploring further afield – and there are some wonderful towns and villages in this region of France, notably the medieval walled town of Provins to the south-east. The road links are good (France also has a superb system of toll roads) and rarely subjected to the kind of congestion we experience in the UK – apart from in central Paris, of course.

BRITTIP

In keeping with Disney's seasonal approach, the New Year period from January to Easter has become the great Family Value time to visit, with plenty of Kids Go Free (with each adult) deals.

You can also stock up on some wonderful food and wine along the way, as well as in Val d'Europe, where the **Auchan hypermarket** is a highly civilised alternative to the rather tired supermarkets of Calais.

All Cast Members speak at least two languages

© Disney

Speaking French

The resort has been a multi-lingual operation since day one and all Disney employees (or Cast Members) should be able to speak at least two languages (many speak four or five). This means you shouldn't have any trouble being understood. However, it is still good practice (and simple good manners) to try to remember a few words of French from time to time. All Cast Members wear a badge with their name and home country, so you can easily spot the occasional Brit working here but, for those who can't remember their basic school French, here is a quick guide to those handy vital words:

ENGLISH	FRENCH
Do you speak English?	Parlez-vous Anglais?
Good morning/Hello	Bonjour
Good evening	Bonsoir
Please	S'il vous plaît
Thank you	Merci
I would like…	Je voudrais…
Do you have…?	Avez-vous…?
How much is…?	Quel est le prix de…?
How much?	C'est combien?
A receipt	Un reçu
The bill, please	L'addition, s'il vous plaît
Coffee	Café
White coffee	Café au lait
Where are the toilets?	Où sont les toilettes?
Toll booths	Les péages
Motorway service areas	Aires
Autoroutes (toll roads)	Autoroutes des péages
Hypermarket	Hypermarché

The main focus, however, should be the theme parks themselves. The original *Disneyland Park* remains the heart and soul of the Magic, especially for families with children under 10, while the *Walt Disney* Studios Park adds an element of excitement and thrills for the older

© Disney

Mickey and Minnie get in the spirit of St Patrick's Day

age group. These provide a complementary experience, but the time requirements of each are slightly different. Don't be fooled into thinking you can spend 2 days here and do it all, even during off-peak times. The original park will require at least 2 days to ensure you've seen and done most of what is on offer, while the Studios will need a full day when all its new attractions are up and running in 2010.

Seasonal fun

Disneyland Paris is unique in the Disney empire of theme parks in providing a huge range of seasonal celebrations. While all its other resorts lay on a brilliantly themed backdrop for Christmas Season and Halloween Festival, only here will you find a real in-depth and broadly arranged series of attractions throughout the year. There are special winter festivities, St Patrick's and St David's Day events each March, extra summer entertainment, a Bastille Day extravaganza, the amazing transformation of Frontierland to Halloweenland in October, a bonfire spectacular in November and the Disney-style magic of Christmas.

Rain and shine

This is still Western Europe and the climate can be depressingly like our own at times – wet, grey and cold. However, much of both parks has been built with rain and wind in mind, which means there is nearly always somewhere you can escape to if the weather turns nasty – indeed, almost 80% of *Walt Disney Studios Park* is under cover. Providing you pack a light raincoat you will be well prepared to carry on enjoying the fun. In fact, spring and autumn can offer some of the best times for visiting *Disneyland Paris* as they rarely come up with any seriously anti-social weather, the crowds are more

A magical day at Disneyland

© Disney

Top 10 campaign tips

1 Decide what you want to do and try to plan a rough daily schedule (especially in summer).

2 Work out if you want to Do It All (opening hours are longest in summer, everything is available but queues are longer, too) or have a quieter time (in spring or autumn with shorter hours and more unpredictable weather).

3 Stay in the resort or outside? The former offers unequalled convenience and essential 'Magic', but the latter is usually cheaper.

4 Choose your mode of transport – Eurostar, car, coach or air. Where you stay will determine which one is the most convenient (see Chapter 3).

5 Long weekend or holiday? The temptation is to pack it all into a weekend, and the ease of the Eurostar makes this appealing. But the weekends are busier and going for 4–5 days instead allows you more variety (see page 28).

6 Take a break. Whether you have a day in Paris, an outing to Provins or Versailles or just a shopping expedition to Val d'Europe, you'll benefit from a Disney break at some stage.

7 Stop and admire the scenery – often.

8 Enjoy the fact you can have a glass of wine or a beer in the Disneyland Park. Alcohol is not served in Walt Disney World's *Magic Kingdom Park* in Florida.

9 Try a little French. The locals are usually more hospitable and forthcoming if you make a polite effort to speak their language.

10 Get everyone in your party to read this book!

manageable and the queues shorter. And, while the delight of Paris in the springtime is a wonderful cliché, that doesn't mean it isn't true – in fact the months of April (after Easter) and May are just about the best time to visit, with a heavenly combination of pleasant weather, convivial atmosphere and generally lower-than-average attendances.

Yes, this is the biggest tourist attraction in Europe – with more than 12m visitors a year, some 2m from the UK alone – but it can easily be a breeze of a place to visit if you get your tactics right.

And so, with that in mind, it's time to move on to the subject of Planning …

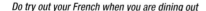

Do try out your French when you are dining out

© Disney

Planning

or How to Do It All and Stay Sane!

It used to be the case just a few years ago that you could pop across the Channel to Marne-la-Vallée, have a fun day out and be back home again for tea the next day, safe in the knowledge you had 'done' Disney. Not any more.

The addition of the *Walt Disney Studios Park* in March 2002, the expansion of the surrounding area and continuing influx of visitors mean this is now somewhere you need to consider carefully before you set out for that 'perfect' holiday. It is not quite the same as *Walt Disney World Resort* in Florida, where any visit has to be planned like a military campaign, but you must have a good idea of what you're letting yourself in for and plan to ensure you avoid the pitfalls that await the unwary.

First of all, the 2 parks – the original *Disneyland Park* and the newer *Walt Disney Studios Park* – are a complete contrast from each other, with different sizes, time requirements and appeal. They provide a complementary experience for all but the youngest children (the Studios has fewer attractions for under 5s, although this is being addressed with new additions in 2010). You'll probably need 2 full days to explore *Disneyland Park* plus a day for the *Studios*.

> **BRITTIP**
> Can't find the characters? Check out Main Street USA in the *Disneyland Park* in the morning and Animation Courtyard at *Walt Disney Studios Park* throughout the day. Better still, book one of the character meals at a restaurant like Café Mickey or the Lucky Nugget Saloon.

On the way to Disney on Eurostar

Disneyland Park

The *Disneyland Park* follows the rough formula of the *Magic Kingdom Park* in Orlando, and *Disneyland California* in Anaheim, Los Angeles. It is subdivided into 5 'lands' around a central hub and features almost 50 attractions in the form of rides, shows, parades and other live entertainment. There is an impressive choice of shops and restaurants, all themed to the various lands and offering useful browsing opportunities. At 57ha/140 acres, it requires some serious legwork to see it all. You'll be amazed at how time-consuming it can be to get from one land to another, especially with the number of diversions on the way.

This is the park that families with younger children tend to focus on (although there are terrific thrill rides, like Space Mountain: Mission 2 and Indiana Jones and the Temple of Peril). There is a huge choice of dining and some wonderful character meal opportunities (that kids adore), but you need to pace yourself as it's easy to get worn to a frazzle – and end up with fractious children – with too much to-ing and fro-ing.

Space Mountain: Mission 2

Meet 'n' Greet at Walt Disney Studios

Walt Disney Studios Park

This park is subdivided into 4 areas and, at slightly less than half the size of its sister park, it is easier to negotiate. As the name suggests, it is themed around the magic of the film world, but it is a different proposition to *Disney's Hollywood Studios* in Orlando (although 3 of the rides are similar and another is a transplant from Orlando's *Magic Kingdom Park*). It is more show-based, hence its attractions take place at specific times of the day (like the amazing Stunt Show), and more of it is indoors, which is handy when the weather is bad! The dining options are pretty ordinary, but you still have the all-important Disney characters and some wonderful live entertainment.

Beyond the theme parks

Once you have visited the parks, the delights of *Disney Village* await you. You can dine, dance, shop, go to the cinema or catch a dinner show in this lively, bustling hub, which is great at night. The choice of dining is terrific, with the superb theming of international duo Planet Hollywood (one of our favourites) and Rainforest Café, the unique Steakhouse and the fun Bavarian-style of King Ludwig's Castle the pick of the bunch. Then there is the 1950s' Americana of Annette's Diner, the country and western style of Billy Bob's Saloon, an all-day character-fest at Café Mickey

© Disney

The breathtaking Panoramagique

(with excellent food, too), a Sports Bar and a New York Sandwiches deli, not forgetting a large McDonald's, a new Starbuck's and a forthcoming Earl of Sandwich café.

Live bands are an outstanding feature of Billy Bob's, while Hurricanes disco (free entry to Disney resort guests) starts bopping around midnight (although it can be quiet Sun–Thurs out of season).

⚓ BRITTIP

Too crowded for lunch in the theme parks? Step outside to enjoy a more relaxed meal in *Disney Village*, with none of the long queues, at restaurants like Planet Hollywood, Café Mickey and Annette's Diner.

Eight boutique stores stay open usually until midnight and there is periodic live entertainment, notably in the busier seasons. The **Gaumont Cinema** is a 15-screen complex showing the latest movies but there is only one English-language presentation on a Monday night, the rest are in French. The large-screen IMAX theatre adds an extra dimension here as they should now be able to provide multi-lingual headphones for all performances (but check before you book). There is also the inevitable video arcade, with a variety of high-tech games.

For live entertainment, **Buffalo Bill's Wild West Show … with Mickey and Friends** is a *Disney Village* institution, a corny but fun dinner show that is usually a huge hit with kids (even grown-up ones!). It offers the chance to shout, cheer and wave your (free) cowboy hat in support of the various acts, who perform in the indoor auditorium during a typical cowboy dinner, accompanied by Mickey and Co. In the summer there is a daily Wild West parade outside before the first of the 2 shows (around 6pm).

Panoramagique is something different again, a breathtaking tethered balloon ride over the Village that soars to some 180m/600ft and provides an awesome view of the surrounding area. Add pedal boats, bungee trampolines and other hands-on activities (including cycling and, in winter, ice-skating) and you have an interactive playground that will keep everyone amused for at least half a day. For the full details on *Disney Village*, see Chapter 8.

As if all that were not enough, you will find the additional lure of **Val d'Europe** quite strong (it continues to develop as a major business centre) as there is some excellent shopping here and at the adjoining La Vallée outlet village. This is just 5 minutes away on the RER train (free buses run between the Disney resorts and La Vallée at various times) and can provide a refreshing break from the world of the Mouse after a few days.

The Gaumont Cinema

© Disney

Paris

- ☐ Average Daily Temperature Min (°C)
- ▨ Average Daily Temperature Max (°C)
- - - Average Monthly Rainfall (mm)

Month

Birmingham

- ☐ Average Daily Temperature Min (°C)
- ▨ Average Daily Temperature Max (°C)
- - - Average Monthly Rainfall (mm)

Month

Inside the Sea Life Centre

Here you will find a huge indoor shopping mall, some excellent restaurants in an upmarket food court and the exceedingly child-friendly **Sea Life Centre**, a major aquarium run by the chain that owns 27 similar attractions throughout Europe. It is a great diversion for kids aged 2–12 especially and provides a good 2-hour lure if mum or dad want to go shopping!

The 5-day test

Leger Holidays is the UK's largest tour operator to *Disneyland Paris*, with the biggest variety of packages and travel options. Its stock-in-trade is a 4-night holiday using coach transport to and from the resort, with Disney accommodation. Here is a typical example, using a family of 4 (with children aged 4 and 6) and leaving from the south-east:

DAY ONE: Arrive at *Disney's Hotel Santa Fe* at 9.30pm after 8½-hour journey, including P&O Ferry crossing.

DAY TWO: Up at 8am for hotel breakfast and off to the *Disneyland Park* soon after. Full day in the theme park, with lunch (pre-booked) at The Lucky Nugget Saloon. Take a break after the 3pm parade back at the hotel (nap time for younger children). Dinner at Planet Hollywood at 6.30pm, followed by a slow wander back to the hotel through *Disney Village* (with much to sidetrack the children).

DAY THREE: A later start, with hotel breakfast at 10am, then off to the *Walt Disney Studios* just in time to catch the 11am Stunt Show. Take in 2 more shows before lunch at Blockbuster Café (self-service), then complete the full range of attractions by 6pm. Switch to *Disneyland Park* for dinner at Silver Spur Steakhouse at 6.30pm (pre-booked), then one last ride before catching bus back to hotel.

DAY FOUR: An 8am hotel breakfast followed by a return visit to the *Disneyland Park*. Spend 2 hours doing many of the rides in Fantasyland, then leave park to take RER one stop to Val d'Europe and visit the Sea Life Centre*. Have lunch and shop, and let children loose in La Vallée play area before catching the train back. Revisit the *Studios* for another chance to see the Stunt Show and Animagique before heading back to the other park for a planned late night. Dinner at 8pm watching the film at Videopolis, and then keep going on various rides until the 10.30 evening parade and fireworks.

DAY FIVE: An 8am breakfast, then time to pack and load luggage back on the coach. Visit the petrol station (next to *Disney's Hotel Santa Fe*) to grab a few snacks for the journey back to Calais. Coach departs at 10am, non-stop to Calais hypermarket. Home again – tired but with very happy children! – at 4.30pm UK time.

*With older children you might consider the full-day Paris sightseeing tour with Cityrama (see Chapter 9) for a break from the theme parks.

When to go

The majority of people who visit do so in full family mode, so they are usually here in the school holidays. This is unfortunate because both the cost and the crowds increase during these times, while the summer can also be uncomfortably hot – in excess of 30ºC/86ºF (and 2 of the resort hotels, *Disney's Hotel Cheyenne* and *Disney's Hotel Santa Fe*, plus the non-suite rooms at the Explorers Hotel, do not have air-conditioning). So you need to consider your options.

If you are confined to the school holidays, try to opt for late Easter or late summer. The spring and autumn half-term holidays are also prime opportunities, although, once again, the cost increases at these times. The big pay-off with a summer visit is the bonus of **extended opening hours** (usually to 11pm) and a full show and parade schedule. If you can avoid 'Le Weekend' crowds, you still benefit from the pure magic of long nights in the *Disneyland Park* with the evening

Pony riding at Disney's Hotel Cheyenne

© Disney

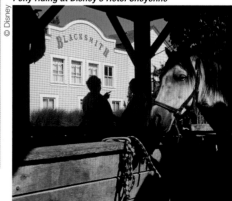

fireworks finale. As ever, it is a case of swings and roundabouts, and you need to consider what works best for you.

Busy times

It is usually better to visit in the non-peak periods, in which we include weekdays rather than weekends. While the locals didn't embrace Disney at the beginning, the theme parks (and *Disney Village*) have developed into a major source of local recreation, so French attendance on a Saturday and Sunday can be 50% or more. This is where much of suburban Paris comes to play at the weekend, and Saturdays can be especially hectic.

Both parks cope pretty well with the thousands who pour in during the first few hours of the day, but the queues build up quickly at the main rides (and just about everywhere in Fantasyland in the *Disneyland Park*). The wait time for rides like Peter Pan's Flight and Dumbo can easily top an hour, which means an uncomfortable period in a queue, especially when it's hot. However, Disney has a nifty virtual queuing system called **FastPass** (see page 122), which takes some of the sting out of the waits for many attractions. But even that has its limitations, and so during Easter,

Character Meet 'n' Greet in Adventureland

© Disney

France on holiday

France has 11 public holidays when government departments, banks and shops are usually closed: 1 January, Easter Monday, 1 May, 8 May, Ascension Day, Whit Monday, 14 July, 15 August, 1 November, 11 November and Christmas Day. French schoolchildren also have 5 holidays a year: a week at the end of October, 2 weeks at Christmas, 2 in February, 2 in spring and the whole of July and August. Consequently, *Disneyland Paris* is noticeably busier then. More details on French school holidays at **education.gouv. fr/pid184/le-calendrier-scolaire.html**. You may also want to negotiate around some of the other main European school holidays; see **eurydice.org**.

summer and Christmas (and any sunny weekend), you'll spend a LOT of time on your feet.

⚓ BRITTIP

Disney's FastPass system is an invaluable aid to your visit, but many people overlook it because they don't understand it. It is FREE to use and simply gives you a time to return to the ride and bypass the main queue with only a short wait. It is fully explained in Chapter 5.

If you prefer to avoid school holidays, most of the summer and the weekends, when should you go? Well, the spring usually sees Paris at its best, and this tends to rub off on *Disneyland Paris* too. Of all Disney's resorts around the world, this is designed and landscaped with distinctly European tastes in mind. There is a greater emphasis on plants and greenery, providing a naturalistic element to the Disneyland Park in particular, which is beautiful in the spring and early summer. Both parks have year-round charm, of course, and you can have as much fun on the rides in winter as you can in spring. But, there is something special about a bright spring day that sets off the Magic provided by Disney's

© Disney

Town Square at Christmas

Imagineers. The grand design and wonderful creativity of Adventureland is a prime example.

Visiting off-peak

The weather in Paris in the spring tends to be more consistent than in the UK – compare the temperature and rainfall charts for Paris and Birmingham on page 20. However, the winters can be just as cold and wet, so there are several factors to bear in mind if you opt to visit Nov–Feb. The most obvious is the downturn in business, with not only the crowds dropping off appreciably, but some of the restaurants and attractions closing, too. All Disney's rides, shows and attractions are regularly refurbished, often in winter, so you may find several things shut down. For example, if you enjoyed the Lion King-style dining at Hakuna Matata (in the *Disneyland Park*) during a summer visit, be aware it is frequently closed at off-peak times.

Some entertainment takes place only during peak periods, when the theme parks are open longer. A nightly Enchanted Fireworks show and a special evening parade extravaganza

in the *Disneyland Park* are real highlights in summer and at Christmas, while the Winnie The Pooh & Friends show is high season only. Bad weather (notably heavy rain) can scupper some of the outdoor entertainment at any time, but this is more likely in the winter. However, the Disney team is adept at creating extra Magic in the form of shows and theming at various times of the year, which make **Halloween** and **Christmas** especially appealing and provides an extra reason to visit at these times (see pages 24 and 27).

The obvious advantage of visiting out of season is the shorter queues. Nothing beats being able to wander around Fantasyland and Discoveryland with the choice of any ride without queuing (and without running into hordes of pushchairs!). The Cast Members have more time for you and the atmosphere is less frenetic, which adds to the enjoyment.

The other big bonus is the regular **'Kids Go Free'** season, usually early Jan–end Mar (another unique feature here), whereby, with any Disney hotel package, every child under 12 stays free with a full fare-paying adult, including continental breakfast and park entry.

'Kids Go Free' is a great Disney bonus

© Disney

> **BRITTIP**
>
> The excellent website **dlrpmagic.com** includes a section on Closures & Refurbishments, which lists rides due for a revamp up to 4 months in advance (go to Calendar, click on the Closures & Refurbishments tab).

Park hours are shorter at this time of year (usually 10am–8pm at the *Disneyland Park* and 10am–7pm at the *Walt Disney Studios Park*), but it is easier to get around, so you shouldn't feel short-changed (8pm is late enough for many children anyway).

A weather eye

'Ah, but what about the weather?' you might well ask. *Disneyland Paris* can organise many things, but it has yet to discover how to keep the rain at bay. But the park designers took the weather firmly into consideration when they were busy Imagineering and you will find more attractions protected from the elements than at any other theme park in the world. It is even possible to walk deep into the *Disneyland Park* mainly under cover (follow the route in Chapter 6).

The provision of arcades down both sides of Main Street USA (the entrance to the main park), some capacious indoor restaurants and few real 'outdoor' rides (not to mention all the shops, which can provide welcome shelter) means much of your enjoyment should be unspoilt by the vagaries of the weather. In addition, if you bring a waterproof (or buy one of the cheap plastic ponchos on sale throughout the resort) you will be able to continue enjoying the rides with fewer people around.

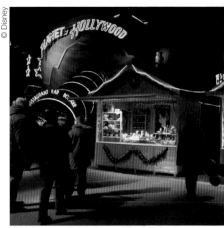
Christmas market in Disney Village

Christmas events

Foremost among the seasonal events you may want to take into consideration when planning your visit is the Christmas programme, which features special shows, parades, fireworks, characters, decorations and other events in the theme parks, hotels and *Disney Village* early Nov–early Jan.

Main Street USA in the *Disneyland Park* becomes the focus of the festive fun as it is transformed into a winter wonderland. There is a Yule overtone to the daily **Once Upon A Dream Parade** with the addition of the 'Dreams of Christmas' float (with toy

Geysers in the snow at Frontierland

© Disney

Meeting the Cast Members

soldiers, Father Christmas and his reindeer, plus the regular Disney characters in festive costume), along with a guaranteed **snowfall** up to 5 times a day. **Disney Characters Christmas Express** is a mini-parade several times a day from Town Square to the Central Plaza, while Main Street is also illuminated with a series of glittering street lamps representing the Disney Princesses. Other highlights are **Belle's Christmas Village** – a charming medieval village themed on *Beauty and the Beast*, with a chance to meet favourite characters from Disney's animated classic (and sample some Yuletide fare!) and **Mickey's Winter Wonderland** – a 20-minute song-and-dance ice-skating frolic with Mickey and the Gang at the Chaparral Theatre in Frontierland (the one Christmas element that usually continues until early Mar). In Fantasyland, look out for **Winnie The Pooh and Christmas, Too**, as the Hundred Acre Wood gang adds a seasonal twist to its indoor show. New in 2007 were **Minnie's Jolly Holiday**, a merry musical revue on the 'snow-covered' gardens of the Central Plaza, and the **Father Christmas Village**, deep in the heart of Frontierland, while **Mickey's Christmas Let's Party** is a truly magical finale to each festive evening, with everyone's favourite Mouse leading an all-signing, all-dancing extravaganza. A nightly performance of the grand **Disney's Fantillusion** parade rounds out the festive events.

At the *Walt Disney Studios Park*, the theme is a glamorous Hollywood festivity, with a seasonal celebration centred on the entrance courtyard. Inside **Disney Studio 1**, the Christmas Ciné Folies invite park-goers to be the 'stars' of their seasonally themed movie productions, while the whole of this indoor 'movie set' is decked out in tinsel-clad style to make it 'Lights! Camera! Christmas!' The travelling show **Toons en Scène pour les Fêtes** departs Toon Studio daily for Production Courtyard, with Chip 'n' Dale, Pluto and Lilo & Stitch in the starring roles, concluding with a big character meet 'n' greet. Finally, at the Umbrellas of Cherbourg in the Backlot area, the normal sprinkling of rain turns to snow for the holiday season.

The highly decorated theme is recurrent through all areas of the resort, including a special **Christmas market** in *Disney Village* and a chance to sample a host of traditional culinary specialities, including mulled wine. If you have seen how brilliantly Disney prepares its

Mickey's Winter Wonderland

© Disney

© Disney

Skating at Disney's Hotel New York

Orlando theme parks for the festive season, we can assure you it takes it to new heights in *Disneyland Paris* and it is definitely worth braving the wintry elements for the experience.

BRITTIP

If you can visit in late Nov or the first 2 weeks of Dec, you will benefit from the full Christmas festivities but without the heavy crowds they attract later in the month.

You can enjoy another great winter touch at *Disney's Hotel New York*, with a clever **ice-skating rink** outside, while all the Disney resorts feature a spectacular **Christmas Tree** in the lobby area with more decorations

Disney's Fantillusion parade

© Disney

than you can shake a Mickey wand at. During 21–31 Dec, *Disney's Newport Bay Club* hotel also features a special musical gala dinner, **Mickey's Holiday Dinner Show** aboard HMS *Newport*, with Mickey, Minnie and Co setting off on a journey of song and dance around the globe. To enjoy it, book from the UK on 00 33 1 60 30 40 50, but be aware prices range from £79–£108 for adults and £29–£40 for 3–11s. There is even a **Merry Christmas Lunch** with characters on Christmas Day (£79 and £29), **Disney Character Christmas Buffet** (24 and 25 Dec) and **Times Square Dinner Buffet Party** (31 Dec) all at *Disney's Hotel New York*.

BRITTIP

The *Disneyland Park* stays open until 10pm 22 Dec–New Year and until 1am on New Year's Eve, when there are party festivities throughout the park and *Disney Village*.

Summer season

From mid-Jul to end Aug, the full range of park entertainment is up and running. The *Disneyland Park* is open until 11pm and crowds are at their highest. At this time of year the **Fantillusion** parade is one of the main highlights, followed by the fabulous **Enchanted Fireworks** show, which bring down the curtain each evening. **Goofy's Summer Camp** is the live show throughout the season at the Chaparral Theatre in

Party time

Disney knows how to throw a good party, and you should keep an eye out for several notable one-off events. **St David's Day** will be celebrated 5–7 Mar 2010, with Welsh-themed festivities in both the *Disneyland Park* and *Disney Village* (including a traditional Welsh choir, face-painting, live bands, a Welsh food and craft market, fireworks and a true 'red, white and green' spirit) while 17 Mar sees the high jinks of the annual **St Patrick's Day** celebration in *Disney Village*. Then 14 Jul is the big **Bastille Day** event, mixing spectacular fireworks and music in the *Disneyland Park*. Both parks celebrate their 'birthdays' in enchanting fashion too – the *Disneyland Park* on 12 Apr and the *Walt Disney Studios Park* on 16 Mar. The resort's 20th anniversary is also on the horizon (2012), so expect to see some early signs of both parks gearing up to celebrate that in style.

Halloween fireworks

Frontierland. The *Studios* also features the **Good Morning Walt Disney Studios** event, a mini-parade with a big character meet 'n' greet.

Halloween

The next great festive period is Halloween, and Disney makes a big feature of this. While the idea is certainly more American than European, the style with which *Disneyland Paris* has adopted this tradition is quite breathtaking. Not only is there a daily **Halloween Parade** (the main Once Upon A Dream parade, given a heavy 'bewitching' makeover) and **Minnie's Halloween Train** several times a day along Mainstreet USA but the whole of Frontierland becomes Halloweenland for all of Oct, with a wonderfully imaginative series of tableaux (amusing rather than scary for young children). Kids automatically gravitate towards the Halloween **face-painting** stalls, while the nightly **Let's Party** show gets 'invaded' by the various Disney villains, including Jack Skellington from Tim Burton's *The Nightmare Before Christmas*. There are also 4 **Mickey's Not-So-Scary Halloween Parties** 8–11pm (at around £20 per person, with park entry possible from 5pm) to give young 'uns their own fun evening out. Special events include the Not-So-Scary show, the Merlin

Mickey's Not-So-Scary Halloween Party

and The Witch Academy, Disney characters in special costume and a special parade, plus all the rides of Fantasyland are open, along with a few in Frontierland and Adventureland. There is also the one-off **Halloween Party** (31 Oct, £25 per person) 8.30pm–1am for more ghostly goings-on (see Brit Tip on page 142), including more live entertainment and a Fantillusion parade plus a late-night party in *Disney Village*.

Finally, the **Bonfire Night specials** run for 3–4 nights each year around 5 Nov in best Guy Fawkes tradition. This magnificent fireworks and special effects spectacular takes place on and above Lake Disney, adjacent to *Disney Village*.

How long do you need?

First-time visitors should opt for the maximum time they can afford, especially at busy periods. The standard packages now offer 2-, 3- and 4-night stays and, as indicated on page 21, the 4-night duration is only just enough, especially if you have young children. If you can afford a week in summer, you will have the ideal amount of time to explore *Disneyland Paris* fully and see some of the surrounding area and Paris too (and not return home too frazzled!). However, because we know the majority of people book one of the

standard packages, we have drawn up an example of how to plan for each length of stay in **Your Holiday Planner** in Chapter 10.

If you're already familiar with the *Disneyland Park* but have yet to see the *Walt Disney Studios Park*, you will probably be comfortable with a 2-night stay, concentrating on the newer park during your full day on site. Couples without children or with older kids who can safely survive the demands of a bit of hectic park-hopping can probably negotiate both parks and, perhaps, Val d'Europe, on a 3-night package. But let us stress – you simply will not be able to 'do it all' in one of the peak periods!

The perfect 4-night visit would run Mon–Thurs, returning on Fri before the place starts to get seriously busy. However, if you can't go for this long or if you have to include a weekend, you can still have a great time. We'll tell you the dodges, tips and short cuts that will give you a head start over the rest of the crowds.

BRITTIP

Lots of little girls like to dress up in their princess outfits to visit the parks so if your princess already has a dress, make sure you pack it. They are more expensive in the park stores than at home

Clothing and comfort

The most important part of your holiday wardrobe is footwear – you will spend a LOT of time on your feet, even during off-peak periods. The parks may not be gigantic but that is irrelevant to the amount of time you'll spend walking and standing in queues. This is not the time to break in new sandals or trainers; comfortable shoes or trainers are essential. Otherwise, you need dress only as the climate dictates. T-shirts and shorts are quite acceptable in both parks when it's warm enough and most restaurants accept informal

Halloween make-up workshop

© Disney

PLANNING

Disneyland Resort Paris calendar

Jan–Mar: Kids Go Free season

5–7 Mar: St David's Day festivities

16 Mar: Birthday of *Walt Disney Studios Park*

17 Mar: St Patrick's Day

12 Apr: Birthday of *Disneyland Resort Paris*

14 Jul: French National Day fireworks

Mid-Jul–end Aug: Summer season

Oct: Disney's Halloween Festival

3–9 Nov: Bonfire Night Specials

Late Nov–end Dec: Christmas season

31 Dec: New Year's Eve festivities in *Disneyland Park* and *Disney Village*

dress, although shoes and shirts must be worn at all times. In summer, bring a mac for those sudden showers. Warm, waterproof footwear is best in winter, along with extra-thick (or thermal) socks.

If you feel you will need a change of clothes after a long day or some extra layers for the evening, you can leave them in a bag at the Luggage Check next to Guest Relations in both parks (€2 per bag) when you arrive. Both parks are well equipped with pushchairs for a small charge and baby-changing areas can be found in most toilets.

Disney with children

We are often asked what we think is the perfect age to take children to Disney for the first time, but there is no hard and fast answer. Some toddlers take to it instantly, while some 6- or even 7-year-olds are left rather bemused. Quite often, the best attractions for young children are the hotel swimming pool or the kiddie rides in *Disney Village*! Some love the Disney characters at first sight, while others find their size frightening. There is simply no predicting how they will react, but Simon's eldest boy (then 4½) loved just about every

second of his first experience (apart from the fireworks). A 3-year-old may not remember much, but you can be sure they WILL have fun and provide YOU with great memories and photos.

Here are a few tips, put together from personal experience and with advice from other parents.

The journey: Try to look calm (even if you don't feel it) and relaxed. Small children soon pick up on any anxieties, which makes them worse! Pack a bag with plenty of little bits for them (comics, sweets, colouring books, small surprise toys, etc.) and keep vital 'extras' like Calpol® (in sachets, if possible), change of clothes, small first-aid kit (plasters, antiseptic cream, baby wipes), sunglasses, hat and suncream in your hand luggage – but remember to check on the latest security advice with regard to liquids. If they are fussy with their food, you may want to take a bottle of their favourite squash, etc. Ribena® is unheard of in European supermarkets, for example.

Once there: Take things slowly and let the children dictate the pace to a large extent. Remember to carry your small first-aid kit with you. Things like baby wipes always come in handy and it is

Goofy in Frontierland

© Disney

© Disney

The Lucky Nugget Saloon in Frontierland

BRITTIP

Pushchairs are essential, even if your children have been out of them for a year or so. The distances involved around *Disneyland Paris* can still wear kids out quickly and a pushchair can save a lot of discomfort (for dads especially!). You can take your own, hire them at the theme parks or even buy one relatively cheaply at the Auchan supermarket in Val d'Europe.

a good idea to take spare clothes, which you can leave at the Luggage Check at both parks. Going back to the hotel for an afternoon break is a good idea – the late afternoon and early evening are usually the best times to be at the parks in terms of

Restaurant Des Stars

© Disney

cooler temperatures (in summer), fewer crowds and pure enjoyment. Both parks have a Lost Children meeting place (see page 124).

In the summer: Carry suncream and sunblock at all times and use it frequently – in queues, on buses, etc. A children's after-sun cream is also a good idea and don't forget to get them to drink lots of water or non-fizzy drinks. Tiredness and irritability are often symptoms of mild dehydration.

BRITTIP

The summer heat can make children irritable in no time, so take breaks for drinks and visit indoor attractions that have air-conditioning.

Dining out: Look for the all-you-can-eat buffets as these are a great way to fill the family up (you may get away with 2 meals a day) and cater for picky eaters. The Lucky Nugget Saloon, Plaza Gardens Restaurant (in the *Disneyland Park*), Restaurant Des Stars (*Walt Disney Studios Park*) and Billy Bob's (*Disney Village*) all offer some serious buffets. Try to let your children get used to the size of the Characters before you eat at a restaurant where they visit.

BRITTIP

Baby Care Centres (for changing, preparing food and feeding, with nappies and baby food for sale) are behind the Studio Services, just inside the entrance to the *Walt Disney Studios* Park and next door to the Plaza Gardens Restaurant in the *Disneyland Park*.

Having fun: Try to involve your children in some of the decision-making and be prepared to go with the flow if they find something unexpected they like (the Pocahontas Indian Village playground in the *Disneyland Park* is a good example). With young children, you are unlikely to see and do *everything*, so just take your time and make the most of what you can all do together.

Minnie's Party Train

Travellers with disabilities

Disney pays close attention to the needs of guests with disabilities, and there are few rides and attractions that cannot cater for them, while wheelchair availability and access is almost always good. As the *Walt Disney Studios Park* is so recent, much thought and care has gone into the arrangements for people with various disabilities (from the wheelchair-bound to those with autism and epileptic concerns). It is worth taking time to familiarise yourself with all the ways in which you can take advantage of the facilities. The Cast Members should be fully prepared to help and assist, ensuring you get full value from all the thoughtful extra touches. The main car park also has areas closer to the park entrances set aside for guests with reduced mobility and you should ask for one of these on arrival. There are even specially adapted minibuses for transfers from the Disney hotels to the parks (on request at your hotel reception desk and at Guest Relations in the parks).

All Disney hotels (except *Disney's Davy Crockett Ranch*) have rooms accessible for guests with disabilities, while they also publish a free *Guide for Guests with Special Needs*, which is available at hotel receptions and Guest Services at both parks. The

guide can be sent to you in advance from: *Disneyland Paris*, Guest Communication, PO Box 100, 77777 Marne-la-Vallée, Cedex, France.

Guidebooks in Braille are also provided and guide dogs are allowed in (although they are not permitted on certain attractions). You can also ask for an **Assisted Access Card** that allows access to special waiting areas for many attractions for a person with disabilities and up to 3 companions (although this does not provide special access to the rides, as most queues have been made wheelchair-accessible). There are also special areas at the many shows and parades for the disabled. However, not all rides at the *Disneyland Park* are fully accessible to the disabled as some require transfer and therefore the help of a companion is needed.

Visitors with hearing disabilities are not terribly well catered for, apart from a handful of attractions that have subtitles on video screens rather than bilingual commentaries or headphone translators (Animagique and Cinemagique in the *Walt Disney Studios* both have induction loops, for example). The multi-lingual nature of the resort makes it difficult to use a close-captioning system effectively, as in Disney's American parks, and it still seems to be some way from solving this problem.

Fantasyland façades

Disney for grown-ups

You don't need to have children in tow to enjoy *Disneyland Paris*. In fact, we've often felt the place is actually too good for kids! There is so much clever detail and creativity that the majority of youngsters miss in their eagerness for the next ride, it is usually the grown-ups who get the most out of the experience. In fact, there are just as many couples without children and young adults on their own visiting the theme parks, making it a legitimate holiday for all ages. Certainly, when you look at some of the sophisticated dining on offer and the evening entertainment at places like Billy Bob's and Hurricanes in *Disney Village*, it is easy to see the attraction for those aged over 21.

Paris obviously makes a wonderful honeymoon destination and newly-weds are just as likely to visit one of Disney's parks as the Eiffel Tower. Restaurants like the Blue Lagoon and Auberge de Cendrillon in the *Disneyland Park*, The Steakhouse in *Disney Village*, Hunter's Grill Restaurant at *Disney's Sequoia Lodge* and the superb California Grill at the *Disneyland Hotel* all offer a genuine romantic touch to dining à la Disney.

© Disney

Auberge de Cendrillon

Being practical

When it comes to the practicalities of your holiday, your obvious needs include **passports** for all the family (double-check that the name on your passport matches that on your travel tickets) and remember that all children must now have their own passport. All British subjects MUST have a full, valid 10-year passport that will not expire for at least 3 months after you enter France. Non-British subjects should check their visa requirements in advance. For UK passport enquiries, call 08705 210410 or look up **passport.gov.uk**.

The Blue Lagoon

© Disney

Top 10 must-do things in Disneyland Paris

1 Have a character meal.

2 See the daily parades (especially if Fantillusion is running).

3 Take a stroll around Lake Disney.

4 Have dinner at Planet Hollywood and then check out the live music at Billy Bob's Saloon in *Disney Village*.

5 See Buffalo Bill's Wild West Show with Mickey and Friends.

6 Have a drink in the Redwood Bar and Lounge at *Disney's Sequoia Lodge*.

7 Go shopping at La Vallée.

8 Try the Panoramagique balloon ride at *Disney Village*.

9 See the unique CinéMagique show in *Walt Disney Studios Park*.

10 Dine at the California Grill restaurant.

Travel insurance

You can get free or reduced cost treatment in all EU countries. However, you must possess a European Health Insurance Card (EHIC), which replaced the old E111 in 2006. You can apply for the free EHIC online at **dh.gov.uk/travellers**, by phone on 0845 606 2030 or 0845 605 0707, or by post – you can obtain a form at the Post Office. You need to know your NHS/National Insurance number. The EHIC does not cover all medical expenses, however, or the cost of bringing a person back to the UK in the event of illness or death, so it is essential to have adequate travel insurance cover as well.

You should never travel without good insurance, but you should also not pay over the odds for it. Tour operators may imply you need to buy their insurance policy, which you don't and their policies can be expensive. Make sure your policy covers you for: **medical treatment** up to £1m; **personal liability** up to £1m;

cancellation or curtailment up to £3,000; **personal property** up to £1,500 (but check on expensive items, as most policies limit single articles to £250); **cash and documents**, including your passport and tickets; and finally that the policy gives you a **24-hour emergency helpline**.

Shop around at reputable dealers like **American Express** (0800 028 7573, **americanexpress.com/uk**); **AA** (0845 492 1677, **theaa.com**); **Direct Travel** (0845 605 2700, **direct-travel.co.uk**); **Club Direct** (0800 083 2466, **clubdirect.com**); **Columbus** (0870 033 9988, **columbusdirect.com**); **Egg** (08451 222 888, **http://new.egg.com**); **Norwich Union** (0800 051 3606, **norwich union.com**); **Worldwide Travel Insurance** (01892 833338, **worldwide insure.com**).

 BRITTIP

The new **TinyTotsAway** has travel insurance especially for families, with free cover for youngsters, through Infinity Insurance. Look up more at **tinytotsaway.co.uk** or call Infinity on 0871 250 7500.

MoneySupermarket also compares different travel insurers at **money supermarket.com/insurance**.

Medical matters

There are 2 fully English-speaking hospitals in Paris: the **American Hospital in Neuilly**: 63 Boulevard Victor Hugo, 92200 Neuilly-sur-Seine (Métro Porte Maillot); tel. (in Paris) 01

Fantillusion Parade

© Disney

Disney for seniors

If Simon's parents are anything to go by, the over-60s can also get a huge amount of enjoyment from the Disney experience. The greater ease of getting here (as opposed to the American parks) is high on their list of plus factors, while the convenience of just about everything being within walking distance or a short bus or train ride away scores highly, too. They preferred the *Disney Village* and hotel areas during the day when crowds were lighter. Within 2 days they were fully *au fait* with the whole resort and extremely comfortable with the set-up. Here is their own top 10 attractions suitable for the over-60s.

1 CinéMagique (*Walt Disney Studios Park*).

2 Star Tours (*Disneyland Park*).

3 Pirates of the Caribbean (*Disneyland Park*).

4 Moteurs … Action! Stunt Show (*Walt Disney Studios Park*).

5 Studio Tram Tour (*Walt Disney Studios Park*).

6 Phantom Manor (*Disneyland Park*).

7 Animagique (*Walt Disney Studios Park*).

8 Once Upon A Dream Parade (*Disneyland Park*).

9 'it's a small world' (*Disneyland Park*).

10 Flying Carpets Over Agrabah (*Walt Disney Studios Park*).

They would even go as far as listing the walk around Lake Disney as an attraction in its own right, while they also felt the more show-based style of the *Walt Disney Studios Park* suited them better than the rather more hectic ride-orientated nature of the original park. However, they still acknowledge that the essential Magic of the latter is totally unmissable.

46 41 25 25, **american-hospital.org**; and the **Hertford British Hospital**, 3 Rue Barbès, 92300 Levallois-Perret (Métro Anatole France); tel. 01 46 39 22 22, **british-hospital.org**.

Once Upon A Dream parade

© Disney

For an after-hours chemist, the **Drugstore Champs-Elysées** at 133 Avenue des Champs-Elysées (Métro Charles de Gaulle-Etoile); tel. 01 47 20 39 25, is open until 2am daily, while the **Pharmacie Dhery** at 84 Avenue des Champs-Elysées (by Métro Georges V); tel. 01 45 62 02 41, is open around the clock. There is also a pharmacy at the entrance to the big Val d'Europe shopping mall, closest to the RER station entrance, open 10am–9pm Mon–Sat.

Emergency contacts

- **Police:** 17 or 112.
- **Fire brigade:** 18 or 112.
- **24-hour doctor:** 01 47 07 77 77.
- **24-hour medical emergencies:** 15 or 112.
- **Less serious medical incidents:** 18 or 112.
- **Public ambulance service:** 01 45 13 67 89.

© Disney

Mickey and Minnie on Main Street USA

Safety first

Crime has never been a major issue at *Disneyland Paris*, but you should still use your common sense as you would in any city (especially around the RER station, where pickpockets sometimes operate). Keep your hotel door locked at all times (even if you are just popping down the corridor) and don't leave things like cameras or camcorders on view in the car when you leave it parked. Both parks have a Lost and Found office and Guest Services can advise you of any additional security requirements (only the *Disneyland Hotel, Disney's Hotel New York* and *Disney's Newport Bay Club* have rooms equipped with safety deposit boxes).

The Paris **lost property office** is located at the Préfecture de Police, 36 Rue des Morillons, 75015 Paris (Métro Convention); 08 21 00 25 25. It is open Mon, Wed and Fri 8.30am–5pm, Tues and Thurs 8.30am–8pm. If for any reason you need to contact the **British Embassy** in Paris, it can be found at 35 rue du Faubourg St Honore, 75363, Cedex 08, Paris; 01 44 51 31 00.

Money

As ever on a foreign holiday, it is advisable not to carry too much cash with you. Travellers' cheques are easier to replace if lost or stolen (make a note of the serial numbers), but, generally speaking, cash and credit cards are almost universally accepted (although not by many small hotels and cafés in some areas of France). You can also use Switch, Visa and Mastercard at the several cash dispensers around the resort.

Snow White on parade

© Disney

The currency, of course, is the euro. At the time of writing, £1 = €1.13, or €1 = 88 pence, so, roughly speaking, £10 would be a touch less than €12.

BRITTIP

Want the best exchange rate for your holiday cash? Check out **comparetravelmoney.co.uk** for the best deals on a day-by-day basis.

Perhaps the best option, though, is the convenient, simple **FairFX card**, a debit card which you charge in advance and use as a credit card to your pre-paid limit. The exchange rate is fixed at loading and you can save 5–10% on High Street currency rates. Look up more at **fairfx.com**. For those who have yet to encounter the euro, there are eight coins – 1 and 2 euros, and 1, 2, 5, 10, 20 and 50 cents – and seven notes in 5, 10, 20, 50, 100 and 200 denominations.

Tipping: In France, a 15% service charge is sometimes added to restaurant and hotel bills but the usual practice of tipping is simply to leave a few euros at the end of a meal. A taxi driver would expect a 10–15% tip, while a porter would expect €1 a bag.

Phone calls

If you need to **phone home**, avoid using the hotel phones as they are fiendishly expensive (and Disney

La Pont Suspendu in Adventureland

hotels are no exception). Your mobile phone will probably also have expensive connection charges for calling from abroad (or even for receiving calls). It is better to use a public payphone and pay via your BT Chargecard or another kind of phone card. To call the UK from France, dial 00 44 and then the UK number (omit the first 0 from the area code).

BRITTIP

Look for a character meet 'n' greet without the crowds – in the first-floor lobby of the *Disneyland Hotel* twice a day, usually at 11am and at teatime. Ask at the hotel's Guest Relations desk for exact times.

Disney's Fantillusion Parade

Top 10 'hidden secrets' of Disneyland Paris

Look out for the many special 'extras' that may not be so obvious to the busy visitor. Here is our guide to the best.

1 La Tanière Du Dragon – the 'Dragon's Lair' under the Castle at the *Disneyland Park*, which many people miss.

2 Lighting effects – you can change the lights inside Studio 1 at the *Walt Disney Studios Park*, in front of Club Swankadero and in the Liki Tiki Lounge.

3 Take a phone call – pick up the phone next to Walt's bureau inside the Photo Shop on the corner of the *Disneyland Park*'s Town Square and listen for a message!

4 Get breezy – approach the giant fan at the exit to the Armageddon attraction in the *Walt Disney Studios Park*; it works via a motion sensor.

5 Heavy rock – sit on the large stone underneath the suspended bridge in Adventure Isle (*Disneyland Park*) – it rocks from side to side!

6 Puppet parade – be outside 'it's a small world' on the hour for a fun parade of ride characters on the 'clock tower'.

7 Take a ride – sit on the motorcycle outside the Café des Cascadeurs in the *Walt Disney Studios Park* and be startled by the sound effects!

8 Get a haircut – in Dapper Dan's, the period barber's shop on Main Street USA in the *Disneyland Park*.

9 Make it rain – stand under the Umbrellas de Cherbourg next to the Backlot Express restaurant in the *Walt Disney Studios Park*.

10 Make some music – try out the working keyboard in the back of the technician's van outside Rock 'n' Roller Coaster starring Aerosmith, again at the *Walt Disney Studios Park*.

Plus, it's not exactly 'hidden,' but Cinema Mickey inside the Videopolis restaurant/theatre in Discoveryland (in the *Disneyland Park*) is a charming opportunity to sit and watch some of the classic cartoons that made Walt's most iconic creation famous. It is fully air-conditioned and makes for a great break during hotter (or wetter) periods.

Adventure Isle

© Disney

Tourist info

If you are out and about in France, look for the local **Offices du Tourism** and **Syndicats d'Initiative** for maps, advice and info on the local sights and attractions. Most tourist attractions are open 10am–5pm, with one late opening day per week but, surprisingly, many close on public holidays (although not in *Disneyland Paris*).

A question of characters – where are they?

The biggest question on most visitors' lips (especially those with children!) is usually 'Where can we find the characters?' Invariably, some that leave frustrated because they simply miss out on this essential photo and autograph opportunity. So here's a head start on where you can usually meet Mickey and Co.

Disneyland Park:

- Various characters at the top of Main Street USA for the Main Street Park Opening at 9–9.30am (or 10–10.30am on later opening hours) every day.

- Mickey in front of the upper exit of the Liberty Arcade by Casey's Corner.

- Minnie under the Gazebo on Main Street USA periodically throughout the day.

Meeting Cinderella in Fantasyland

© Disney

- Mary Poppins and friends after their *Step In Time* show in Town Square, after Minnie's Party Train, which runs along Main Street to the Central Plaza 4 or 5 times a day.

- Winnie the Pooh and Friends periodically outside the Fantasy Festival Stage in Fantasyland OR at Casey's Corner on Mainstreet USA.

- Disney Princesses on the Castle Stage (usually 11.30am–1.30pm) to the right of the Castle at the entrance to Fantasyland (you'll need to queue); Sleeping Beauty also appears in the Castle Courtyard for the *Once Upon A Time* show several times a day.

- Mickey and/or Minnie, plus *Toy Story* friends Woody, Jessica and Bullseye at Woody's Roundup Village in Frontierland (usually in the afternoon).

- Jungle Book characters or Captain Hook and Mr Smee periodically outside Colonel Hathi's Pizza Outpost in Adventureland.

- Captain Jack Sparrow outside the Blue Lagoon restaurant.

- A wide variety of characters can often be found outside 'it's a small world' in Fantasyland; at lunch or dinner in the Lucky Nugget Saloon in Frontierland or Auberge de Cendrillon (with various Disney Princes and Princesses, plus Suzy and Perla, the mice from *Cinderella*) in Fantasyland; or for tea at Lucky Nugget Saloon (or, occasionally, the Plaza Gardens Restaurant on Main Street USA).

Walt Disney Studios Park:

- Mickey, Minnie and many classic characters in the entrance courtyard in front of Studio 1 for the first hour of the day and periodically thereafter (usually from opening to 3pm), notably after the Toon Train, which runs 3 or 4 times a day.

- Mickey and Friends in Place des Stars in Production Courtyard.

Key contacts

Here are the principal contact numbers for all the main agencies at *Disneyland Paris* (from the UK, omit the first 0 and add 00 33 to the number, e.g. to call Seine-et-Marne Tourist Office, dial 00 33 1 60 39 60 39):

Annual Passport Hotline: 01 60 30 60 69

Baby Care Centre: 01 64 74 26 00

Billy Bob's Wild West Country Western Saloon: 01 60 30 40 50

Buffalo Bill's Wild West Show: 01 60 45 71 00

Café Mickey: 01 60 30 40 50

Davy Crockett Ranch: 01 60 45 69 00

Davy Crockett's Adventure: 0825 150 280

Disneyland Hotel: 01 60 45 65 00

Disneyland Paris First Aid Centre: 01 64 74 23 03

Disneyland Paris Lost Children: 01 64 74 24 00

Disney Village: 01 60 30 20 20

Disney Village Tourist Office: 01 60 43 33 33

Euro Disney SCA, Shareholders Info & Club: 01 64 74 56 30 (or e-mail dlp.actionnaires@disney.com)

France Tourist Office, London: 09068 244 123 (60p/min) or info.uk@franceguide.com

Golf Disneyland: 01 60 45 68 90

Hotel Cheyenne: 01 60 45 62 00

Hotel New York: 01 60 45 73 00

Hotel Santa Fe: 01 60 45 78 00

King Ludwig's Castle: 01 60 42 71 80

Lost and Found: 01 64 74 25 00

Mail Order Service: 01 64 74 48 48 (or e-mail dlp.mail.order@disney.com)

Newport Bay Club Hotel: 01 60 45 55 00

Panoramagique: 01 60 45 70 52

Planet Hollywood: 01 60 43 78 27

Rainforest Café: 01 60 43 65 65

Resort Guest Relations: 01 60 30 60 53 (or e-mail dlp.guest.communication.@disney.com)

Resort Restaurant Reservations (up to 2 months in advance): 01 60 30 40 50

Sea Life Aquarium: 01 60 42 33 66

Seine-et-Marne Tourist Office: 01 60 39 60 39 or cdt@tourisme77.fr

Sequoia Lodge Hotel: 01 60 45 51 00

The Steakhouse: 01 60 45 70 45

UK bookings (to book a Disneyland Resort Paris stay from the UK): 08705 030 303

VEA Airport Shuttle Bus: 01 55 28 98 05

VIP Guided Tours: 01 64 74 21 26

Write to *Disneyland Resort Paris* Guest Relations: *Disneyland Resort Paris*, Communication Visiteurs, BP 100, 77777 Marne-la-Vallée, Cedex 4, France.

PLANNING

- Chip 'n Dale and others occasionally by Les Parapluies de Cherbourg in the Backlot.

- Meet Remy from *Ratatouille* in the Restaurant Des Stars periodically.

- The latest Pixar Films stars at the character scenes next to the Cars Road Rally ride in Toon Studio.

- Buzz Lightyear and other Pixar classics in the central plaza of Toon Studio.

- Monsters Inc characters at the set-piece display in Toon Studio next to Studio 1; and after the *Good Morning Walt Disney Studios Parade* shortly after opening in peak season.

✠ BRITTIP

To check when and where to meet the characters in the parks, always call in at City Hall at the *Disneyland Park* or Guest Relations at the *Walt Disney Studios Park* for an exact timing and location schedule.

Disney Village:

- At one of the character meals served throughout the day at Café Mickey (7.30 and 9.30am for breakfast, noon–2.30pm for lunch and 3–11pm for dinner); and also for Sunday brunch at The Steakhouse (midday–3pm).

- For all character meals you need to make a reservation either when you book your Disney package, through reception at your Disney hotel or in advance by phoning (from the UK) 00 33 1 60 30 40 50 (just 01 60 30 40 50 in France) up to 2 months in advance.

Disneyland Hotel:

- At dinner at the Inventions Restaurant, and in the foyer in the morning and late afternoon.

All Disney Hotels (including Disney's Davy Crockett Ranch):

- In the lobby area at regular intervals throughout the morning.

Know before you go

As hard as we work to keep this guide up to date, there are always things that change after our deadlines or areas we can't cover fully in this relatively small volume. There are a number of websites to help you stay up to date.

disneylandparis.co.uk: First and foremost is the official Disney website with the opportunity to book online and save money (although it can be hard to navigate).

dlp.info: The English translation of a superb German fan site, this is easier to navigate and provides a more comprehensive approach. It also has a handy News/Blog section.

dlrpmagic.com: Another sharp site with great photos, videos and maps, in-depth dining and ride detail. It has separate sections, **dlrptoday.com** for News, Rumours & Updates, **dlpfoodguide.com** for dining, as well as a lively discussion forum.

clickmagique.com: Some of the best photos and other news.

photosmagiques.com: More excellent photos.

thedibb.co.uk: This is the top UK site dedicated to all things Disney and has its own *Disneyland Paris* forum.

disboards.com: This site also has a special forum on the Paris resort.

Other general tourist information websites are: http://uk.franceguide.com, new-paris-ile-de-france.co.uk, http://en.parisinfo.com, paris.org and tourism77.co.uk.

Well, that should give you enough food for thought in the Planning stage for now. Let's move on to another vital subject in your preparations, that of actually Getting There…

3 Getting There

In many ways, your choice of **when to go to** *Disneyland Paris* **pales into insignificance compared with the issue of how to get there. The options for travel for this relatively short journey are almost as wide-ranging as the resort itself.**

Obviously, your location in the UK plays a large part in your decision. The Eurostar service may be a wonderful method of transport but it is not ideal if you live in Newcastle or Bangor. Equally, going by coach and letting someone else do all the driving has a lot of appeal but it can seem the long way of doing things if you live in the south-east (where Eurostar and Eurotunnel are quicker options). Flying is increasingly popular and affordable with the low-cost airlines, and the advantages are especially noticeable from regional airports like Newcastle, Aberdeen, Bristol and even Southampton. So here is an outline of the pros and cons of each of the main possibilities.

By car

With the opening of the Channel Tunnel in 1994, the dream of quick, reliable transport to the Continent became a reality. A permanent link was established along with a whole new realm of Channel-hopping possibilities. Some 85m people used

the longest undersea tunnel in the world (50km/31mls in total, 39km/24mls of them under the sea itself) in the first 10 years alone. In 2008, the figures were: 1,907,484 cars, 55,751 coaches and 9,113,371 Eurostar passengers.

BRITTIP

If you exceed the speed limit by more than 40kph/25mph, the French police have the power to take your driving licence immediately, so you won't be able to drive. For serious offences they can confiscate your car.

While the Channel Tunnel obviously opened in direct competition with cross-Channel ferry businesses, it actually served to increase the total traffic between the UK and Europe. Not only did the day-tripping habit pick up (as did the number of British-

The Channel Tunnel

© www.answers.com

9

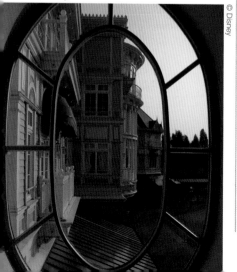

A map showing routes from England to France:

- **ENGLAND** with LONDON (M25), M2, A2, Dover, M20, Ashford, Folkestone, Newhaven, Portsmouth, Hull
- **FRANCE** with Calais (A25, E42), Dunkerque, Zeebrugge, Lille (A1, E17), Boulogne, A26, E15, A16, Dieppe (N27), Amiens (A1, E15, E19), Le Havre, A150, A151, Ouistreham, Caen, Rouen (N15), A13, A16, A104, PARIS (A4), Disneyland Paris

Legend:
- ⋯⋯⋯ Eurostar
- ——— Ferry Route
- ▪▪▪▪ Eurotunnel Crossing

orientated supermarkets in the Calais vicinity), but driving holidays to France, Belgium, Holland, Spain, Germany and even Italy also received a major boost. So, just 2 years after the opening of *Disneyland Paris*, it stands to reason the Tunnel would become a prime route to get there (in fact, it was one of the many reasons why Disney eventually settled on the Paris site).

The combination of the Tunnel and the well-established ferry links from Dover, Newhaven and Portsmouth now provide a wealth of opportunity for routes into France by car and coach, and more people travel by car than any other mode of transport. France is also blessed with well-organised and relatively smooth-flowing motorways (certainly compared to our M25), many of which are toll-road autoroutes (*autoroutes des péages*). In autumn 2009, the tolls amounted to just €20.20 one way to use this quickest and most convenient of routes (A26 from Calais, then A1, A104 and A4 – see maps above and opposite). Basically, it is 104km/65mls on the A26, 156km/97mls on the A1, 25km/16mls on the A104 and then another 11.5km/7mls on the A4 before the turn-off (Exit 14) for 'Les Parcs Disneyland'.

Toll roads and routes: The toll-road system in France is split into 8 privately owned networks, although

Disneyland Hotel

© Disney

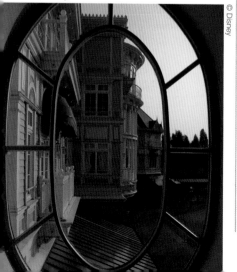

✚ BRITTIP

Watch out for the A26 junction with the A1, as the signposting is not very clear and it is easy to miss. The motorway turn-off signs are in white (and set off to the right-hand side) and you need to follow the big blue overhead destination signs for Paris.

Autoroutes des péages

Tickets are issued at the beginning of each of the paid motorway networks. Payments are then calculated on the distance you travel and must be paid on leaving the motorway. You pay at the *péages* (toll-gates) with either cash or credit card. For short local journeys it is a good idea to keep some small change handy to avoid the hassle of using your credit card. Payments vary according to the type of vehicle, with different price bands for cars, vans, cars with trailers, lorries and motorbikes.

the one from Calais to Marne-la-Vallée is all under the control of SANEF (**sanef.com/en/**).

Check out:

- **autoroutes.fr** for more details on your journey, a handy route planner and real-time traffic info

- **eurotunnel.com** for helpful route advice

- **multimap.com** and **mapquest.co.uk** for maps and directions

- **theaa.com** for a good route planner.

BRITTIP

The autoroute speed limit is 130kph/80mph, but 110kph/68mph when it is wet. It is 110kph/68mph on non-toll motorways and 90kph/56mph on other roads, 80kph/50mph when wet and 50kph/30mph in towns.

Driving from Calais: Most people drive from Calais. From Calais ferry port, you are directed straight on to the A26 (via the E15 – follow the clear signs for Paris, Reims), while from the Channel Tunnel you have a short 6km/3½ml stretch south-west on the A16 (signs for Calais) before picking up the A26.

BRITTIP

It is best to navigate by the directional signs rather than the route numbers.

From Calais on the A26, initially follow the signs for Saint-Omer, Arras, Reims, Paris; at the junctions with the A1, follow signs for Paris, Arras Est; immediately after Charles de Gaulle Airport, follow signs for Bordeaux,

Nantes, Lyon, Marne-la-Vallée, Paris Est, Bobigny; once on the A104, look for Lyon, Meaux, Marne-la-Vallée and 'Les Parcs Disneyland'; at the junction with the A4, follow signs for Meaux, Reims.

BRITTIP

Although *Disneyland Paris* is officially located in Marne-la-Vallée, the whole area along the A4 here is designated Marne-la-Vallée, hence it is easy to get sidetracked. From the A104, follow the signs for 'Les Parcs Disneyland'.

The only other area to watch out for is switching from the A1 to the A104 at Charles de Gaulle Airport, although there is a sign for 'Les Parcs Disneyland' just before and after the airport, directing you on to the A104. Immediately after the airport, the autoroute splits and you need to be in the right-hand lanes for Marne-la-Vallée; it then splits again and the 2 right lanes bring you on to the A104 heading south (see map on page 43).

It should take you a shade under 3 hours to drive from Calais. You can save the toll money by taking the Routes Nationales (or N-roads), but that would add nearly an hour to your journey.

The first tollbooths you come to on the A26 are after about 61km/38mls between Exits 4 and 5, and here you simply collect a ticket from the machine, which records the point at which you join the A-route system, and then you pay at the tollbooths just north of Charles de Gaulle Airport (after Exit 7). These are the only tolls

Indiana Jones and the Temple of Peril

Meet Cinderella and Prince Charming

you pay on the direct Calais–Marne-la-Vallée route.

BRITTIP

Speed camera detectors are illegal in France, and if found by police will be confiscated and incur a BIG fine.

Driving from Boulogne: From the ferry port at Boulogne, follow the 'Toutes Directions' signs and these quickly bring you on to the A16 via a stretch of dual carriageway. Once on the A16, head south for 200km/125mls until it becomes the N1, then follow N1 around until it hits the junction with D104 (after about 7.5km/4½mls. Take D104 (La Francilienne) for 16km/10mls to the A1 just north of the airport. Go south on the A1 and follow the same directions as above (A104–A4). Tolls will be about €18.70 and the journey will take 2½–3 hours.

Driving from Caen: If you take the Portsmouth–Caen ferry route, your journey will be around 265km/164mls via the A13, the Paris *périphérique* and the A4, and the tolls will be about €13.90.

Local roads: Once in the Marne-la-Vallée area, your main route to and from the theme parks is likely to be the A4, a busy stretch of motorway at peak periods (especially into Paris itself) but otherwise an easy-to-use arterial. There are no tollbooths on this section, hence you can use the A4 as frequently as you like at no extra

Disneyland Paris

1 Disneyland Hotel
2 Disney's Hotel New York
3 Disney's Newport Bay Club
4 Disney's Sequoia Lodge
5 Disney's Hotel Cheyenne
6 Disney's Hotel Santa Fe
7 Disney's Davy Crocket Ranch
8 Explorers Hotel
9 Vienna International Dream Castle Hotel
10 Holiday Inn at Disneyland Resort Paris
11 Kyriad at Disneyland Resort Paris
12 Pierre & Vacances
13 Radisson Hotel
14 Vinci multi-storey car park
15 IMAX Cinema
16 Panaramagique
17 Davy Crockett's Adventure
18 Hotel L'Elysée

DISNEYLAND PARIS

DISNEYLAND PARK

DISNEY VILLAGE

WALT DISNEY STUDIOS PARK

GOLF DISNEYLAND

VAL D'EUROPE

SEA LIFE

LA VALLÉE

cost. Once you turn off at Exit 14 for the theme parks, everything is well signposted to the hotels and main car parks. A huge ring road encompassing the whole resort (plus Val d'Europe), called the Boulevard de l'Europe, makes an interesting drive as you can get some unusual glimpses of the theme parks from it.

BRITTIP

If a French driver flashes their lights at you, it means they intend to go first, NOT that they are giving you right of way.

Parking and breakdowns: Parking and rest zones are situated every 10–20km/6–12mls on motorways, with 24-hour petrol stations about every 40km/25mls. In addition, you must not park on yellow kerbs.

If you break down, pull up on the right, put on your hazard lights and place a red warning triangle 30m/33yds behind your vehicle (compulsory for vans and cars with trailers). Orange emergency telephones are usually every 2km/1¼mls apart on motorways. If you break down and can't leave your vehicle, there are regular road patrols on all autoroutes.

Both AA and RAC members can take advantage of their organisation's European Breakdown Assistance

Carnival time at Disneyland Paris

© Disney

Disney characters in Frontierland

service, invaluable when travelling on the Continent. Visit **theaa.com** (0800 085 2721) or **rac.co.uk** (08705 722 722).

Service areas: French motorway service areas (or *aires*) are generally open 24 hours and offer a combination of facilities way beyond anything in the UK in terms of quality. There are two types: one has full fuel, catering and shopping facilities, while the other is a picnic area with toilets. The latter are often pretty places to stop, but bring your own toilet paper (for some reason it is not a standard French provision!).

BRITTIP

Buying petrol in motorway service stations in France is as exorbitant as it is in the UK. You can save 12–15% (more on diesel) by filling up at the nearest hypermarket (*hypermarché*) in Calais or Le Havre.

Maps: For maps, the AA's *Touring Map France* series (£4.49 each) are among the best available. Look for *Paris & The North* for the full route from Calais to Marne-la-Vallée, while you would need *Normandy* and *Paris & The North* to cover the journey from Caen. Online, the website **viamichelin.co.uk** also offers some valuable maps and info. All autoroutes have an information radio station. In northern France, English-language bulletins are on 107.7FM on the hour and half-hour.

Driving in France

There are no major differences in the traffic rules in France (other than driving on the right!), but driving with dipped headlights is compulsory in poor visibility – so don't leave home without a pair of headlight beam adjusters. It is also advisable to take a set of spare bulbs, while a red hazard warning triangle is compulsory (for vans and cars with trailers) in case of a breakdown. You should take your vehicle registration document and insurance certificate, as well as your driving licence (it is a legal requirement to have it with you whenever you are driving). Check with your insurance company to ensure you have full cover while driving in France. Green cards are no longer required, but some insurance companies issue them anyway as they are a sure way of convincing local police you are properly insured. Road signs are pretty much universal, but additional signs or warnings to watch for are:

Allumez vos phares/feux	Switch on your lights	*Interdit aux piétons*	Forbidden to pedestrians
Attention au feu	Fire hazard	*Rappael*	Remember (often on speed limit signs)
Attention travaux	Beware roadworks		
Cedée le passage	Give way	*Route barrée*	Road closed
Chaussée déformée	Uneven road surface	*Sens interdit*	No entry
Essence sans plomb	Unleaded petrol	*Sens unique*	One way
Fin d'interdiction de stationner	End of prohibited parking	*Supercarburant*	Lead replacement petrol
Gazole	Diesel	*Verglas*	Black ice

By ferry

You need to decide which method of cross-Channel travel you prefer – the various ferry services from one of 3 south coast ports or the Eurotunnel service from Folkestone. If you opt for the more traditional ferry route, you can go from Dover, Portsmouth and Newhaven, or even Hull to Zeebrugge in Belgium.

French driving rules

- Children under 10 are forbidden to travel in the front seat.

- On-the-spot fines or deposits (in cash – and you should get an official receipt) can be demanded for not wearing seat-belts (which are compulsory front AND back).

- Drink-driving, driving on a provisional licence and speeding offences will also incur heavy fines (and French police are pretty hot on the latter).

- The use of mobile phones while driving is strictly prohibited.

Dover

To start with, Dover is an easy port to get to by road – either straight down the M2/A2 in north Kent or (our preferred route) via the M20/A20, both of which come off the M25. It is about 1¾ hours from central London (given a relatively traffic-free run) and you need to head to the Eastern

View across Paris from the Eiffel Tower

Docks for the main ferry operators. Dover is a modern, well-organised port and should get you aboard your ferry with the minimum of fuss.

The main passenger terminal includes a bureau de change, a bank and cashpoint, an AA shop, a café and newsagent, information desks, phones, toilets and baby-changing facilities. Also, once you have driven into the terminal area itself, there are 2 mini food villages offering another café, a Burger King, a bar, bureau de change and cashpoint, a shop, plus toilets, baby-changing facilities and phones. You should arrive at least 30 minutes before your sailing time and have passports ready as you drive in.

If you have booked in advance (which is highly advisable), you proceed straight through to your ferry operator's check-in. If you don't have a ticket, you can park up in the short-stay parking area at the main entrance to the passenger terminal and buy one from the Travel Centre (6am–9pm). Alternatively, you can pass straight to check-in and purchase a ticket there. There are NO services by any operator on Christmas Day.

Once through the Eastern Docks' main reception area, follow the 'Ferry' signs to Border Control, where you will need to show your passports. Remember, all British subjects MUST have a full, valid 10-year passport that

P&O Pride of Dover

will not expire for at least 3 months after you return. Non-British subjects should check their visa requirements in advance. Then follow the ferry operator signs to check-in, where you will be allocated a numbered embarkation lane to proceed to, from where you will be directed to the ferry when it is ready to board. While waiting, you can take advantage of the food villages and facilities.

Four main companies operate from this busy cross-Channel hub, all using the well-provisioned Eastern Docks.

P&O Ferries: Dover's biggest and most sophisticated operator, with up to 46 crossings to Calais a day on 5 ships, 364 days a year, it operates the most frequent services on this route and in a high degree of comfort and quality. The crossing time from Dover is 90 minutes, although you mustn't forget to put your watches forward an hour on arrival in France.

BRITTIP

Visit P&O's website **poferries.com** to take advantage of its Best Fare Sailings, which offer cheaper fares the earlier you book.

Once settled aboard, you have a good choice of bars, shops, lounges and cafés in which to while away the time. All P&O Ferries' ships include an International Food Court (usually the busiest area on board, especially just after embarkation), a **First Base** fast-food counter, the **Costa Coffee**

Lounge café on a Norfolkline ferry

GETTING THERE

Join the club

P&O Ferries offers 3 distinct extra services, which can be pre-booked or, in the case of the Club Lounge, booked onboard at an additional cost.

The **Club Lounge** is an exclusive quiet lounge, complete with comfy leather armchairs, where you are greeted with a complimentary glass of champagne and offered tea and coffee, biscuits, fruit and newspapers by its own waiter/waitress service. There is also a business area where laptops can be used.

The **Priorité** service is a pre-booked priority loading system, which allows you to embark early and unload first, which is highly worthwhile when time is of the essence.

These can be combined in a **Club Plus** service, which provides use of the Club Lounge and the priority loading/unloading as well. At the time of writing, the prices were: £12/person each way for the Club Lounge, if booked in advance (£14 if booked onboard); £12/vehicle each way for Priorité; if opting for Club Plus, £12/person each way plus £6/vehicle. For 2 people, Club Plus would be £60 return.

From Dec 2010, P&O Ferries will have a new vessel operating this route and a second from Sept 2011, the largest Dover–Calais ferries ever built at 49,000 tons (replacing *Pride of Dover* and *Pride of Calais*). They will offer more capacity, more comfort and more facilities, as well as being the most environmentally-friendly ferries at sea (08716 645 645, **poferries.com**).

company, **The Bar** and a shop selling sweets and other snacks. **Langan's Brasserie** offers a more upmarket choice for a meal mid-Channel and, if you opted for Club Plus when you booked, you also get the benefit of the Club Lounge and its personalised service, as well as priority embarkation and unloading at the other end. For the young ones, there are children's entertainers during the school holidays, along with soft play areas, while children eat at half-price in the International Food Court. Provisions for the youngest members of the family now extend to free Heinz baby food. There is also a good video games centre, the Megadrome, to keep older children amused.

For shoppers, some of the biggest savings available are on fragrances, at up to 50% off UK high-street prices. Top brand designer sunglasses at up to 20% cheaper include Gucci, Prada, Ray Ban and Police. Wines start from just £12 for 6 bottles and an extensive range of spirits is available at 2l for £22.

BRITTIP

You can save money on P&O Ferries by booking a night crossing. Some onboard services are closed (Club Lounge and Langan's Brasserie, for example) but prices are reduced for these 'Lite Night' crossings.

SeaFrance: This is the only French ferry operator on the Dover-Calais route, offering up to 15 daily crossings, 364 days of the year (not Christmas Day). All of these crossings, which take just 75 minutes, are operated by its superferries, award-winning *SeaFrance Berlioz*, sister ship *SeaFrance Rodin* and the newest addition to the fleet *SeaFrance Molière*.

Across the fleet, SeaFrance provides a wide range of restaurants and onboard activities. Each ship offers a choice of restaurant areas: Le Relais, a

P&O Ferries Club Lounge

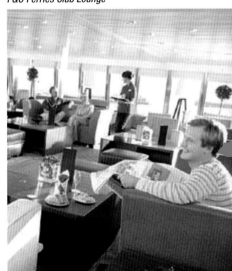

self-service restaurant; Le Parisien, a French café; Le Pub, a traditional bar; and La Brasserie, a fine-dining restaurant serving gourmet French cuisine. All ships have a well-stocked shop, with major discounts on high street prices and at least one lounge area, plus a good children's play area and video arcade.

Prices fluctuate depending on the month of travel and early booking is strongly advised, with discounts often available. SeaFrance's website displays prices next to each crossing and alternative crossing times, so passengers can see which will suit them best. It also offers 2 types of ticket: *Saver*, its lowest-rate, non-refundable fare, with a £5 booking modification fee and 100% cancellation fee; and *Flexible*, with no modification fees. 0871 423 7119, **seafrance.com**.

Norfolkline: An alternative to the occasionally hectic Calais crossings, with up to 12 sailings a day to Dunkerque, just over 40km/25mls along the French coast from Calais. The crossing time is a slightly long 2 hours but the Dunkerque port facilities are well run, usually uncongested and easy to negotiate. There is a distinctive Norfolkline travel centre within the Dover Ferry Terminal, while the Dunkerque Terminal has a lounge area with facilities for the disabled and a snack bar, La Véranda, offering non-alcoholic drinks and food 9.30am–5.30pm (Sat–Thurs).

Norfolkline also has a fleet of 3 modern ferries, each of 35,293 tons, which have added significantly to their onboard facilities. They include relaxation areas, gaming areas, a cinema, 2 playrooms for children (the Games Castle and Little Nippers), a full-service restaurant, fast-food restaurant and bistro. Freight drivers also have a separate restaurant and relaxation area. You can upgrade (for £12/person on board or £9.60 if booked in advance online) to the **Executive Lounge**, which has an exclusive seating area, free internet access and complimentary tea, coffee, soft drinks and pastries. All Norfolkline ferries' interior facilities are smoke-free but there is an outside deck area for smokers.

For the tourist market, Norfolkline continues to focus on the needs of the motorist by carrying only cars, caravans and trailers, motorhomes and motorcycles, not coaches and foot passengers. The gift shop (taking advantage of French duty-paid prices) offers fairly standard fare but is worth a visit, especially on your return, to grab a last-minute bargain in wines, spirits, beers, tobacco and perfumes.

You are advised to check in 1–2 hours before your departure time. From Dunkerque, Marne-la-Vallée is just over 300km/186mls away – follow the signs for the A16, then take the E42 to the A25 all the way to Lille and pick up the A1 to Paris. 0870 870 1020, **norfolkline.com**.

Norfolkline

With a new direct link to the A16 motorway from the port of Boulogne, this now offers the fastest road link to Paris. The history-rich town of Boulogne also makes a good stopping point for its 13th-century Old Town and the modern National Sea Centre, plus an array of outstanding seafood restaurants. The town is only a few minutes' walk from the port, but has limited parking, so it is better to park and walk in. Visit **tourisme-boulognesurmer.com**.

LD Lines: Dover's most recent player, starting in Feb 2009, is French, offering another attractive alternative, this time to Boulogne. It is due to increase the frequency from 4 to 5 daily crossings each way in early 2010, using the latest high-speed ferry – the *Norman Arrow* – for a 1-hour journey time (the largest fast-ferry ever to operate on the cross-Channel route). The sleek 11,000-ton Incat Catamaran can take up to 1,200 passengers and 417 cars and also features an exclusive Premium Lounge for **Priority Service** passengers, with reclining seats, complementary drink, newspapers and magazines. There are 3 other bars and lounges, the Horizon Bar (with panoramic views of the Channel), the Bistro du Norman restaurant (with a large selection of meals, drinks and snacks) and the main Blue Mountain Café. The Wave Shop provides the onboard selection of spirits, wines, perfumes and toys. There is also an outside deck on the *Arrow* (mainly for smokers), but you cannot return to your car during the crossing. Priority Service – for priority embarkation and disembarkation, plus use of the Premium Lounge – costs £7/person (every passenger in vehicle must purchase service to qualify). LD Lines is able to utilise the new Hub Port Terminal in the port of Boulogne, meaning a swift and efficient loading and unloading process. It also has plans to introduce a second high-speed ferry on this route in the near future. 0844 576 8836, **ldlines.com**.

For more info on the port of Dover, visit **doverport.co.uk** or call 01304 241427.

Newhaven

Between Brighton and Eastbourne on the Sussex coast is this small, busy port.

Transmanche Ferries: This French sister company of LD Lines is now the only ferry service on the Newhaven–Dieppe route. Newhaven is on the A259 coast road, but is best reached (from London) via the M23, A23, A27 (at Brighton) and A26.

Transmanche brought in a smart new ferry in 2006 (the *Seven Sisters*), with all modern onboard amenities, covering the journey in just 4 hours, with 2 or 3 crossings per day. You can add a cabin to your booking, for £35–48, or just opt to stay in the lounge, bar or café. The *Seven Sisters* has an extensive choice of shops and a video lounge, while it also boasts a full-service restaurant, bar, games arcade and children's playroom. Check-in begins 2 hours before sailing and passengers must arrive at least 45 minutes before departure. 0800 917 1201, **transmancheferries.com**.

From Dieppe, it is 257km/160mls to *Disneyland Resort Paris*; follow the N27, A151, A150 and N15 before picking up the A13 and the route from Caen.

LD Lines' Norman Arrow

Portsmouth

For the closest port to Paris, head for Caen with Brittany Ferries or Le Havre with LD Lines. The French capital is barely 2 hours from the Normandy ports (see map on page 42) and Portsmouth is more accessible from the Midlands and West Country than Dover or Newhaven. The down side is the much longer crossing.

Brittany Ferries: Brittany's new high-speed *Normandie Express* can do it in 3¾ hours, but their older classic ferry offers either a 6-hour day sailing or 7 hours at night. However, the night crossings have an advantage, arriving in Caen at 6.30am so you can be in *Disneyland Paris* by 9.30am. There are up to 4 sailings a day (one a day with the high-speed ferry, from mid-Mar to mid-Nov), leaving Portsmouth at 7am (high-speed), 7.30am–12.30pm and 10.30–11.30pm, and the port facilities are all new and well organised.

Normandie Express features a self-service café, a bar, shop and open viewing deck, with reclining seats and a video games room, while the older *MV Normandie* and *Mont St Michel* have the extra facilities of cinemas, children's entertainment, a full-service restaurant, a second bar, Wi-Fi internet access and a coffee shop, plus 2- and 4-berth cabins.

⚓ BRITTIP

There is a Carrefour hypermarket in Caen and also one in Herrouville, not far from Ouistreham, if you need to do some last-minute shopping before your return trip home.

Caen is about 2 hours from Paris

Brittany Ferries sail from Portsmouth

The Caen terminal is actually located at Ouistreham, the newest ferry port on the Channel, 15km/9mls to the north of Caen (open 6.30am–11pm), and is well designed to provide a smooth return journey, with easy access and good facilities. To reach Paris, simply follow signs to Caen along the D514 and D515, then pick up the city ring road (N814) and go south-east for 3.5km until you hit the A13. Then it is autoroute all the way to Paris (210km/131mls), with €16.90 in tolls. Stay on the *périphérique* and skirt the city to the south, then pick up the A4 to *Disneyland Paris*. On the return to Caen/Ouistreham, follow the signs for 'Car Ferry'. 0870 907 6103, **brittany-ferries.co.uk**.

LD Lines: Also offering 2 sailings a day from Portsmouth to Le Havre, from where it is only 200km/124mls to Paris, using the N15, A131 and A13. Departures daily are at either 11.15am or midday and 11pm, arriving in Le Havre at 5.45 or 6.30pm and 8am. They offer two different, modern ferries, the *Norman Spirit* and *Norman Voyager*, both featuring a bar, restaurant, cinema, Wi-Fi access and a choice of comfortable lounges. They also dock at the exclusive, modern Citadelle terminal in Le Havre, making for a smooth departure or embarkation. 0844 576 8836, **ldlines.com**.

Portsmouth (**portsmouth-port.co.uk**) itself is also served by excellent road links, with the port at the base of the M275 having its own exit on to the motorway. It is actually closer to London than either Dover or the

Thank you ferry much

We asked Britain's leading cruise and ferry website, Seaview (**seaview.co.uk**), to pass on their top tips for getting the most out of your cross-Channel journey – at the best price. Here's what they said:

To thwart those gendarmes eager to penalise Brits, drivers would do well to carry an emergency triangle and a high-visibility warning jacket. But do NOT use a radar warning device. You will be fined about €750, lose the device and risk having your licence confiscated

Don't leave your booking until the last minute. Prices rarely improve by waiting.

Don't try to pull a fast one by buying a day-trip ticket when you plan to stay longer. Ferry operators have a knack of finding out and take a very dim view.

Most ferry companies make it easy to book online and offer discounts for doing so.

If you book online, keep the confirmation e-mail with its unique reference number. Short crossings are often ticketless, so a booking reference is vital. And look after it – you'll have to produce it at the ferry terminal.

Read the reservation details carefully – twice! Mistakes do happen.

Make sure you give the correct details when booking, such as names as they appear on passports, exact length of car, etc. It can save vital minutes at check-in.

If there is a person with disabilities in your party, enquire about priority on-and-off arrangements.

Try to book a sailing time that you can make without having to dash. However, don't panic if you miss it. Nowadays, there's usually room on the next sailing. If you are ahead of schedule, there's a chance you'll be put on an earlier sailing.

If you are taking your dog on holiday, the train is best. Eurotunnel has areas for dogs to excuse themselves before travelling and, unlike the ferry, they have the pleasure of their owners' company on the journey.

If you sail with SeaFrance, opt for its new trio of *Berlioz*, *Rodin* or *Molière*, by far the best in the fleet.

If you prefer P&O Ferries and can afford the extra, treat yourself to the Club Lounge. It's comfortable, usually quiet, and soft drinks, coffee and tea, etc. are complimentary. You can also pamper yourself with a meal at Langan's Brasserie.

Be aware that, should an emergency arise, Apex bargain tickets are non-refundable, while full-price tickets usually are.

Remember you lose an hour on arrival in France, so take this into account when you are considering sailing times.

Channel Tunnel and is arguably Britain's best-connected ferry port. The Newbury bypass on the A34 has also cut down the journey time from the Midlands, West and North.

Hull

One final possibility for those living in the north who don't fancy the long drive down the M1, M25 and M3 or M2/A2 is to take the **P&O Ferries** overnight route from Hull to Zeebrugge in Belgium. The *Pride of Rotterdam* and *Pride of Hull* are both big, modern propositions (at 60,000 tons apiece), offering 3 categories of

cabin as well as a good choice of bars and dining – including the trademark Langan's Brasserie – and excellent children's facilities. It is a 13¾-hour ferry journey but then only a 3¼-hour drive from Zeebrugge to *Disneyland Paris*, via the N31, A17, A14, A22,

Pride of Hull

GETTING THERE

D656, A1, A104 and A4 (with €14.60 in tolls).

Useful websites: To help you with ferry crossings and road access after you arrive, the following are helpful, starting with the essential **seaview.co.uk**. Then there's **ferrybooker.com** (with lots of useful info on driving in France, the ports and working out your route). When it comes to driving, **auto routes.fr**, **viamichelin.com** and **sytadin.tm.fr/** (for Paris traffic reports) are useful and worth checking in advance.

By Eurotunnel

Need to get to Calais fast, conveniently and with a choice of services 24 hours a day? Eurotunnel is the answer. This versatile shuttle service from Folkestone in Kent has up to 3 departures an hour, with a crossing time of just 35 minutes. In fact, it can take just 45 minutes from the time of loading to driving off at the other end, making it easily the quickest vehicle crossing time of any cross-Channel service. Finding Eurotunnel also couldn't be easier as the terminal is just off Junction 11A on the M20, about a 45-minute drive from its intersection with the M25, and is well signposted.

BRITTIP

For the latest travel, weather and road news for the area, call Eurotunnel's information line on 0800 096 9992.

Heading for the Eurotunnel

© Disney

Aboard the Eurotunnel train

After arriving at the Eurotunnel terminal, proceed straight to check-in and quote your booking reference number (or use its new self-check-in facility, which you can practise online). You can just arrive on spec, but you will be allocated a space on the next available shuttle, and may have to wait a while. It will also usually be more expensive than booking in advance. In busy periods a booking is highly advisable to avoid a wait of more than an hour. You are requested to arrive at least 35 minutes before your booked departure time. You can stop off in its extremely smart and spacious main terminal building, grab a bite to eat and do a bit of pre-trip shopping. Once checked in, you drive through both British and French passport controls (there are no checks on arrival, as with the ferry). Please note LPG vehicles are NOT allowed on Eurotunnel trains.

Eurotunnel recognises it is not always possible to plan your arrival time accurately. So, if you arrive late but within 2 hours of your booked departure time, it transfers you to a space on the next available shuttle at no extra charge (although this could take a while if it's busy). If you arrive 2–24 hours after your departure time, you will be charged only the difference between the price paid originally and that applicable to your new departure. If you arrive more than 24 hours late, you will need to buy a new ticket.

Eurotunnel is quick and convenient

BRITTIP

Don't forget the necessary documentation for your vehicle, insurance and any breakdown cover you have for the journey.

For an even quicker and smoother passage, travel **FlexiPlus** and benefit from a priority lane at check-in and a guaranteed space on the next available shuttle. There is an exclusive lounge (open 6am–10pm) to allow you to freshen up, enjoy a light meal, complimentary tea, coffee and newspapers, and use the phone, fax or internet. There is even a free take-away snack service. The extra speed, convenience and service this provides is highly worthwhile, especially on a short trip. For direct access to the lounge, go straight to passport control, then follow the FlexiPlus signs (in Folkestone, keep to the right-hand lane, in Calais, keep left). Stay in the respective lane until you reach the Eurotunnel FlexiPlus barrier, then use the PIN number given to you at check-in to gain access to car parking for the lounge. You will also be given a paper hanger at check-in, which you need to display on your rearview mirror. From the lounge, you will be given priority boarding on the next available shuttle.

Once you're ready to board, you just drive straight on to the shuttle where you stay in your car. You can get out to stretch your legs in the carriage (and there are toilets, usually in every third carriage). On arriving at the other end, you drive off (in Calais/Coquelles) practically straight on to the A16 autoroute. From there, you head for the A26 (signposted initially to Calais and then to Saint-Omer, Arras, Reims and Paris) before picking up the A1 at Arras (see map on page 42). On the return journey, you come off the A16 at Junction 13 (look for the signs for Tunnel Sous La Manche). If you have time to spare, you can visit the huge **Cité Europe** shopping mall, which has some 200 shops and offers the usual great deals on things like wine, beer, spirits and food, notably at Tesco Vin Plus. And there are clothing stores such as Armand Thierry, H&M, Andiamo, Mango and Zara, as well as other well-known chains like Footlocker, Sephora, Yves Rocher and even a Disney Store.

BRITTIP

Check out **day-tripper.net** for more details on Cité Europe, the bargains to be had and an excellent map.

All in all, the Eurotunnel operation really is as simple as it sounds, and the ease with which you are suddenly off and running in France comes as quite a surprise the first time, so don't forget to drive on the right! It is also a relatively cheap option, with Short Stay Saver fares (2–5 days) from £84/car (at 2009 prices) and Standard Fares (more than 5 days) from £106. A 5-Day FlexiPlus costs £149 each way and a Standard FlexiPlus £199 each

High-speed Eurotunnel trains

way (you can also 'mix and match' FlexiPlus and Standard fares).

The other great benefit of Eurotunnel as opposed to the ferries (apart from it suiting more independent-minded travellers) is the fact the shuttle service is never affected by the weather and you are unlikely to get seasick on a train! 08705 353 535, **eurotunnel.com**.

BRITTIP

An excellent route-planning facility can be found at **eurotunnel.com**. Just type in your route details and you get easy-to-follow instructions to your destination. It even provides the total cost of the tolls en route. Click on 'Passenger Travel,' then 'Travel With Us' and 'Route Planner'.

By rail – Eurostar

The fastest direct route from London to Paris these days is via the smooth Eurostar operation from the new St Pancras International station. There are up to 18 services a day to the Gare du Nord station in Paris, with a fastest journey time of 2¼ hours (usually quicker than flying, once you take into account time negotiating the airports to get into the city centres). You can go to Gare du Nord and then use the RER rail service to get to *Disneyland Paris* (at the Marne-la-

Leaving on Eurostar

Aboard Eurostar

Vallée station). But you are much better off waiting for the **daily direct service** – 2 hours 34 minutes from London to Mickey! This is literally the fast-track service – at up to 300kph/ 186mph – especially as it's just 2 hours from Ashford International station in Kent. (Not available on Tues and Sat except during school holidays.) It is a high-speed link with great comfort, style and convenience.

Put aside any preconceptions (and real misgivings) of the British rail system, because this is how modern rail travel *should* be. You are guaranteed a seat (no mean feat for some regional rail services), the trains are clean and comfortable and their time-keeping is second to none in the UK (okay, the latter is not saying a lot, but Eurostar really does have an excellent punctuality record). The opening of the final section of the new high-speed rail link trimmed almost 30 minutes off the rather pedestrian journey from London to the tunnel itself, while the whizz through northern France remains a breathtaking experience. The move from Waterloo to St Pancras in 2007 brought a wonderful range of purpose-built facilities to this high-quality experience.

Add to this the excellence of all the other terminal facilities – at the brand new Ebbsfleet Station in Kent (although this is not on the direct route to *Disneyland Paris*), Ashford,

Super St Pancras

The original Victorian structure of St Pancras station has been given a major contemporary makeover – inspired by New York's iconic Grand Central Station – to accommodate the Eurostar trains and their facilities. The array of shops, bars and restaurants include a world-class brasserie and Europe's longest champagne bar – all 90m/295ft of it! There is even a Sourced Market offering fresh produce from nearby Borough Market. The shops alone are a mixture of one-off boutiques and big-name brands, including Fossil, Thomas Pink, LK Bennett and Hamley's, making for a retail selection unequalled at any station in Europe. There is Wi-Fi connectivity, including an exclusive lounge for Business Premier customers, while the main Departure Lounge still boasts plenty of options for relaxing, dining or a quick drink. In all, there are 6 platforms for the Eurostar services, instead of 5 at its old Waterloo location, with the capacity to operate far more services. There are also outstanding connections to St Pancras International, with 6 underground lines and 7 rail companies operating from here or nearby King's Cross and Euston.

Gare du Nord and Marne-la-Vallée – and you have an operation of the highest order and user-friendliness. For anyone living within 2 hours' drive of Ashford, this is a highly worthwhile alternative to the London station, as the ease and efficiency with which you can park and walk across to your train makes for a hassle-free journey, especially with children.

Eurostar operates a daily service direct to Marne-la-Vallée during school holiday periods, departing from St Pancras at 9.53am and Ashford at 10.26am, arriving in the heart of the Disney Magic at 1.31pm (with the 1-hour time change). There are also direct services to Lille, Brussels, Avignon and the French Alps, while connections are possible to more than 100 destinations in France, Belgium, Germany and Holland (NB: there are no Eurostar services on Christmas Day. Sunday train times also vary slightly – consult **eurostar.com** for the latest timetables). Outside school holidays, the service does not run on Tues and Sat, but it is still possible to travel direct with one change at Lille or going to Gare du Nord and using the RER line.

RER-ing to go

Using the RER system to get to and from *Disneyland Paris* is a doddle. This largely overground train link takes about 35–40 minutes to get from the resort into central Paris and runs until after midnight. While the trains may not be the cleanest (the graffiti menace has been here with a vengeance!), they run at regular intervals every hour and scrupulously to time. The RER goes underground through central Paris, where it links up with the *Métro* underground system. You do not need to use the Métro – or the well-organised bus system, which links with both – unless you are on a serious sightseeing tour of the city.

Marne-la-Vallée is at the end of the (Red) Line A4, which runs basically east–west through Paris. Gare du Nord is at a junction of the (Green) Line D, which runs largely north to south and (Blue) Line B, which bisects the city from north-east to south-west, and has the **Charles de Gaulle Airport** at the end of the B3 link (north-east). **Orly Airport** is on a special branch line – the Orlyval – connecting to the Antony station on the (Blue) Line B4.

St Pancras arrivals

If you choose the Gare du Nord route (or are unable to take advantage of the Disney direct service), you should find it relatively easy to transfer to Marne-la-Vallée via the RER train link on Line D (although the trains are seriously crowded in the morning and evening rush hour). Just follow the (Green) signs to Melun. From Gare du Nord, you change trains at Châtelet Les Halles to switch from Line D to Line A for Marne-la-Vallée.

Another alternative (and a worthwhile tip if you miss the direct service) is to take one of the Eurostar trains to **Lille** and change there for a TGV train to Marne-la-Vallée (about 65 minutes). You do not even have to change platforms at Lille, just wait (usually no more than half an hour) for the French high-speed train and you're off to the heart of the Magic once more.

Ticket types: With the Eurostar service to Paris and Lille (or any of its other regular destinations), you have the choice of 3 classes, **Standard**, **Leisure Select** or **Business Premier**. If you are used to using your local train service, Standard will feel like travelling first class – the individual seats are all comfortable, with decent elbow room, carriages are roomy and there is easy access to the 2 buffet cars. With Leisure Select and Business Premier, the service is seriously upgraded.

BRITTIP

A special fare applies for both wheelchair users and a travelling companion on Eurostar – priced at the lowest available Standard class fare – and there are toilets and an area adapted especially for wheelchairs in Leisure Select or Business Premier. Blind people travelling with companions also benefit from the same deal.

Leisure Select fares offer a 3-course meal at your (extra-width, reclining) seat and complimentary newspapers and magazines. There is plenty of space if you need to work en route (or keep the kids amused with board games etc.) and uniformed staff are always on hand. Business Premier, as you would expect, is the most expensive and affords complete flexibility for travel any day of the week from London to Paris, as well as other perks like a 10-minute check-in and exclusive lounge access. However, if you are interested only in the direct service to Disneyland Paris, your choice is just Leisure Select or Standard fares. There are always 2 buffet cars per train and a smattering of Disney fun to whet your appetite, with Disney Cast Members onboard to assist with hotel arrangements and provide some entertainment for the children, ensuring your visit gets off to a flying start. Baby-changing facilities and bottle-warming are

Marne-la-Vallée station

A Disneyland day trip?

The high-speed nature and regularity of the Eurostar service means you could opt for just a **day-trip** to *Disneyland Paris*. Taking the 5.25am from London would put you in Paris by 8.50am. Taking the RER to the resort would get you to the theme parks by around 10am. The direct return service is at 7.25pm from Marne-la-Vallée, arriving back in Ashford at 8.37pm and St Pancras at 9.13pm. But, if that does not suit you, the last train from the Gare du Nord station in Paris to London is usually at 9.13pm, which means you could still have until 7.30pm in the parks before catching the RER service into Paris.

available, along with activity packs for children if you ask at the terminal. Plenty of ramps, passenger conveyors and lifts are provided as well.

BRITTIP

Using the RER from Gare du Nord to get to *Disneyland Paris*? Change at Châtelet Les Halles, as you simply need to switch platforms rather than go up and down a potentially confusing set of escalators – the RER signposting takes a bit of getting used to.

On the direct St Pancras–Ashford–Marne-la-Vallée route, Standard fares start from £59 return/adults and £44/under-12s. Leisure Select fares start from £146 and £94 (under-4s travel free without an assigned seat). Its cheapest fares are also *non-flexible*, which means there are no refunds or exchanges; you need to choose a (more expensive) *semi-flexible* ticket for leeway with exchanges and refunds. With the London–Paris Leisure Select variety, all trips (except the Weekend Day Return) must include a Sat night stay. But there is NO stay-away condition if tickets are booked more than 21 days in advance.

Eurostar fares compare extremely favourably with airline prices (even the low-cost carriers) and, for the extra convenience of arriving right in

the heart of the Disney fun, they take some beating.

BRITTIP

It is possible to travel one way in Leisure Select and the other in Standard. It is definitely worth considering Leisure Select on the way home to give yourself room to wind down after all that exhausting fun!

Eurostar services: At the main Eurostar **terminals**, you should find everything efficient and easy to use. At London's **St Pancras International** mainline station, the Eurostar services operate on the main level from platforms 5–10. The departure terminal is built into an upper level in the old station's undercroft and here you will find the impressive range of purpose-built facilities – shops, cafés and bars, along with a cash machine that dispenses both euros and sterling. There is not much car parking nearby, though, and it's a whopping £25 a day at the NCP station car park.

At **Ashford International**, the main concourse offers a pleasant café, plus shops, currency exchange and left luggage, while passing into the departure lounge gives you more chances to grab a drink or bite to eat, another shop and currency exchange, plus a Eurostar information desk. The multi-storey car park here holds 2,000 cars and parking is £11.50 a day (an alternative, open-air car park is

The Eurostar leaves Ashford

available nearby at £10 a day, although it involves about a 100m/109yd walk to the station). To plan a rail journey to Ashford (or any other UK station), look up details on **nationalrail.co.uk** or **thetrainline.com**.

If you are returning from **Gare du Nord**, the Eurostar service is upstairs on the first level (it's surprising how many people don't notice this when they arrive), where there is again a good range of cafés and shops once you pass into the departure area. You have to check in at least 30 minutes before your departure to allow plenty of time for security screening.

BRITTIP

At Ashford International, go through to the second café as you enter the departure lounge as it is usually less congested.

Marne-la-Vallée is the least exciting of the main Eurostar terminals (but then it can afford to be with its situation). You arrive at the lowest level of the station and take the escalator or lift up to the main concourse. If you are heading straight for the theme parks, there should be a Disney Cast Member to direct you to the nearest exit. If you are heading for your hotel first, go out of the main doors straight ahead of you, and the bus stop for all the Disney hotels (except *Disney's Davy Crockett Ranch*, which does not have a bus service) and those of the 4 Selected Hotels

Gare du Nord

Sharing breakfast with Mickey

(the Explorers, Vienna International Dream Castle, Vienna International Circus Hotel and Kyriad) are immediately in front of the station.

BRITTIP

If you haven't already bought your RER ticket to get from Gare du Nord to Marne-la-Vallée (which you can do at any Eurostar station), avoid the often crowded main ticket offices on the Paris station concourse. Instead, wait until you reach the last, smaller ticket office just before the entrance to the (Green) Line D of the RER as there is rarely much of a queue there.

The Eurostar service includes the considerable bonus of the **Disney Express** baggage arrangement, which enables you to go straight to the theme parks on arrival while your bags are taken to your hotel. This has to be organised before you travel either through your tour operator or at the St Pancras terminal if you have booked Disney accommodation independently (you need to be able to show confirmation of your hotel booking to do this at St Pancras).

Once you have the correct baggage tags (and Disney Cast Members will be on the direct service to assist you and provide the right tags if you have not been sent them with your tickets), you simply attach them to your luggage and take them to the first-floor *Disney Express* baggage office when you arrive at Marne-la-Vallée.

Meet Captain Hook!

For our money, this is the most efficient and stress-free form of travel we have encountered, especially in Europe. When travelling with children it provides much to ease parents' minds (as well as the bonus of children's general fascination with trains). The onboard buffet food has improved a lot recently and Eurostar is a completely non-smoking service.

Eurostar also now features **packages** to *Disneyland Paris*, with a full range of Disney hotels and others nearby on the RER line to Marne-la-Vallée. Go to **eurostar.com** and click on the *Latest Deals* link, but you must add Disneyland tickets to your booking as they are not included automatically.

Remember that all Eurostar journeys are carbon neutral (unlike flights) and you can also take advantage of regional connecting fares from outside London starting at £59.

🇬🇧 BRITTIP

Several low-cost airlines use Beauvais as their 'Paris' airport, even though it is more than 60km/37mls north of Paris itself. The airport does provide a shuttle bus to Porte Maillot RER and Métro station in west Paris for €15/person but look for the new **VEA Navette** shuttle for the best way to get to *Disneyland Paris*. This runs 3 times a day via Charles de Gaulle airport and Disney at €25/adults (€20 for children) one way and takes 2½ hours.

By air

If the Eurostar route is the most time-efficient way of getting to the heart of the Magic, where does that leave air travel? Well, if you live anywhere outside the south-east, it provides the best alternative, especially using the 2 main Paris airports of Charles de Gaulle and Orly. The proliferation of low-cost airlines in recent years has broadened the choice considerably.

All of the regional airports around the UK have at least one daily service to the French capital and, with the likes of **EasyJet** (Luton, Liverpool, Bristol, Belfast, Glasgow, Edinburgh, Newcastle), **flybe** (Manchester, Birmingham, Cardiff, Exeter, Glasgow, Jersey, Southampton), **Ryanair** (Glasgow Prestwick, Dublin and Shannon to Paris Beauvais), **Jet2.com** (Leeds Bradford) and **bmi baby** (East Midlands) all offering variations on the low-cost alternative, it means your choice of flights has never been greater. Add the scheduled services of **Air France** (from eight UK airports, including Aberdeen, Bristol and Newcastle) and **British Airways** (up to 10 flights a day from Heathrow) and you have almost 20 regional flight gateways to Paris.

Paris Charles de Gaulle Airport: (CDG) is by far the bigger (and more complex) of the 2 Paris airports (it is the main international terminus, whereas Orly has more domestic flights). Situated some 23km/14mls to the north-east of the city centre, it actually consists of Terminals 1, 2 and 3. Terminal 2 is subdivided into 2A, 2B, 2C, 2D, 2E and 2F, with the RER station (Aéroport Charles-de-Gaulle 2) and TGV station situated between 2C/2D and 2E/2F. From Terminal 1, the nearest RER station (Aéroport

CDG Terminal 2F

Charles-de-Gaulle 1) is located next to Terminal 3. A new Satellite 4 (S4) next to 2E and 2F is due to open in 2012 to handle the giant Airbus 380, while a 2G terminal (purely for local traffic) opened in 2008.

BRITTIP

It's about a 10-minute walk from the RER station to the Air France departure gates in Terminal 2F and from the station to Terminals 2A and 2B.

There is also an automated shuttle train that links all 3 main terminals, in a straight line fashion, from Terminal 1 to Parking PR, Terminal 3 (for the RER), Parking PX and Terminal 2 (for the TGV station and second RER stop), then back again. It covers the full 3.5km/2¼mls distance in 8 minutes and the service runs every 4 minutes.

VEA Navette: The shuttle offers a direct service from Terminal 2 (from 2E/2F, with a linking shuttle service from all the other terminals) to the hotels of *Disneyland Paris* 8.30am–7.45pm (10pm on Fri) daily, either to the 6 Disney hotels and the Marne-la-Vallée bus station OR (4 times a day) to the 4 partner hotels of the Val de France area (if no direct Val de France

VEA Navette

service is scheduled, take the Disney hotels service and change at the bus station for the free shuttle bus). It is a fairly plodding coach service, taking a good 45 minutes to reach the first stop, but it does have the great benefit of being door to door and runs at 20–40-minute intervals throughout the main part of the day. It costs €17/adult and €13/3–11s (under-3s free). The Shuttle will take a credit card payment, so don't worry if you don't have any euros to hand yet. 00 33 1 55 28 98 05, **vea-shuttle.co.uk**.

RER: Alternatively, you can take the RER service on Line B all the way in to Châtelet Les Halles (about 40 minutes), then change there for Line

Adventureland in spring

© Disney

Indiana Jones and the Temple of Peril

D to Marne-la-Vallée (another 35–40 minutes). It is a simple enough route at off-peak times but much harder to negotiate with luggage in the morning or evening rush hour. 00 33 1 58 76 45 91, **ratp.fr** and click on the UK flag for the English version.

BRITTIP

If you arrive at the new Terminal G, take the N2 airport shuttle that goes to Terminal 2F for the VEA Navette shuttle.

TGV: Another alternative is to take the TGV train from the airport to Marne-la-Vallée, which can work out slightly cheaper than the VEA shuttle (although services are fewer). There are 9 trains from 6.54 to 11.43am, then another 8 from 12.58 to 5.51pm and 8 in the evening from 6.24 to 9.55pm. At off-peak times the ticket is €15.60 one way but it rises to €24.30 at peak times. The big benefit though, is that it takes just 12 minutes and you can walk out of the station to pick up the shuttle bus to any Disney hotel right outside. For the return journey to the airport there are 11 services from 7.25am to 12.27pm, then another 13 from 3.11 to 10.56pm (be warned – if you miss the Charles de Gaulle stop, you will end up in Lille or even Brussels!).

Taxis: You can also get taxis outside all the terminals, although it will cost around €90 one way to any Disney hotel.

BRITTIP

For information on both Paris airports – including terminal maps, flight times and services – visit **aeroportsdeparis.fr** and click on 'In English' in the top right-hand corner.

Paris Orly Airport: 15km/9mls to the south of the city centre, Orly is divided into Sud (South) and Ouest (West) terminals, and there is a free shuttle service operating every 5 minutes or so over the 2-minute journey between them (from the South terminal, look for Exit K and

Euro Limo Shuttle offer luxury airport transfers

from the West terminal, go to the departure level and Exit W). With good direct links into the city, Orly makes a reasonable alternative to Charles de Gaulle.

RER: Unfortunately the RER route is a little more complicated (take the airport link to Antony on Line B, then go to Châtelet Les Halles and change to Line A for Marne-la-Vallée). At Orly South, take Exit G on the ground floor (platform 1 to Paris), and at Orly West, also take Exit G.

VEA Navette: This direct shuttle bus to all the Disney hotels is the best choice (8.30am–7.30pm daily, journey time 45–50 minutes) for €17/adult, €13/3–11s (under-3s free). At Orly South, head for the Bus Station, platform 2 for the VEA bus and at Orly West, go to Level 0, Gate C.

Taxis: A taxi from Paris Orly to any of the Disney hotels will cost about €45–50.

Airlines: Then it comes to the airlines themselves.

- **Air France** (**airfrance.co.uk**) is the biggest carrier in terms of daily flights, using both main Paris airports. At Charles de Gaulle,

Disney's Hotel Cheyenne

its UK destinations fly into Terminal 2E.

- **British Airways** (**britishairways.com**) flies to Terminal 2A.

- **flybe** (**flybe.com**) and **bmi baby** (**bmibaby.com**) both use Terminal 1.

- **EasyJet** (**easyjet.com**) operates at Terminal 2B.

Disney Village

© Disney

Once Upon A Dream Parade

- **Jet2.com** (**jet2.com**) flies into Terminal 3.

- You could also try *Alitalia* (**alitalia.com/gb_en**), which flies from Aberdeen, Birmingham, Dublin, Edinburgh, Manchester, Newcastle and Shannon to Terminal 2E and **American Airlines** (**american airlines.co.uk**), which flies from Heathrow to 2A.

There are few direct flights to **Orly** from the UK, although **Air France** flies there from London City Airport (to Orly West). **EasyJet** also uses it as a base, but only for operations elsewhere in Europe, not the UK.

Choosing a tour operator

While it is perfectly possible – and sometimes cheaper – to book a DIY holiday by putting together your own hotel and travel arrangements, the tour operators to *Disneyland Paris* have developed a sophisticated, not to mention exceptionally good value,

Meet n' Greet in Discoveryland

© Disney

Vienna International Dream Castle Hotel

raft of packages that make booking with them (especially if you book direct) highly worthwhile. Add the number of internet travel companies like **ebookers.com** and **lastminute.com**, and there is a bewildering variety on offer for you to choose from.

The first thing to do is to shop around and get an idea of the prices for the different types of package. Most tour operators in this market are the big, well-known brands, who all feature some of the keenest pricing thanks to their ability to deal in bulk (notably Leger Holidays, Cresta and Thomas

Enjoying the pool at the Dream Castle Hotel

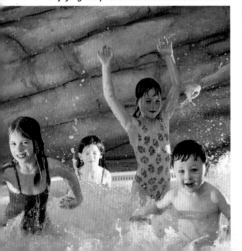

Cook), but several out-and-out Paris specialists are worth considering.

When it comes to simple price comparisons, it is more the method of travel that makes the main difference, hence a coach-based trip is usually the cheapest on offer, followed by Eurotunnel or ferry self-drive, then Eurostar and finally flying. But there are often special deals to be found – particularly at off-peak times – and it definitely pays to keep your wits about you when looking for a bargain. So you need to know what the general going rate is before you plunge in!

Look for the *Kids Go Free* season (usually Jan–Mar) when under-12s travel, stay and play for free (return travel, hotel accommodation with continental breakfast and park tickets); or the more limited season for *Kids Under 7 Free*, when children aged 4–6 benefit from free accommodation and park tickets (in 2009, this extended until 2 January, plus periodic extra days for free. Look out also for periodic **'All your meals free'** offers, as Disney has used this in recent years to boost quieter times of the year, adding 2 free meal vouchers per person for each night booked (on a minimum 3-day/2-night stay).

Leger Holidays luxury coach

Here is a look at the main national tour operators on the *Disneyland* beat. With all of them, Disney accommodation usually comes with theme park passes for the full length of your visit (but check full details before booking).

Harry Shaw: A popular and busy Midlands coach-tour specialist, this company's speciality is 2- and 3-night trips, with either 1 or 2 full days in the theme parks. It features primarily Disney accommodation at the *Santa Fe, Cheyenne, Newport Bay* and *Sequoia Lodge* hotels, inclusive of park tickets and breakfast. The 2-day tour picks up during the morning at 38 points in the Midlands (variously from Tamworth to Newport Pagnell and Milton Keynes) and 4 in the South East (Luton, Thurrock, South Mimms and Dartford), arriving in *Disneyland Paris* in the evening. You then have a full day in the parks before returning in the afternoon of the third day after more park time (arriving back in the Midlands in the early hours). The 3-night option adds a second full day in the parks before returning on the morning of the fourth day. There are also some tempting packages for the special occasions like Christmas and New Year. 024 7645 5544, **harryshaw.co.uk**.

Transport: Coach via P&O Ferries or Eurotunnel.

Leger Holidays: The biggest coach-tour operator to *Disneyland Paris* (although it also offers all the main package opportunities), Leger has a countrywide network of routes, with more than 400 joining points in England and Wales, taking customers

Sleeping Beauty Castle

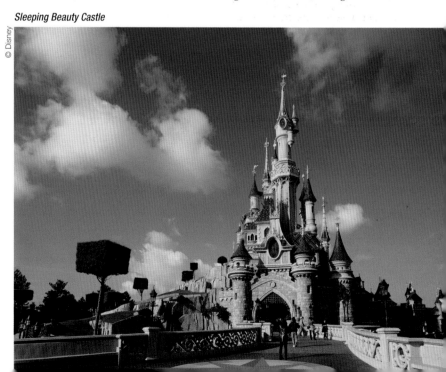

to Dover and crossing the Channel for the 4-hour drive to the resort (with 1 refreshment stop). It operates a mixture of its own branded coaches plus those of well-known companies from all over the country. All are modern and comfortable, with toilets and drinks facility and they reduce travel hassles to the minimum, which goes down well with families. There are also activity packs for kids and age-appropriate films. The 4-day package features 2 full days in the parks, with departure after breakfast on the fourth day and the 5-day trip offers 2 full days in the parks and an all-day Paris tour on the fourth day, or the option to stay in the parks (extra day's park admission not always included). Leger also offers rooms at the Magic Circus Hotel during Christmas week, with its 5-day departures having a 2-Day Park Hopper ticket. Arrival time aims to be between 8 and 10pm on the first evening.

Leger is the only UK tour operator to offer all 4 modes of transport, with increased departures of coach, self-drive, Eurostar and air packages, and a huge choice for all budgets. Included is a range of early booking offers – from room discounts, hotel

Disney's Newport Bay Club

upgrades and single-parent discounts – to enhance its value-for-money family prices. It also packages it extremely well, using its most popular hotel, the 3-star Explorers Hotel (see page 98), which is wonderfully family-friendly and the only one that will accommodate 6 to a room. The Explorers is Leger's base price accommodation and comes in slightly cheaper than Disney's most budget-orientated offering, the *Hotel Santa Fe*, which is 2-star. It has the option to upgrade to *Disney's Hotel*

Davy Crockett's Adventure next door to Disney's Davy Crockett Ranch

© Disney

Halloween is a great time to visit

Cheyenne, *Sequoia Lodge* or *Newport Bay Club.* The Kids Go Free season (for 3–11s, Jan–Mar) is available with all 4 transport options (based on 1 adult to 1 child). The self-drive alternative is *Disney's Davy Crockett Ranch*, which offers self-catering accommodation. Its brochures also highlight special events like Bonfire Night, Halloween and Christmas extremely well.

Leger's innovative flight programme features scheduled and low-cost airlines from 15 UK airports, including Birmingham, Manchester, Newcastle, Aberdeen, Glasgow, Belfast and Cardiff. Transfers are provided with all flights, either using the VEA Navette shuttle or a Leger coach.

Summer is easily the busiest period and the 5-day package has caught on really well since the opening of *Walt Disney Studios Park*. The Explorers Hotel always proves popular but Leger has also added the 4-star Magic Circus Hotel in recent brochures as it offers large family rooms and is located just 8 minutes (by the free shuttle) from the parks. This reflects a demand for another quality hotel that is still well priced compared to Disney's 3-star range, with higher standards of service and the bonus of a swimming pool.

Leger has a year-round programme to Disney. The majority use P&O Ferries

from Dover but some dates are served via Eurotunnel. We describe a typical Leger 5-day break in Chapter 2 (see page 21), which shows how hard it is to fit everything in! 0845 408 1093, **http://tothemagic.leger.co.uk**.

Transport: Coach via P&O Ferries or Eurotunnel; Eurostar; self-drive with P&O Ferries or Eurotunnel; flights (Air France, BA and various low-cost carriers).

Red Garter Saloon, Hotel Cheyenne

© Disney

Newmarket: A specialist tour operator you won't find in any travel agency, its Magical Breaks packages appear in many local and national newspapers, plus a range of direct-sell holidays by either coach or car. From Aberdeen to Plymouth, you are likely to see its newspaper-endorsed reader offers and usually at eye-catching prices (even for Eurostar packages). It offers mainly off-site hotels (hence the budget-orientated operation) with good, reliable coach services (most of which use P&O Ferries from Dover). Its Paris expertise dates back to the opening of *Euro Disney*, hence it has a knowledgeable staff (including its own in-resort reps), and also do big business with special interest groups and schools' Study Experiences (for students of information and communications technology, plus other curriculum-driven subjects). With its coach tours (the vast majority), it has some 500 pick-up points all over the UK and the coach is your mode of transport throughout the trip at the off-site hotels, which tend to be in the greater Paris area (usually of the Campanile,

Plan with Eurostar

While Eurostar now offers full travel agent packages to *Disneyland Paris*, its latest website addition is its **Trip Planner**, which provides a terrific range of ideas, opportunities and itineraries for any visit to Paris itself. Choose from the likes of Paris for Romantics, Half-Day Paris, An Older Look, and Paris with Kids, and don't forget to check its Useful To Know section, with a variety of tips for visiting the area. Check it out at **eurostartripplanner.com**.

Ibis, Novotel standard – a basic but comfortable 2- and 3-star). The only drawback is you're restricted to the coach's one trip to and from the hotel (you have to make your own way back if you want to return from the parks earlier). Occasionally, it does use Disney hotels, which provides greater convenience.

All are on a bed and (continental) breakfast basis, and they feature either 3- or 4-day trips. On coach tours, the 3-day trips feature 2 1-Day Passports for the theme parks (you

Disneyland Hotel

© Disney

Top 10 romantic options for Disneyland Paris

Although it's well known as a family destination, *Disneyland Paris* is also popular for honeymoons, anniversaries and other special couples-only celebrations. Here is our guide to the best things to do when it is just the 2 of you, so you can really make the most of your visit.

1   Stay in one of the Tinker Bell suites at the *Disneyland Hotel*.

2   Or stay in the Roosevelt Suite at *Disney's Hotel New York*.

3   Failing either of those, *Disney's Newport Bay Club* offers a genuinely lovely Honeymoon Suite.

4   Take one of Cityrama's Illuminations evening tours of Paris.

5   Have dinner at the California Grill at the *Disneyland Hotel*.

6   Take an evening stroll around Lake Disney and stop for a drink at the Redwood Bar at *Disney's Sequoia Lodge*.

7   Have lunch at the wonderful Blue Lagoon restaurant inside the Pirates of the Caribbean ride at the *Disneyland Park*.

8   Enjoy a drink in the Fantasia Bar at the *Disneyland Hotel*, listening to the relaxing sounds of their pianist.

9   Try the dinner buffet al fresco at the Vienna International Dream Castle Hotel.

10 In winter, stop at *Disney's Hotel New York* to watch the ice-skating and grab a mug of hot cocoa from the nearby drinks stall.

arrive mid-evening on the first day, have one full day there, then return early afternoon on the third day), while the 4-day version has a 3-Day Passport included (as you have 2 full days for the theme parks, plus part of the final day before an afternoon return; Scottish departures leave earlier on the final day). It also offers a good range of Disney breaks for specific events such as Christmas, New Year, Bonfire Night and Halloween.

Transport: Coach or self-drive via P&O Ferries or Eurotunnel.

Other operators: There are other regional companies that all feature *Disneyland Resort Paris*, including: **Applebys** of Lincolnshire (01507 357900, **applebystravel.co.uk**), which features coach tours of 3 and 4 days, some using P&O ferries from Hull to Zeebrugge; Yorkshire's **Gold Crest Holidays** (01943 433 457, **gold-crest.com**), with 3-, 4- and 5-day coach tours staying at a standard off-site hotel; York-based **Superbreak** (0871 221 3344, **superbreak.com**); and

Middlesbrough-based **Siesta International Holidays** (0845 217 2443, **siesta holidays.co.uk**), with 3-night coach-tours staying at Disney hotels.

Finally, to use some of the best online search engines (that seek out deals and special offers from a wide range of tour operators) for flights or holidays, try any of the following: **lastminute.com, expedia.co.uk, travelo city.co.uk, opodo.co.uk, ebookers.com**.

And, while Thomas Cook no longer offers its own tour operator service to *Disneyland Paris*, you can still book packages at its high street travel agents **Thomas Cook** and **Going Places**.

Book direct

Of course, you can always book directly with Disney if you have an idea of what you want to do. The resort offers a full range of packages with all the usual methods of transport and it even features a good range of off-site accommodation, with the 9 nearby hotels in Val D'Europe and Val de France, including the new Adagio City Aparthotel, with apartments for up to 7. Disney's brochure is worth getting just for all the lavish photography and large-scale maps, and it highlights all the extras, free nights and Kids Go Free deals. The pricing system and dizzying array of supplements for the different forms of transport can take some deciphering, but basically every possible permutation is open to you.

The brochure is designed so you begin by choosing your *accommodation* (inclusive of local taxes, breakfast and park tickets in most cases); then how *long* you want to stay (from 1–5 nights, with discounted extra nights possible); decide your mode of transport (from Eurostar, flights or self-drive using P&O Ferries or Eurotunnel); whether to opt for the *Half Board Meal Plan* (which adds a lunch or dinner a day for the duration of your stay, see also page 77) and finally select any *additional features* (such as character meals, shows, excursions or even birthday celebrations). Hotline 08705 030303, **disneylandparis.co.uk**.

Transport: Eurostar; flights (Air France, British Airways, bmi baby, EasyJet, Ryanair, Jet 2 and flybe); self-drive via Eurotunnel or P&O Ferries.

But wait, before you can make a fully informed choice, you need to have a good idea of the array of accommodation that awaits you, both in the form of the Disney resorts themselves and the usually cheaper alternatives for staying off-site. So, read on and we will reveal all about how to choose your hotel...

Take a promenade by Lake Disney

© Disney

4 Staying There

or How to Play the Hotel Game

When it comes to where to stay in and around *Disneyland Paris*, you will not be surprised to know there is a bewildering variety. Disney alone has 6 very different and entertaining hotels on site, while *Disney's Davy Crockett Ranch*, about a 15-minute drive away, offers an alternative for those with a car. There are another 8 hotels near the Magic, which benefit from being close to the resort, and several dozen more within a 15- to 25-minute drive.

The key is the combination of location and price. All the Disney resorts offer the huge convenience of being just minutes from the essential theme park Magic, but their hotels do tend to be on the expensive side. If you are staying on-site, the chances are you won't need any other form of transport. But you can also get away without a car elsewhere, as the easy-to-use RER rail line makes staying in somewhere like Bussy-St-Georges, Noisiel or even Bercy, towards the centre of Paris, a perfectly viable proposition.

The section on the tour operators in the previous chapter shows the great range of packages on offer. Many operators feature off-site hotels, as the demand for Disney hotels is high and they are at virtually 100% capacity in peak periods like summer and Christmas. The area along the RER corridor makes a handy base for tackling Disney (and Paris, for that matter), and the general standard of hotels is sound if unspectacular. Their star-rating system is pretty accurate and virtually every hotel works on a bed and breakfast basis (a continental breakfast with cereal, pastries, cold meats, cheese and tea/coffee – the Vienna International Dream Castle and Magic Circus Hotels are rarities in providing a full breakfast). It is advisable to stay off-site during the summer when Disney's prices are at their highest, while the price difference between on- and off-site properties is less in the winter.

BRITTIP

The quoted price rates of hotels in France are always per *room* and not per *person*.

Explorers Hotel

STAYING THERE

Off-site: Staying off-site can actually provide you with more flexibility if you want to use the hotel just as a base and not part of the holiday itself (Disney hotels play an important role in the holiday experience). You'll have more incentive to get out and about if you stay off-site and it's convenient for seeing more of Paris, while many hotels offer 'extra night free' deals.

You should certainly check in advance, however, whether or not you'll need a car. If you are not close to an RER station – or the hotel does not have a shuttle service to the nearest station – you will struggle without your own transport.

✦ BRITTIP

As of January 2008, France was officially a public **No Smoking** zone. All public places have been declared smoke-free, which means restaurants, bars, museums, offices and shops – and the theme parks – are off limits to smokers. However, hotel rooms are excluded from this law, so you still need to specify if you want a non-smoking room. And, from our observations, it is not universally enforced!

Disneyland Hotel

© Disney

© Disney

Disney's Newport Bay Club

Disney hotels

When it comes to getting the maximum out of your trip, you can't beat the full and all-encompassing experience of staying **on-site** (see maps on pages 83 and 94). The majority of Brits choose this option; yet, curiously, only a small percentage of other nationalities do, so Disney hotels are often mainly occupied by British guests. Just the simple fact of being able to walk into the parks in the morning, through *Disney Village*, is one of the great pleasures of staying here. Even from *Disney's Hotel Santa Fe*, which is the furthest away of the 6 on-site resorts, it is no more than a 20-minute stroll and, on a sunny morning, a delightful one. The old estate agent adage of 'location, location, location' is just as true here.

Extra Magic Hours: There are also other significant benefits to staying *chez* Mickey for the duration of your visit, most notably the Extra Magic Hours perk. This allows guests staying at the 7 Disney resorts and the Hotel L'Élysée Val d'Europe (plus Dream Annual Passport holders) to enjoy specific attractions in Fantasyland and Discoveryland at the *Disneyland Park* on certain dates, 2 hours before park opening. On Extra Magic mornings, follow the signs for 'Extra Magic Hour' or 'Disney Hotel Guests' to bypass the ordinary queue. Just show your Disney Hotel EasyPass (which you collect when you check in at the hotel).

Extra Magic Rides

The **Extra Magic Hours** perk for Disney hotel guests (and those at the Disney-owned Hotel L'Élysée, and Dream Annual Pass holders) is great if you have specific rides you'd like to do without the queues you often encounter later in the day. Here's the full list of what is usually open for these extra 2 hours in the morning (presuming you can always get up and get breakfast that early!):

Rides: *Fantasyland* – Le Chateau de la Belle au Bois Dormant; Les Voyages de Pinocchio; Le Carrousel de Lancelot; Peter Pan's Flight; Dumbo; Mad Hatter's Tea Cups. *Discoveryland* – Buzz Lightyear Laser Blast; Orbitron – Machines Volantes; Space Mountain: Mission 2.

Restaurants: Market House Deli, Cable Car Bake Shop, Au Chalet de la Marionnette, Pizzeria Bella Notte.

Evening Magic Hours often add Phantom Manor, Big Thunder Mountain, Indiana Jones and the Temple of Peril and Pirates of the Caribbean.

Character interaction: This is another important perk, especially for families, you get at all 6 hotels in the morning and evening. At least one character will always be 'on parade' in the hotel foyer and kids are virtually guaranteed to get their autograph books off to a flying start.

Disney's service and hospitality: This adds significantly to everyone's enjoyment, while all resort guests get their own **Identification Card** that can be used as a charge card in both parks and at *Disney Village* (apart from the Rainforest Café, Planet Hollywood, McDonald's and the Gaumont Cinema complex).

Resort guests also benefit from **free parking** at the hotels, theme parks and *Disney Village*; the free shuttle bus service; free entry to **Hurricanes disco** in *Disney Village* and a whole range of recreational activities, from swimming and tennis to outdoor playgrounds, video games and even ice-skating (outside *Disney's Hotel New York*, but open to all Disney hotel guests for a small fee). The 2 outdoor **tennis courts** at *Disney's Hotel New York* are available to all Disney hotel guests (there is a small fee for balls and racket hire), on production of your Disney resort ID card.

There is a **shopping service** for hotel guests, whereby you can have anything you buy in one of the theme parks delivered to the Disney shop in your hotel, for collection from 8pm that day. Each hotel also organises regular **children's activities** and all have Disney TV and a computer games console in their play area. You can even pre-book pirate and princess costume packs for your kids (at £31 and £38 respectively) with a stay at any of Disney's hotels! Hotline 08705 030303, **disneylandparis.co.uk**.

BRITTIP

The character dining options can be booked through your hotel concierge in the foyer (see Brit Tip on page 82), and it is advisable to do this as soon as you check in.

Disney's Hotel New York

© Disney

Character breakfast: Finally, and highly importantly for those with children, you can book a character breakfast at one of 3 locations – the Inventions restaurant for guests at the *Disneyland Hotel* or either Café Mickey or The Steakhouse in *Disney Village* (there is, as you would expect, an additional charge). These feature an American buffet breakfast with breads, pastries, scrambled eggs, ham, sausages, cereals, fruit juices and hot drinks, and are priced at €17/adult and €13/3–11s for Disney hotel guests (it counts as a supplement against the normal hotel breakfast). They are also available for non-Disney hotel guests, but the prices are €26 and €18.

BRITTIP

Although there is no extra charge for the Good Morning Fantasyland breakfast, you need to specify whether you would like to do it when you book your package, as it is likely to be fully subscribed when you check in.

Good Morning Fantasyland: An additional (non-character) feature at peak times for guests at *Disney's Newport Bay Club, Disney's Sequoia Lodge, Disney's Hotel Cheyenne* and *Disney's Hotel Santa Fe* offers hotel guests the option of entering the *Disneyland Park* an hour early and boarding the Disneyland Railroad train (or just walking) to Fantasyland, where a basic continental buffet breakfast is served in one of the restaurants (usually Au Chalet de la Marionette).

If you arrive as early as possible, you will then be in pole position to ride the likes of Dumbo and Peter Pan or the Carrousel, up to 30 minutes before regular park opening, with little or no wait. This is especially useful on non-Extra Magic Hour mornings.

Park Hopper: In nearly all cases, when booking a Disney hotel or one of Disney's partner hotels, you are obliged to accept a Park Hopper Ticket for the duration of your stay as part of the package (or a 3-Day ticket if you opt for the minimum 2-night/3-day package), which obviously suits most people as it keeps you up and running in the theme parks from first minute to last. However, it may not be suitable if you plan on doing some non-Disney sightseeing as well, so you need to weigh up whether an off-site hotel might be the better option. The main exception to the Disney hotel rule is if you are an Annual Passport holder, in which case you can book just bed and breakfast packages through the central reservations office on 00 33 1 60 30 60 69 from the UK.

BRITTIP

If you are on the Plus or Premium Dining Plans, You will need to make sure you dine in one of the top restaurants each day to get full value for your vouchers.

Le Carrousel du Lancelot

The Half-Board option

One extra feature available for all Disney's on-site resort guests (except at the *Disneyland Hotel*) is the **Half Board Meal Plan** – pre-paid meal vouchers that can be used in a wide variety of Disney restaurants for a saving of up to 15% off menu prices. Designed to encourage guests to try more than just the counter-service dining options, it is has proved a highly popular plan, but it takes a bit of explaining and you need to be aware of your voucher use to get full value for money.

To start with, you MUST purchase the vouchers prior to arrival for all members of your party and for every night of your stay. Each adult voucher is valid for a starter, main course and dessert or an All-You-Can-Eat Buffet, plus one soft drink or mineral water. Children's vouchers are valid for a main course and dessert *or* an All-you-Can-Eat Buffet, plus one soft drink.

There are 3 basic plans that provide different levels of dining choice, getting more expensive each time. The **Half Board Standard** meal plan is designed for guests staying at the *Hotel Santa Fe*, *Hotel Cheyenne* and *Davy Crockett Ranch*, including the restaurants at those hotels plus 4 in the parks and one in *Disney Village*. This costs £17.30/adult and £8.20/3–11s per night. The **Half Board Plus** is designed for guests staying at *Hotel New York*, *Newport Bay Club* and *Sequoia Lodge*, so it includes their restaurants (but NOT the *Manhattan* and *Yacht Club*), the 8 standard restaurants, another 3 in the *Disneyland Park* and 2 more in *Disney Village*). This costs £23/adult and £9.90/3–11s per night. The **Half Board Premium** is designed for anyone staying at the *Disneyland Hotel* or *Hotel New York* as it includes all the restaurants at those hotels, all those in the Standard and Plus plans, as well as the big Princess character meal in the *Disneyland Park* and Buffalo Bill's Wild West Show. This costs £39.50/adult and £15.70/3–11s per night.

You can **upgrade** the Standard or Plus vouchers to **Plus** or **Premium** on any night to try dining not included in those plans (at the specific restaurants only), simply by exchanging your voucher for its face value when you dine. You can combine 2 Half Board Plus vouchers for the Grand Princess character lunch or dinner at Auberge du Cendrillon in the *Disneyland Park*.

You can book vouchers up to 3 months in advance on 08705 03 03 03 and they can be used for lunch or dinner.

The restaurants

Half-Board **Standard** entitles guests to eat at: La Cantina (*Hotel Santa Fe*), Chuck Wagon Café (*Hotel Cheyenne*), Crockett's Tavern (*Davy Crockett Ranch*), Silver Spur Steakhouse and Plaza Gardens Restaurant (*Disneyland Park*), Restaurant des Stars (*Walt Disney Studios Park*), Annette's Diner (*Disney Village*).

Half Board **Plus** includes the above, plus: Hunter's Grill and Beaver Creek Tavern (*Sequoia Lodge*), Cape Cod (*Newport Bay Club*), Parkside Diner (lunch only; *Hotel New York*), Lucky Nugget Saloon, Blue Lagoon and Walt's – An American Restaurant (*Disneyland Park*), The Steakhouse and La Grange at Billy Bob's (*Disney Village*).

Premium includes the above, plus: California Grill and Inventions (*Disneyland Hotel*), Manhattan Restaurant (*Hotel New York*), Yacht Club (*Newport Bay Club*), Auberge du Cendrillon (*Disneyland Park*), Café Mickey and Buffalo Bill's Wild West Show (*Disney Village*).

The pros and cons

With the Half-Board vouchers, you can budget for meals in advance, avoid having to carry too much cash and not be tempted to try too many restaurants. You do also save up to 15% on the full menu prices.

Disney benefit because you will probably eat in a table service or buffet restaurant more often that you would have done otherwise. It is also *essential* to book your restaurants in advance to avoid queuing or, more importantly, not being able to get in to some restaurants. This means being more organised than those who can decide where to eat as they go along. Having to have the vouchers for every day CAN still work out quite expensive – staying for 3 nights at the Newport Bay Club with Plus vouchers would cost a family of 4 (with children under 12) £197.40, and they will still need to fund another meal at some point during the day (this is Half Board, not Full Board, remember). A typical counter service meal is around £32 for that same family of 4 (£96 over those same 3 days), so this is not a cheap option. Vouchers cannot be used at McDonald's, Starbucks, Planet Hollywood, Rainforest Café or King Ludwig's Castle, and they are NOT valid December 24 or 31. Some restaurants can also be closed from time to time.

NB: You receive the Half Board Meal vouchers themselves when you check in to your Disney hotel but they do NOT guarantee a table reservation. Restaurant reservations must still be made separately. See your hotel concierge desk on arrival or call the Dining Reservation Service (in France) on 01 60 30 40 50 or from the UK on 00 33 1 60 30 40 50 (listen for the English option). Premium vouchers can be used at 2nd sitting of Buffalo Bill's only. Present your vouchers when you are ready to pay (all voucher prices correct as at 01/04/10).

Rooms: Most will accommodate a family of 4 comfortably, but you are limited for choice with 5 or more (although some rooms can accommodate a cot if required). Basically, you have only 4 choices in this instance: *Disney's Davy Crockett Ranch*, where the cabins can house up to 6 (but you must have your own transport); 2 connecting rooms in one of the 6 hotels; the family rooms in the (expensive) *Disneyland Hotel*, which can sleep 5; or one of the 15 family rooms, which can accommodate up to 6, at *Disney's Newport Bay Club*, although these rooms are more expensive and are at a premium, so you would need to book early.

Looking outside the resort, the Pierre & Vacances Residence Val d'Europe is an ultra-smart apartment block in the town which can accommodate up to 7, while the Explorers Hotel can take family groups of up to 10 and the new Adagio City Aparthotel, also in Val D'Europe, can take 5–9).

Rooms for guests with disabilities are available in all 6 hotels, but not *Disney's Davy Crockett Ranch*.

All rooms feature a telephone, international TV channels and radio, and a shower/bath. *Disney's Hotel Cheyenne, Disney's Hotel Santa Fe* and *Disney's Davy Crockett Ranch* do NOT have air-conditioning (although the former 2 have ceiling fans), while only

Parkside Diner at Disney's Hotel New York

Disneyland Hotel

the *Disneyland Hotel* and *Disney's Hotel New York* have hairdryers fitted as standard in the bathrooms (the others have hairdryers available on request). The *Disneyland Hotel, Disney's Hotel New York* and *Disney's Newport Bay Club* all have mini-bars, as does *Disney's Sequoia Lodge* in its Montana rooms only, while the former trio also have room safes. All hotels can offer non-smoking rooms and a left-luggage service (except *Disney's Davy Crockett Ranch*).

Other details: When checking in, you will be given your park tickets, any vouchers for various options you might have booked (for meals or Buffalo Bill's Wild West Show), park maps, an information guide to the hotel (these are well written and highly collectable), a *Disney Village* programme and your Resort ID card, while children also get a name badge to wear (if they wish!).

BRITTIP

If you arrive at Hotel New York between noon and 2pm, have lunch there before heading off to the theme parks; you will get served much quicker.

Each resort hotel should be able to supply a cot on request and all feature **children's menus** in their main restaurants. **Room service** is available at the *Disneyland Hotel, Disney's Hotel New York* and the Admiral's Floor of *Disney's Newport Bay Club*. There is no official in-house **babysitting** service for any of the hotels, although there is a private firm that can arrange in-room babysitting for you via the front desk.

In all cases, check-in time is 3pm (although rooms are occasionally available from 1pm. Take advantage of the left-luggage provision and you can still head straight for the theme parks), while check-out is 11am.

BRITTIP

If you have booked Eurostar's Disney Express service (see page 60), you simply leave your bags, cases, etc. in the left-luggage office at your hotel when you check out, and they will be transferred for you to collect at the Disney Express office at the Marne-la-Vallée station. Whether or not you've booked, Disney Express labels ARE available for your return journey for a few extra euros from the hotel check-in.

Suites: Finally, almost the ultimate perk of staying onsite comes if you opt for one of the suites at the *Disneyland Hotel, Hotel New York, Sequoia Lodge* or *Newport Bay Club*. All guests at these accommodations receive **VIP FastPasses** providing all-day front-of-line access to all the rides that have the FastPass system (see page 122). All guests at the *Disneyland Hotel* also receive one free FastPass per day, for use on any FP ride of their choice.

Disneyland Hotel

Disadvantages: The pros of staying on-site are substantial, but what of the cons? Well, the price difference is the obvious issue. You can save a good 20–30% by opting for one of the smaller hotels nearby, and the 7 official nearby hotels (4 in the **Val de France** area) all represent significant savings while offering much of the convenience, facilities and service. In fact, we rate the Vienna International Dream Castle and Explorers Hotels as possibly the best all-round value.

Breakfast at the Disney resorts can also be something of a bunfight at peak periods. You are allocated a set time-slot (that may not be terribly convenient in the first place) but you may still find queues just to get in, even at more upmarket hotels like *Sequoia Lodge* and *Newport Bay Club*. If you're looking to be in the parks by 9am, you may struggle to get through breakfast in time, unless you have the 7.30am time-slot (not everyone's idea of a holiday rise-and-shine!). The off-site hotels are noticeably less frenetic (with the possible exception of the busy Explorers Hotel), and often provide a welcome break from the hustle and bustle in early evening.

Those in the Val de France area benefit from a beautiful countryside location, with a large lake that backs on to the 4 hotels, which provides a pleasant way to unwind after a day at the parks. However, the (free) shuttle bus service can be a bit of a trial at peak times (half an hour before park opening and at park closing). It calls at all 4 hotels in turn, which means either an uncomfortable 10–15-minute ride or, occasionally, having to wait for another bus if the first is full. The Dream Castle in particular suffers from this as it is the last pick-up point on the 4-hotel circuit.

Having underlined the price differential, Disney's 6 hotels (amounting to 5,200 rooms, plus the 535 cabins and 60 caravan sites of *Disney's Davy Crockett Ranch*) do offer a range of prices to suit most pockets, from the more budget-priced *Disney's Hotel Santa Fe* to the opulent 4-star *Disneyland Hotel*.

We at the *Brit Guide* have our own ratings system for the hotels, too, allocating €s in the following price ranges:

€€€€€	=	More than €150/night
€€€€	=	€100–150/night
€€€	=	€75–100/night
€€	=	€50–75/night
€	=	Less than €50/night

We also award CCCs out of 5 for the extra facilities at each property. Hence you can be sure a CCCCC hotel should have all the creature comforts you can think of, including a swimming pool and a choice of restaurants, while a CC would be of the more basic, motel-type. Here are Disney's magnificent 7 in detail.

The Chuck Wagon at Disney's Hotel Cheyenne

© Disney

Disneyland Paris Hotels

1 Disney's Hotel Cheyenne
2 Disney's Hotel Santa Fe
3 Disney's Sequoia Lodge
4 Disney's Davy Crockett Ranch
5 Disney's Newport Bay Club
6 Lake Disney
7 Disney's Hotel New York
8 RER/TGV/bus station
9 Disneyland Hotel
10 Disneyland Park
11 Walt Disney Studios Park
12 Vinci Car Park
13 Disney Village

DISNEYLAND PARIS HOTELS

BRITTIP

Each Disney hotel has a concierge desk in the foyer specially for booking meals and shows in any of the hotels, parks or *Disney Village*. Try to plan day by day and visit the desk first thing in the morning to make your bookings, especially at peak times. If you can book for your whole stay straight away, you will be one step ahead of the masses.

Disneyland Hotel

The resort's signature hotel, right at the entrance to the *Disneyland Park* (and otherwise known as the Pink Palace), is a massive mock-Victorian edifice featuring the most comfortable and spacious rooms, sumptuous decor and one of the best restaurants in the whole area. The Disney theming is at its most discreet here (you have to look closely at the wallpaper to realise the built-in Mickey subtlety) and there is some elegant furniture sprinkled around (witness the 4 classic grandfather clocks along one corridor that display the times at each of the Disney resorts around the world – they also play Disney tunes on the hour and half-hour!).

Rooms and suites: Standard rooms feature either a king-size bed and a fold-out or 2 doubles, plus a highly elaborate TV/video cabinet with mini-bar, and all have the high ceilings reminiscent of Victorian buildings.

The top 2 floors feature the exclusive **Castle Club**, with a private lift (straight to the theme park!) and reception desk, a lounge bar for breakfast, afternoon tea and light refreshments, plus a fabulous view out over the *Disneyland Park*. There are spacious Junior Suites (58m²/ 624ft² as opposed to the 34m²/ 366ft² of standard rooms), plus 4 Tinker Bell Suites (69m²/743ft m²) with a lounge and a separate walk-in shower as well as a bath. In addition there are 3 one-off suites of truly exceptional order – Walt's Apartment, the (Cinderella) Vice-Presidential Suite and the (Sleeping Beauty) Presidential Suite.

BRITTIP

If you find *Disney Village* a touch too frenetic in the evening, head for the City Bar at *Disney's Hotel New York*, which offers the perfect surroundings for relaxing and enjoying a drink.

Shopping and dining: From the 3-storey lobby right through to the Celestia Spa, the period theming is impressive but not overwhelming. There is a **Galerie Mickey** selling souvenirs and travel essentials, the main bar area **Café Fantasia** (with inventive decor geared to the film of the same name) as well as 2 restaurants. **Inventions** is themed on the great technical creations of the early 20th century and offers an excellent dinner buffet, in addition to the character breakfasts. The

Celestial spa at the Disneyland Hotel

Manhattan Restaurant

California Grill is the hotel's fine-dining option and the quality on offer is superb, with a conservatory-style motif and an open kitchen at one end. At the other end, a lounge affords more great views of the theme park.

Facilities: The indoor pool area is equally smart, with a medium-sized pool, jacuzzi, gym and face and body treatment rooms, as well as a sauna, steam room and solarium. The inevitable video games room is fully geared up for kids of the requisite age, while the Minnie Club activity centre includes TV, video and computer games. The only thing it doesn't have is an outdoor play area, but then the *Disneyland Park* is right on the doorstep! However, there is a supplement for a standard room with a park view. The Celestia Spa offers a fabulous array of spa, massage and beauty treatments, including couples treatments (€195/2 hours) and adds the ultimate relaxation after the parks! Call 01 60 45 66 05 to book, or 6605 from a Disney hotel phone.

In all, there are 496 rooms, plus 18 suites and it really is the pinnacle of the on-site accommodation.

Official rating ****; our rating €€€€€, CCCCC.

Disney's Hotel New York

Welcome to the Big Apple! While this is a Disney hotel, it is a wonderfully themed hotel in its own right, with an art deco, 1930s' view of New York that extends from the massive 'tower block' façade to individual touches in the rooms and the background jazz throughout the lobby and bar area. There is little overt Mickey-ness about it, but lots of grand style and clever imagery, with the bonus in some rooms of a fabulous view over Lake Disney. It also has, we reckon, the most amazing suite of them all, the 2-storey Presidential Suite, with floor-to-ceiling windows, wonderful furniture, a living room complete with piano and a dining room for up to ten guests. The upstairs double bedroom has a separate lounge and jacuzzi.

BRITTIP

Disney's Hotel New York is a product of American architect Michael Graves, who also designed the Swan and Dolphin Hotels in *Walt Disney World Resort in Florida*. So, if you enjoy the fun-style architecture of those, *Disney's Hotel New York* is bound to appeal to you too.

Disney's Hotel New York

Rooms and suites: There are 565 rooms in all, including 27 spacious suites. Most standard rooms (31 m²/334ft²), with some lovely rosewood cabinets, sleep 4 comfortably, while others offer just one king-size bed. The Resort Suites (56m²/603ft², one on each corner of each floor) have masses of space for a family of 4, with a separate bedroom and living room. There is a beautiful Honeymoon Suite (62m²/667ft²) as well.

Dining: The hotel features 2 restaurants (the intimate, formal atmosphere of the **Manhattan Restaurant** and the more relaxed, cosmopolitan style of the **Parkside Diner**, both of which were completely refurbished in 2009) and a delightfully elegant bar.

⚑ BRITTIP

The elegant (and recently renovated) Manhattan Restaurant in *Disney's Hotel New York* is an oft-overlooked but worthwhile venue for a special dinner, with a terrific Italian-tinged menu.

Facilities: There's a hair salon (the only one on-site), boutique and gift shop, 2 outdoor tennis courts (small fee for racket and ball hire) and an ice-skating rink (an eye-catching facility in winter AND summer).

For kids, there is the indoor **Roger Rabbit Corner**, with themed activities at different times of the day, and the ubiquitous video games room, plus daily appearances of Disney characters in the main hall each morning. The one drawback here is that the hotel is also a big convention facility, and it can draw a sizeable business/conference crowd at times.

A bonus with *Disney's Hotel New York* is the excellent swimming pool complex (the New York Athletic Club), which is among the best of the on-site hotels. The extremely large pool has both an indoor and outdoor aspect, while there is also a jacuzzi, sauna, steam room and a good-sized gymnasium, plus a pleasant outdoor terrace. After the *Disneyland Hotel*, it is also the closest to the theme parks, situated at the opposite end of *Disney Village*, and is barely a 10-minute

The lobby at Disney's Hotel New York

Princess for a day!

Young girls wishing to have the full princess touch should head for the *Disneyland Hotel* where, on the first floor landing, there is a special **'Princess for a day' parlour**, offering different packages of dresses and make-up and a range of accessories sure to please any princess-in-waiting! They start at €60 for Makeover No. 1 (hair, make-up, crown and photo), then there's the €130 Makeover No. 2 (adding dress and magic wand) and finally the Castle Package, Makeover No. 3 (with a feather boa, frame for picture and princess toy figurine), which costs €160. Girls 3 and above can choose from 3 hairstyles – Fairytale, Diva and Pop Princess – and a range of dresses and shoes.

stroll from the gates of the *Disneyland Park*, slightly less for the *Walt Disney Studios Park*.

While it may be a touch too formal for some tastes (mainly due to the conference aspect), *Disney's Hotel New York* does have an exciting feel, especially for young adults and teenagers, and is in a perfect situation looking over Lake Disney but still within an easy stroll of *Disney Village*.

Official rating ****; our rating €€€€, CCCCC.

Disney's Newport Bay Club

Keeping with the American theme, *Disney's Newport Bay Club* has a New England seaside resort feel, with the largest spread of rooms of any of the on-site hotels (or any hotel in Europe, come to that). It may not appeal quite so much to children (it has the most 'grown-up' style of all 6 hotels), but it is well equipped to cater for all the family.

The sheer size of the hotel (1,080 rooms, plus 13 suites) means the foyer can get terribly congested, especially during 9–10am when people are checking out.

Rooms and suites: There is a separate reception desk for the **Admiral's Floor**, which covers the lake side of the top 2 floors (giving wonderful views) and offers a more personal level of service, plus room service and a quieter, more relaxed atmosphere (quite a bonus when the hotel is full). The majority of the spacious, 2-room suites (55m²/592ft²) are at this level, too, with the unusual octagonal Honeymoon Suite (45m²/ 484ft²) being quite stunningly romantic. The main suites also feature some lovely

The pool at Disney's Hotel New York

© Disney

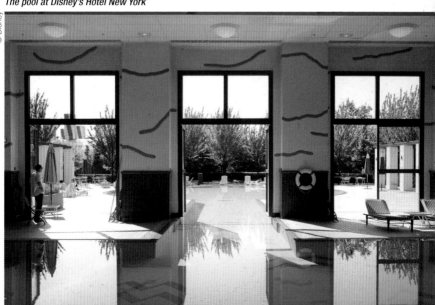

colonial-style furniture and extra nautical touches. Standard rooms (27m²/290ft²) continue the refreshing blue and white colour scheme of the rest of the hotel and all include mini-bars and room safes.

Dining and shopping: The 2 restaurants are semi-formal – the **Cape Cod** serves European cuisine with a touch of Mediterranean flair, while the similar **Yacht Club** specialises in fish, seafood and grilled meats (try the clam chowder for a true taste of New England), plus a handful of Asian-influenced dishes and a children's buffet. You are allocated either one for breakfast when you check in (if the hotel is full – if not, the Cape Cod is used on its own), but the breakfast offerings are the same in both. There are 2 fine bars – **Fisherman's Wharf**, which opens from the foyer and also offers a range of snacks during the day, and the more nautically themed **Captain's Quarters** piano bar – that both look out over Lake Disney. The large **Bay Boutique** offers a good selection of Disney merchandise and travel essentials.

Facilities: It has 2 excellent pools (a large one outdoors and an elaborate one, with a pirate ship centrepiece, inside), a jacuzzi, steam bath and fitness room, an outdoor play area, the

usual video games arcade and **Ariel's Lagoon**, a children's play area with organised activities on certain days. There is also a convention centre here, but the business aspect is less intrusive than at *Disney's Hotel New York*.

✚ BRITTIP

Hairdryers and irons are available free on request from the front desk at most Disney hotels, subject to availability and sometimes a deposit, except for the *Disneyland Hotel* and *Disney's Hotel New York*, where they are provided in the rooms. Some in *Disney's Newport Bay Club* and *Sequoia Lodge* will also have them.

Disney's Newport Bay Club is at the furthest end of Lake Disney, so it is a good 15-minute walk to the theme parks. But, on a pleasant morning, there is not a more delightful walk anywhere in the Ile de France.

Official rating ***; our rating €€€, CCCC.

Disney's Sequoia Lodge

If you like to be surrounded by gardens and greenery, head straight for *Disney's Sequoia Lodge*. Here you will be transported to one of the great American national parks. The main aspect of the hotel is a touch flat and monolithic but the interior and

Disney's Newport Bay Club pool

© Disney

Join the club!

The new **Empire State Club** at *Disney's Hotel New York* is a concierge-level option for guests that bestows some highly tempting privileges (like the Castle Club level at the *Disneyland Hotel* and Admiral's Floor at *Disney's Newport Bay Club*). The 34 top-floor rooms and suites all have their own specialist check-in, an exclusive lounge (with complimentary refreshments) and a buffet breakfast with characters every day. The rooms have also been refurbished in a more luxurious style, with upgraded amenities. More importantly, the Club gives all its guests a valuable **VIP FastPass** (see page 122) for the duration of stay, all for around £26–41 extra per person per day.

landscaping detail are breathtaking, with a fabulous use of stone and hundreds of imported trees and bushes for an authentic feel.

For the ideal warming winter retreat, the **Redwood Bar and Lounge** has a massive open fireplace and cosy furniture. The low, sloping, beamed ceiling and flagstone floor of the lobby set the scene for an outdoor adventure with all the comforts of a luxury resort (well above its 3-star rating, in our opinion). The judicious use of dark woods adds to the rugged feel and, when the weather is good, there is a lovely terrace overlooking Lake Disney where you can sit with a drink.

BRITTIP

Not sure of where to stay at Christmas? *Disney's Sequoia Lodge* is the perfect choice during the winter. It takes on an enchanted atmosphere with all the festive decorations.

Rooms and suites: The 1,011 rooms (including 16 suites) are split between the huge main building and 5 lodges spread throughout the gardens. Standard rooms (22m²/237ft²) have either a lakeside or gardens/car park view, large windows and a few extra themed touches like rocking chairs and rustic light fittings, which

combine well with the dark wood furniture and the dark bedspreads and curtains to provide that American backwoods ambience.

The cabin lodges offer exactly the same room space and facilities as the main building (Montana) rooms, apart from a mini-bar (so they are slightly cheaper). A lakeside view carries a supplement but is well worth while (and should be requested when you make your booking). The spacious 2-room suites (55m²/592ft²) all have a lake view, and the Honeymoon Suite features an open-plan arrangement with no door between the bedroom and living room.

Dining and shopping: *Disney's Sequoia Lodge* has 2 mouth-watering diners, the **Beaver Creek Tavern** and **Hunter's Grill**. The former is the more family-orientated option, with a varied menu to suit those with a big appetite and an outstanding dessert buffet. Within the restaurant is a kids' area with a TV showing Disney cartoons. The Hunter's Grill continues the hotel's outdoors theme in magnificent style, with a huntin', shootin', fishin' motif that boasts a feature kitchen serving up a fabulous international buffet option (€28/adults, €13/children). Neither restaurant is open for lunch.

Disney's Sequoia Lodge

© Disney

BRITTIP

Our suggestion for the Hunter's Grill at *Disney's Sequoia Lodge* is the Ranger's Rotisserie – a Yosemite Salad, followed by a marinated roast chicken thigh, a herb sausage and prime roast rump steak, sliced at your table, plus dessert. Outstanding!

The gift shop, **The Northwest Passage**, sells a standard range of toiletries, snacks, drinks and souvenirs.

Facilities: The **Little Prairie** is the kids' corner, with a TV and video, games station and an elaborate character photo area (available 5 days a week to either take your own snaps or use the official Disney photographer). There is the usual video games room, plus an outdoor play area, with slides and a sandpit, set among some beautiful gardens, full of unique (for Western Europe) foliage, a waterfall and even a mock beaver dam. Stroll the paths along the 'Rio Grande' and you come to the hotel's pool lodge, an indoor/outdoor facility that features a water-slide, freeform leisure pool (great for kids), large jacuzzi, sauna, steam room and gymnasium.

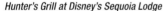
A room at Sequoia Lodge

At a first look, *Disney's Sequoia Lodge* may seem more of an adult environment, but children usually love the 'outdoorsy' feel. The great extras of the pool, gardens and play area make it an excellent family base but you may have trouble persuading the kids to leave when the characters are in residence! It takes 10–15 minutes to walk into the theme parks, or you can take the free 5-minute shuttle bus ride.

Official rating *; our rating €€€, CCCC½.**

Hunter's Grill at Disney's Sequoia Lodge

Disney's Hotel Cheyenne

Howdy partners, welcome to the Wild West – or Disney's version of it at least (safer and a lot more comfortable!). This imaginative hotel is usually a huge hit with children and is therefore a popular family choice (although it can be a little raucous at times when the kids re-enact Custer's Last Stand at regular intervals, armed with rifles and bows and arrows from the hotel shop!). The theming is comprehensive and convincing, from the wonderful period-style entrance lobby (complete with 2 striking bronze horse and rider statues) to the rooms and their rustic, kid-friendly bunk-beds. It is also quite extensive, as all the rooms are low-rise (no more than 2 storeys) to give the feel of a Wild West town.

The level of creature comforts is not quite the same as elsewhere – no swimming pool or air-conditioning, no luggage delivery to the rooms and only a self-service restaurant. But there are some significant extras aimed at the kids – optional pony rides, mechanical buffalos and 4-wheeled Surrey bikes (spring and summer, for a small fee) and a Fort Apache outdoor play area, plus the Nevada games room.

The lobby is themed like a Goldrush-era claims office, with a Land Claims desk instead of a reception area, a huge stone fireplace and a mock hotel entrance at the opposite end of the vaulted-ceiling foyer. The foyer has a kiddie corner (with organised colouring and drawing on certain days) that has mini-saddles instead of chairs! There's also a video games room.

Step out of the main building and you are in a true cowboy town, with raised, boarded sidewalks, dirt streets and blocks of hotel rooms all disguised as various buildings, such as the Guest House, Blacksmith and Sheriff's Office.

Rooms: The 14 blocks are each named after a famous character like Doc Holliday, Jesse James, Calamity Jane and Running Bear. Blocks 17–19 (they are actually numbered 10–25, omitting 13), Sitting Bull, Wyatt Earp and Billy The Kid are closest to the main building and the bus stop for the free shuttle to the theme parks and *Disney Village*. There are 1,000 identical rooms (all 21m²/226ft²) spread out through the 14 blocks, which have internal access only and most feature a double bed and 2 bunks.

The in-room theming is more limited here and the bathrooms slightly more spartan compared to the other resorts, but then it is designed for more budget-conscious visitors (no air-conditioning, just ceiling fans).

Dining and shopping: Western paraphernalia abounds and the cowboy theme continues into the bar and restaurant areas, with saloon-style doors, wooden tables, chairs, balustrades and ceiling beams. The **Red Garter Saloon** features live country music in the evening and has an outdoor terrace. The 750-seat **Chuck Wagon Café**, which also has its own **Saddle Bar** and wagon play area, is a cafeteria-style eaterie dressed up like a Texan pioneer marketplace. It serves a good mixture of international dishes, from barbecue-smoked chicken and beef to salads, pasta, risottos and fresh wok-fried Chinese specialities (set meal €22/adult and children's buffet €9.90). **The General Store** is the standard gift shop.

Disney's Hotel Cheyenne

© Disney

BRITTIP

If the bus queues are too long when you want to return to *Disney's Hotel Cheyenne*, take the short cut back in less than 10 minutes. Walk out past the train station, cross the bridge to the main road, turn right and you can enter the hotel's main gate (along a walkway) from the car park. You may need to show your hotel ID.

Facilities: As well as the kid-friendly options mentioned at the beginning, the 2 guest launderettes are free to use, although you need to buy washing powder from the General Store. Kettles can also be provided for in-room use with a small deposit.

The regular shuttle bus to the theme parks, *Disney Village* and RER station takes about 5 minutes (queues permitting) or you can walk it (in 15–20 minutes) along a scenic pathway by the Rio Grande river, under the main road and past *Disney's Hotel New York*.

Official rating **; our rating €€, CCC½.

Disney's Hotel Santa Fe

Right at the budget end of the 6-hotel spectrum is this extensive *pueblo-*style resort decked out in best American South West fashion, with Native American, Spanish and Mexican cultures providing the decorative motif, and a giant Clint Eastwood billboard (like a drive-in movie screen) welcoming you 'into

Disney's Hotel Santa Fe in summer

town'. In truth, this is a glorified motel, but that doesn't stop it being fun for kids, reasonable value for money and still well situated to enjoy all the Disney Magic. It gets extremely busy in high season (breakfast sittings are pre-allocated 7–10.30am) and is popular with coach operators, so it gets congested in the morning with large numbers of guests arriving and departing at the same time.

BRITTIP

You need to request a room with bunk-beds when booking at *Disney's Hotel Santa Fe* if that is what your children want (and which is usually a lot more comfortable for children aged 6 plus).

On first impressions, the hotel looks rather dreary with its collection of square, concrete blocks up to 5 storeys high, but the Imagineers have added a few fanciful touches, even if the original 'volcano' is now a derelict grey hulk. There are 4 'trails' through the resort (corresponding to the 4 different room sections – Artefacts, Water, Monuments and Legends), each with their own symbols and icons scattered around – from rusting desert 'vehicles' to outlandish meteorites, water trails, a geyser and even a crashed flying saucer! The smattering of desert scenery is also quite eye-catching.

The main facilities are in the reception building, while the 1,000 rooms are spread out over 41 blocks

A room at Disney's Hotel Santa Fe

© Disney

Disney's Hotel Santa Fe

surrounded by small car parks, so if you are driving, this is the only hotel where you can more or less park outside your room.

Rooms: The identical rooms (21m²/226ft²) are cheerfully decorated, if a little sparse by comparison with the other hotels, but many also come with bunk-beds instead of 2 double beds. As with all Disney accommodation, they can house a family of 4 (or 4 plus one in a cot), although they are a little short of drawer space. There is no in-room air-conditioning, just a ceiling fan.

However, from our most recent visit (summer 2009), we would have to say this is the one hotel in need of extensive refurbishment, with some of the rooms looking decidedly dog-eared and corridors dingy and uninviting.

BRITTIP

As at *Disney's Hotel Cheyenne*, breakfast at *Disney's Hotel Santa Fe* is of the most basic continental kind – cereal, croissants, pastries, juice, tea/coffee – but you can pay a supplement to add bacon, eggs and fresh fruit.

Dining and shopping: The 700-seat **La Cantina** serves up a Tex-Mex dinner buffet (6–10.30pm) in a food-court-style servery. You can make up your own meals (salads, tapas, fajitas, nachos, roast pork, chicken, beef, spaghetti and meatballs) or choose

one of the set meals (€20/adult and €9.90/child), and there is an ice-cream and coffee bar. Imaginative touches have food served from the back of a flat-bed truck and drinks dispensed from 'petrol pumps' – worth highlighting as so many people miss them in their rush to get to the parks. Next door to La Cantina is the **Rio Grande Bar**, with live entertainment and karaoke on certain evenings. **The Trading Post** is the Disney gift shop, with a good range of souvenirs, snacks, drinks and basic toiletries.

BRITTIP

The petrol station next door to Disney's Hotel Santa Fe is one of the few places on-site where you can buy fresh milk and other handy groceries.

Facilities: The children's corner, with organised colouring and drawing activities (in the evenings), is in La Cantina, with a computer console and Disney TV. A video games room is available for the kids, plus an outdoor playground, the Totem Circle, which is handy if they have any energy left at the end of the day! Back in the lobby, characters meet 'n' greet in the morning, which is the ideal way to start the day if you have young autograph hunters. The hotel is next to *Disney's Hotel Cheyenne*, so it is perfectly permissible to pop 'next door' to enjoy some of the facili ties there too, notably, the Fort Apache play area for kids, the pony rides and the Red Garter Saloon.

Disney's Hotel Santa Fe

© Disney

The hotel is a good 20- to 25-minute walk from the parks, but once again, if the weather is fine, it is a lovely way to start the day as you stroll alongside the 'Rio Grande' and up by *Disney's Hotel New York*, around Lake Disney and through *Disney Village*.

Alternatively, the shuttle bus takes about 10 minutes and, while there is usually quite a queue in the morning around the parks' opening times, they run several buses at once on this route (as they do at all the bigger hotels).

Official rating **; our rating €€, CCC.

Disney's Davy Crockett Ranch

If you drive down to *Disneyland Paris* and are happy to use your car to get to the theme parks every day, staying at *Disney's Davy Crockett Ranch* is the best value way to enjoy all the fun and still have a taste of Disney imagination in your accommodation. Here, in 'trapper country', are 535 cabins with 1 or 2 bedrooms accommodating up to 6, plus 60 caravan and camper van sites. The sites all have water supply and connections for electricity and water drainage, plus their own picnic bench and open-air barbecue.

Set in 57ha/140 acres of pretty woodland about a 15-minute drive from the theme parks (where parking is free with your resort ID card), you do get the feeling of being out in the

wilds (see map on page 94). The woods are dotted with imaginative touches such as Native American tepees, while all the main services and facilities are located in a wonderfully fun cowboy 'village' at the heart of the ranch, where you will find a host of great activities and amenities.

The site is completely secured against non-visitor traffic. You check in at the reception area at the main entrance, much as you would for a hotel, and they provide you with your keys, the all-important Disney resort ID cards and the security code to access the site, which you punch in at the gate just past reception. Then, when you depart, you just drop off the keys in a deposit box, so you need not go back into reception.

BRITTIP

The camping sites are particularly popular with the Brits and the Dutch. They sell out well in advance at peak season, so you need to book EARLY in summer.

Rooms: Eight circular 'trails' house all the accommodation. Each trail has its own take-away 'cottage', where breakfast is served (7–11am) for you to take back to your cabin, caravan or tent. The 1-bedroom cabins (all 36m²/388ft²) feature a spacious lounge with TV, a kitchen complete with 2 hot-plates, dishwasher, fridge, microwave, kettle, coffee machine and all the necessary cutlery, crockery and cooking utensils. There is also a breakfast bar area. The bathroom (fully stocked with towels) includes the toilet but the 2 are separate in the 2-bedroom cabins. Some have a pull-down double bed in the lounge, others a convertible sofa, while the bedroom has a double bed and 2 bunks. Many of the 1-bedroom cabins do look their age (more than 12 years old), hence it is a basic 2-star property. Outside, each has its own brick-built barbecue and picnic bench, plus parking.

Disney's Davy Crockett Ranch

© Disney

> **BRITTIP**
>
> The ranch's 60 2-bedroom cabins are all newer than the 1-bed ones, and come at a slight premium. They also go quickly (although more are due to be built), so it's best to book early.

The 2-bed cabins ($39m^2/420ft^2$) have the 2 bunk-beds in their own room, giving mum and dad a little privacy. The living quarters are arranged slightly differently and the general fixtures and fittings are a bit smarter. The difference in price is minimal, so these are the better option.

The caravan and camp sites are on Moccasin Trail (the others are named after similar cowboy icons – Wagon Wheel, Big Bear, Tomahawk, etc.) and you'll find toilets, showers and a launderette at the centre of this area. At peak times, a mini-train/tram runs around all the trails, ferrying guests between the accommodation units and village area.

Dining and shopping: The 'village' is actually a fully fledged resort in its own right, centred on the **Trading Post** and **Crockett's Tavern**, a log-cabin restaurant serving dinner plus a take-away service (but not lunch any more). The buffet-style servery offers up a good variety of dishes, from salad, fish and chips, roast chicken and pasta to entrecôte steak and even a vegetarian meal, while there is a choice of 4 kids' meals (€9.90). Across the street is the authentic (if rather small) **Saloon** (5pm–midnight) serving beer, wine and cocktails, with live entertainment and karaoke at peak times, plus outdoor seating and a large-screen TV in summer. The **Alamo Trading Post** is the gift shop and grocery store (8am–11pm).

Facilities: Bowie's Bike Barn, the information centre (8am–6pm, 8am–10pm seasonally), houses the children's activity corner, with a computer play station, video console and colouring sets for kids, all set up around a large table with clever mini-

saddles to sit on. Disney characters make an appearance every evening, while there is grown-up entertainment too, with themed evenings, line dancing and discos, plus organised sports, from jogging and aerobics to petanque and archery.

> **BRITTIP**
>
> It is advisable, especially in summer when the resort can hold around 4,000 people, to book a table for dinner at Crockett's Tavern. Lunch is rarely over-subscribed.

The **Lucky Raccoon** video games room adds that essential amenity for kids, and they are then spoiled for choice with the likes of horse and pony rides (4–11s only; €10), Davy's Farm (a petting zoo with reindeer, goats, sheep, rabbits, birds and ducks), an outdoor play and climbing area, table tennis, volleyball, basketball, archery and mini-golf (the latter for €7 for 9 holes). There are 2 free-to-use indoor tennis courts (one of which is used alternately for archery, table tennis and volleyball in winter) and a nature park with the Indian Meadows village and walking trails.

> **BRITTIP**
>
> The reindeer 'work' in Disney's Christmas Parade at the *Disneyland Park*, but they get 10 months off, which they spend at the ranch!

Tepees at Disney's Davy Crockett Ranch

© Disney

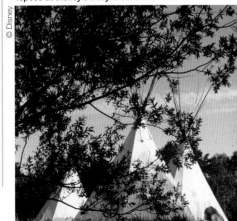

Off-site hotels

1 *Disney's Davy Crockett Ranch*
2 Hotel du Moulin de Paris
3 Hotel l'Elysée
4 Explorers Hotel
5 Vienna International Magic Circus Hotel
6 Hotel Kyriad at *Disneyland Paris*
7 Chanteloup Hotel
8 Best Western Marne-la-Vallée
9 Golf Hotel
10 Novotel Collégien
11 Tulip Inn
12 Adagio City Aparthotel Val d'Europe
13 Hotel Saphir
14 Hotel Abbaye du Golf
15 Hotel St Rémy
16 Vienna International Dream Castle Hotel
17 Marriott's Village d'Ile de France
18 Radisson Blu Hotel at *Disneyland Paris*
19 Camping Le Parc
20 Parc de la Colline
21 Kyriad Chelles
22 Comfort Inn Lagny-sur-Marne
23 Novotel Atria Marne-la-Vallée

= Autoroutes
= Major Roads
= Minor Roads
= RER
⑫ = Autoroute Junctions

Davy Crockett's Adventure

This is an adjacent public forest park with tree-top adventure trails for all ages from 8, for 3 hours of challenging tree-climbing, rope bridges, giant swings, obstacle courses and the feature Tarzan Tree Jump. Look up more on page 211 or (in French only) on **aventure-aventure.com**.

Cycling is another activity for children and adults, with a huge range of bikes and quadri-cycles (Surrey bikes) for hire at €20 for an hour, to be used on the cycle trails throughout the resort and woods. The final outstanding element of the resort is the **Blue Springs Pool**, an extensive indoor water park with a semi-circular paddling pool for toddlers, a large, free-form leisure pool that has a waterfall, long water-slide, fountains, squirt pond and a huge jacuzzi. You can rent towels for a small fee. Under-12s must be accompanied by an adult at all times in the pool area. It is an exceptional facility and you may struggle to get the kids out, even with the lure of the theme parks!

🇬🇧 BRITTIP

To call ANY of Disney's hotels, simply dial the main switchboard – 00 33 1 64 74 40 00 from the UK, or 01 64 74 40 00 in France – and ask for the hotel you require.

The parks and *Disney Village* are about a 15-minute drive from the ranch, which is about 3km/2mls off Exit 13 of the A4 autoroute. To get there, simply come out of the property, take the second exit from the roundabout (signposted A4 Reims) and continue along the A4 to Exit 14 for 'Les Parcs Disneyland'.

Official rating **; our rating €€, CCCC.

Beyond Disney

Once you move beyond Disney for your choice of accommodation, things become simpler. There are few grand theme hotels (the Magic Circus, Dream Castle and Explorers Hotel at Val de France are the only exceptions) and no great variation in style or facilities (almost all are 2- or 3-star). Rooms tend to be small but comfortable and the majority will provide a good, basic continental breakfast. We have toured the Seine-et-Marne region extensively to check the hotels on offer and have been impressed by the generally high standard of cleanliness and friendliness.

A lot of hotels in the immediate vicinity of Marne-la-Vallée are quite modern and pleasant, while all hotels are inspected regularly to ensure they conform to their star rating. Quite a few have swimming pools, but you need to decide if you are likely to use a pool after a long day at the parks to make it worthwhile paying extra.

We have subdivided the off-site hotels into those that are Near the Magic (including the new sub-region of Val de France), those that are a short drive away, and hotel chains that have accommodation in Paris itself (which is not necessarily a bad idea if you want to see a lot of the city, as it is only 35–40 minutes to *Disneyland Paris* by RER).

Disney's Hotel Cheyenne

© Disney

Near the Magic

When it comes to hotels that are within a figurative stone's throw of the theme parks, there are 9 contrasting choices in the Val d'Europe area. These include 4 hotels in an associated development just off the main ring road (which Disney refers to as its Selected Hotels). One of these, the Explorers Hotel, is primarily for the UK market, while all usually host a high percentage of British guests.

Adagio City Aparthotel Val d'Europe: Opened in 2003, this stylish apartment complex (part of the Pierre et Vacances chain) has a good array of flexible accommodation that makes it an ideal base for a longer stay in the region. With 290 apartments and studios, sleeping 2–7, this is a modern and well-furnished offering. All feature a fully equipped kitchenette (cooking hob, fridge, microwave and dishwasher), a living room and either a 1- or 2-bedroom option. The studios offer living/sleeping space for up to 3, while the largest apartments can sleep 3 in the living room and 4 in the 2 bedrooms. All have a bathroom and the larger ones have a shower room, too. There is no daily maid service, however, and linen service only every 7 days.

The resort-style set-up offers a launderette, indoor car park (€15 a day or €60 a week), luggage room, small gym and an outdoor heated swimming pool open May–Sep. A separate charge (on check-in) is made

Hotel l'Elysée

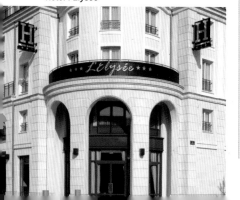

for TV, Wi-Fi and phone use and there is a €15 charge for its 'baby kit' (cot and high chair). A free continental breakfast is served daily in a corner of the big reception area, while it offers a full buffet breakfast at €9/adults and €5/children and a takeaway breakfast at €7.50 and €4. There is a free daily shuttle to the parks. 00 33 1 60 42 82 82 (in France) or 01 55 26 32 00 (UK only), **pv-holidays.com**.

Official rating *; our rating €€€, CC.**

Hotel l'Elysée: At the heart of the Val d'Europe development, and therefore just a 5-minute RER ride to the theme parks, this rather chic 3-star property opened in July 2002. The Hotel l'Elysée features a grand reception lobby and underground parking. It has an extremely quiet ambience, which is a nice contrast after the hurly-burly of the Disney parks. The 152 rooms all accommodate 4, in a double bed and 2 single sofa beds (made up ready for you), while there are 4 spacious junior suites and 5 rooms adapted for the disabled (2 persons maximum). The rooms all have a mini-bar and safe and the marbled bathrooms are extremely smart. Cots are available on request, but they can't add up to a fifth person. However, there are inter-connecting rooms for larger families.

The hotel has a left-luggage room, free shuttle service to the Disney theme parks, a video games room for kids, an elegant bar and a high-quality restaurant and bar, the new **Pop Art** (with a pleasant outdoor terrace in summer), while 24-hour room service is also available. Many packages here include park tickets and there is a daily free shuttle service to both the Disney parks and *Disney Village* a 10-minute drive away. An extra bonus is the fact the hotel benefits from the **Extra Magic Hours** programme, providing access to the *Disneyland Park* 2 hours before official opening time. The last train from Marne-la-Vallée back to Val d'Europe is at 12.12am each day if you need to use the RER line. 00 33 1 64 63 33 33, **hotelelysee.com**.

Official rating ***; our rating €€€€, CCC.

BRITTIP

Anyone visiting Val D'Europe for some shopping or a meal should consider dinner at the Hotel l'Elysée's **Pop Art restaurant**, where the French chef provides an excellent menu featuring local produce. Try the Chocolate Tower dessert!

Hotel Ibis Paris Marne La Vallée Val D'Europe: A recent addition to the smart, budget Ibis chain, this is right in the middle of Val D'Europe and just a short walk from the RER station. With 100 air-conditioned rooms (4 of them disabled accessible), it offers a budget choice in an ideal 'near the Magic' location. With a continental breakfast served 4am–noon you will not go hungry and the Ibis chain also feature 'anytime snacks,' available

24/7 from the bar or reception, just to make sure! The hotel is fully Wi-Fi accessible and, while the facilities are fairly simple – the Pasta Café restaurant (open 7–10.30pm, not weekends) and bar – it is hard to fault its eager-to-please attitude. It is just a 5-minute walk from the big Val D'Europe shopping centre, with its cafés and restaurants, and has its own car park. 00 33 1 60 36 20 06, **ibishotel.com**.

Official rating **; our rating €€€, CC.

Radisson Blu Hotel at Disneyland Paris: This smart property in the Radisson group stands right on the edge of the Golf Disneyland complex in Magny-le-Hongre (and has impressive views over the 3 9-hole courses). The hotel has 250 fully air-conditioned rooms, including 20 suites and 139 family rooms (with convertible sofa-beds) for up to 4 people, some of which are inter-connecting. All have flatscreen TVs and tea and coffee-making facilities.

Pamplemousse restaurant at the Radisson Blu

It is set up, to a large extent, as a convention hotel with excellent business facilities, so you can expect a busy but elegant style. But there is also plenty to attract the Disney holidaymaker. There are 2 restaurants – the casual Brasserie Birdie for breakfast and the gourmet dining of Pamplemousse Restaurant – as well as the Chardon bar (also serving snacks), a Play Club for children and a Wellness & Fitness Centre, including a swimming pool, fully equipped gym and a variety of treatment and massage rooms. Free Wi-Fi is available throughout the hotel. 00 33 1 60 43 64 00, **radissonblu.com/golf resort-paris**.

Official rating****; our rating €€€€, CCCC.

Val de France

This region consists solely of 4 neighbouring hotels that are well worth considering. Disney counts them as official partner hotels, tour operators call them 'Near the Magic' and they can be found just off the Boulevard de l'Europe, about a 10-minute drive from the Marne-la-Vallée station hub for drop-off to the theme parks and *Disney Village* (with a regular free shuttle bus service). It is possible to walk from here, but it takes a good half an hour.

Explorers Hotel: This highly imaginative 390-room hotel – one of the real highlights of this area – is run by tour operator Thomas Cook and is

Special suite at the Explorers Hotel

Explorers Hotel pool

used by a variety of UK companies, notably coach-tour specialists Leger Holidays. It is designed with British visitors in mind (some 70% of guests are usually from the UK), hence there are some smart touches for families. It was the first fully themed off-site hotel (followed by the Magic Circus and Dream Castle) and offers both extra-spacious rooms (with families of 6–10 in mind) and superb children's facilities, although only a handful of rooms have air-conditioning. It is much the same price to eat and drink here as in the parks or *Disney Village*, however, and its fine-dining restaurant can be a touch expensive.

> **BRITTIP**
>
> The shuttle bus serves all 4 Val de France hotels and runs every 15 minutes (5–10 minutes at park opening and closing times). It operates 6.30am–11.30pm Sept–Jun and 6.30am–1am Jul–Aug, and stops at each in turn (Explorers, Kyriad, Magic Circus, Dream Castle). This means the trip to and from the parks from the first stop can take a good 20 minutes at busy times.

Designed like a grand French manor – the preserve of mythical explorer Sir Archibald de Bacle (ouch!) and his various 'discoveries' – it is a fun and spacious creation, from the busy lobby area (complete with a Kids Corner with mini-cinema and 2 rides, plus a novel fountain) to the buffet-style restaurant with its outdoor terrace (wonderful on a sunny morning). Walk through the lobby and you have a great view over the **Tropical Atrium** at the heart of the hotel, which is also home to the Secret Lagoon Swimming Pool, a 20m/66ft heated indoor pool with a separate toddlers' area. The wreck of the Seven Seas Raider pirate ship is beached at one end of the lagoon, allowing kids the chance to explore the decks and passageways or take to the water-slide. A second, more elaborate, dragon-themed water-slide was added in 2005, making this guaranteed fun for kids of all ages. A new **mini-water park** was created for younger children, with smaller slides and water games, in 2008.

BRITTIP

Surprisingly, there is a €1 charge for a pool towel at the Explorers, so take your own towels. The pool also gets VERY busy in late afternoon.

The **Plantation Restaurant** is the main diner, a market-style emporium offering breakfast (7–10.30am) and dinner (6–10.30pm). The plentiful continental-style buffet breakfast offers a good selection for all the family (or you can choose a cooked breakfast for a few extra euros), while dinner is an elaborate all-you-can-eat buffet (salad bar, cooked meats, grills, fish, pasta, vegetables and rice) including soft drinks, at €21/adult (€28 with wine or beer) and €11/child. The salads and desserts are especially good.

BRITTIP

Like the Disney hotels, you are given a time-slot for breakfast each day. You collect these from reception when you check in and it is advisable to pick your times for your whole stay as the most popular ones go quickly.

For more informal dining there is **Marco's Pizza Parlour** where you can order a take-away if you prefer and **Traders Café Bar** for snacks and drinks (both 5–11pm). The **Brioche Dorée** café (5–11pm) offers an elevated view of the Atrium and the chance to sip a speciality tea or coffee and grab a pastry or sandwich. You will also find 3 **internet** terminals here (although there is free Wi-Fi in the rooms). The **Captain's Library** (6–10.30pm) is a themed full-service restaurant, once again offering children's meals, and with a small play area to keep them amused while mum and dad finish dinner. While it is a touch expensive for an off-site restaurant (featuring salads, chicken, salmon, mixed grills and mussels, with kids meals €6.70–12), the food here is outstanding for what is, in theory, a 3-star hotel. Finally, **Smugglers Tavern** (5pm–11pm, 1am in high season) is the hotel's main pub-style bar, with a corner given over to a large-screen TV for sports events. There are pool tables and dartboards, and snacks are available here too. It is highly popular most evenings (you might want to request a room in a different block to the Tavern if you are early-to-bed types).

Traders Café is also brilliantly designed for parents to be able to sit back and watch their offspring expend some energy in the activity areas. **Scally Wagg's Jungle Adventures** is the big indoor soft-play area (in 2 sections, for 2–4s and 5–12s), with all the requisite ladders, ropes, slides and ball pools, while the Seven Seas Raider is also nearby. Then there is a 2-part arcade/games room, a small children's 'fitness room' and Harry's Action Zone for older kids, with the usual (noisy!) video games.

Brioche Dorée Café

BRITTIP

The Explorers' room configurations are the most family-friendly of any hotel here. The use of the 'bunk cabins' and single beds (instead of 2 doubles) give them huge flexibility, especially with older children.

The room choice is definitely a cut above the usual accommodation. Standard rooms, called 'Crew rooms', feature a double bed and 2 singles, with a bath, shower and separate toilet (a useful idea), as well as interactive satellite TV with video games, pay-per-view programmes and films, room safe, hairdryer and ceiling fan (no air-conditioning), plus tea- and coffee-making facilities. Each Crew room can be connected to a 'bunk cabin' for 2 children. Extended families or groups of friends can take 2 interconnecting Crew rooms with the bunk cabin in between and sleep up to 10 (the bunk cabin doors can be closed).

There are 7 Captain's Suites sleeping up to 6 in 2 bedrooms, plus 3 imaginative Themed Suites (Planet Hollywood, Jungle and Sweets), which have superbly equipped kids' quarters (you may struggle to get your youngsters out of these!). All 10 suites have a lake view and air-conditioning for the hot summer months. An additional suite on the top floor is classified as an executive room, and features a plasma TV. Finally, 9 rooms are fitted out for guests with disabilities (arguably the best of their kind in the whole area).

Additional features include free parking at the hotel, the parks and *Disney Village*, picnic lunches (with 24 hours advance notice), currency exchange facilities, an outdoor kids' playground, a Disney store, a concierge and information desk. The Explorers is a non-smoking hotel, apart from areas such as Smugglers Tavern. The hotel is situated just across the resort-encircling Boulevard de l'Europe from *Disney's Hotel Santa Fe* and is the first of the 4 hotels of the Val de France district. 00 33 1 60 42 60 60, **explorershotel.com** (with some online discounts for booking direct).

Official rating ***; our rating €€€€, CCCC½.

Hotel Kyriad at *Disneyland Paris*: Next door to the Magic Circus is the flagship hotel of the budget Louvre Hotels group. With a lovely country house style, it is an excellent option for those who want to watch the pennies but still get a taste of the Magic. The 300 airy and spotlessly clean rooms are all air-conditioned, which is a bonus at this end of the scale, and come with tea- and coffee-making facilities, hairdryer and room safe.

The standard room features a double bed and 2 bunks, while the twin room can be either 2 singles or a double bed. No room can accommodate more than 4, but there are various connecting rooms, bringing the number up to 6 or 8. The rest of the hotel is equally straightforward, with one restaurant and 2 bars in a friendly, relaxing ambience. The small children's play area in the lobby can get quite crowded in the morning. Although it is French owned and run, up to 60% of guests can be British at peak times. The overall feel is fresh and cosmopolitan. 00 33 1 60 43 61 61, **envergure.fr/kyriadfr.html**.

Official rating **; our rating €€€, CC½.

The lobby at the Explorers Hotel

Sans Souci at the Dream Castle Hotel

Vienna International Magic Circus Hotel: If you prefer a more upmarket touch, look no further than one of our favourites in the Seine-et-Marne region (formerly the Holiday Inn and heavily renovated in 2009). Designed in French manorial style with an extensive and stylish circus-themed flavour, this is a cut above the usual tourist fare and scores high marks for families, too. It is also a rarity in being completely non-smoking. At once both chic and cheerful, the 396-room hotel comes as a refreshing change from the usual identikit styling, with bright, fresh colouring to go with the imaginative circus styling. It will appeal to all ages and boasts the extra service touches you would expect from a 4-star property, such as 24-hour room service, Wi-Fi and a business centre.

![BRITTIP] **BRITTIP**

Don't overlook the value of the Magic Circus and Dream Castle's Family Rooms and Kid Suites. They have bags of kiddie appeal and you may have difficulty getting your offspring out of the room because of 'their' area!

The Standard rooms (some interconnecting) feature a double bed; Family rooms have a curtained-off section (like a circus big top) with bunk-beds and a separate TV/games console for the kids; Kid Suites have children's areas built into them in a more elaborate fashion; and a handful of Executive rooms feature a more upmarket and businesslike touch. There are also 9 for disabled guests. All rooms come with a main TV with international channels and internet access, plus room safe, hairdryer and tea- and coffee-making facilities. Even the bathroom amenities (L'Occitane) are a cut above. They are also fully air-conditioned. The hotel offers a sophisticated indoor leisure pool (with toddler area), smart fitness club and an extensive outdoor playground in the park-like gardens for the young 'uns, where they can burn off any excess energy.

The main restaurant, **L'Etoile**, serves a pleasing mix of traditional French and international cuisine, while its buffet breakfast (7–11am, with an extensive array of cereals plus hot and cold

The garden at the Dream Castle Hotel

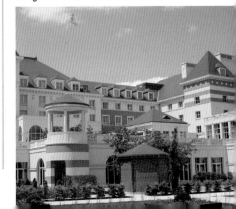

dishes) is possibly the best in the area – including Disney's hotels – and there is no pre-set time allocation either. A bistro-style lunch option was also added during the 2009 renovation. The inner courtyard features an adjoining terrace to the restaurant and, for breakfast, this makes a wonderful start to the day if the weather permits. There is the inevitable Disney Store and an excellent bar/lounge, **Bar des Artistes**, which also serves a good array of family-orientated snacks (salads, sandwiches, omelettes, baguettes) for lunch and dinner.

BRITTIP

If the parks are especially hectic or you just want a quiet break for lunch, head back to the Magic Circus and take advantage of its relaxed and friendly service in Bar des Artistes or the new Bistro.

The hotel has its own bureau de change, and the overall value for money here is top notch. As with the other hotels of Val de France, the VEA Navette airport shuttle for both airports calls 4 times a day and is available without reservation. 00 33 1 64 63 37 37, **magiccircus-hotel.com**.

Official rating ****; our rating €€€€, CCCC.

A room at the Dream Castle Hotel

Vienna International Dream Castle Hotel: This wonderful option opened in August 2004 and is now part of the Vienna International Hotels group, which specialises in independent hotels across Europe. Having stayed here several times, we have no hesitation in pronouncing it our favourite hotel in the area, and the addition in 2009 of the dramatic Royal Suite gives it an extra helping of upmarket style easily equal to any of Disney's grander touches. Next door to the Explorers Hotel and similarly on the free shuttle bus route to the parks, the 397-room property (250 family rooms, 43 'Double Queen' rooms, 76 'King' rooms, including 10 fitted for disabled guests, 27 Baron von Munchhausen and Rapunzel suites, and the Royal Suite, which sleeps up to 7 in regal fashion) exhibits a beautiful castle style, from the elegant lobby, complete with twin 'thrones', a sword-in-the-stone replica and suits of armour, to the well-fitted rooms (200 of which feature curtained-off bunk-beds – a great family touch). All rooms have tea- and coffee-making facilities, mini-fridge and wired internet. There is also a neat children's play area in the lobby, complete with ball pool, plus pool tables.

The restaurant choice is impressive, with the more standard offerings of **Sans Souci** augmented by the expansive style of **The Musketeers**, which features a spectacular themed buffet each evening (the desserts alone are worth stopping in for) at €29 per adult and €15 3–11s. There is also a charming outdoor terrace that makes a lovely setting for dinner on a summer evening. Both restaurants serve breakfast at busy periods, meaning there are no frustrating queues in the morning, as there are at some hotels. Its regular rate also includes a full American-style buffet breakfast (quite a rarity) and, as Vienna International sets great store by the quality of its cuisine, it is a real highlight. The fully themed **Excalibur Bar** (11am–midnight) is a great place

Our top tips

Having stayed at all the hotels at different times, we are happy to pass on our Top 10 of *Disneyland Paris* places to stay, based on what we feel is the best combination of quality, service and value for money.

1   Vienna International Dream Castle Hotel
2   The Explorers Hotel
3   *The Disneyland Hotel*
4   *Disney's Hotel New York*
5   Vienna International Magic Circus Hotel
6   *Disney's Sequoia Lodge*
7   *Disney's Newport Bay Club*
8   Hotel l'Elysée, Val D'Europe
9   Hotel Kyriad at *Disneyland Paris*
10 *Disney's Hotel Cheyenne*

We are fairly confident this selection will provide a pretty good experience, which is not to say others won't, just that these represent the best of the options at or near the parks. *Disney's Hotel Santa Fe* is overdue for a refurbishment while the Adagio City Aparthotel in Val D'Europe is a surprisingly good choice for larger groups (up to 7).

to enjoy a drink after a day in the parks and also serves light lunches and snacks.

BRITTIP

We rate the Excalibur Bar at the Dream Castle one of the most enjoyable places to relax with a drink or two, and at a good price – its alcohol tariff is almost a third less than bars in the *Disney Village.*

Other notable features of the Dream Castle include a fun swimming pool with a jacuzzi, smart fitness facilities, video arcade and a garden overlooking the lake, which backs on to the other hotels in Val de France. It also has an array of its own characters, or 'mascots', which seem to keep children entertained in the lobby and at mealtimes. The hotel boasts its own **Spa**, with sauna, steam bath, jacuzzi and solarium, with a range of Thai and Californian massages, manicures, epilation, facials and other beauty treatments – a blissful tonic after a day pounding the parks! 00 33 1 64 17 90 00 from the UK, **dreamcastle-hotel.com**.

Official rating ****; our rating €€€€–€€€€€, CCCC.

A short drive from the Magic

Hôtel Abbaye Du Golf: A little way to the south, in the older confines of the town of Lésigny, this 12th-century former monastery has been tastefully converted to hold 48 immaculate rooms and a wonderful restaurant. The hotel is right on the edge of a beautiful golf course yet it is still under half an hour's drive from the theme parks. It makes a great base for exploring some of the other villages in this area, but it is some way off the RER routes.

Family rooms offer an extra bed or bunks for children, and all feature satellite TV, Wi-Fi, mini-bar and hairdryer, while the superb traditional-style restaurant has a children's menu. To get there, take Exit 18 off the N104, then continue south on the Avenue des Hyveneaux and turn left after 1km/½ml at the signpost for Golf du Réveillon. 00 33 1 60 02 25 26 from the UK, **parisgolf hotel.com**.

Official rating ***; our rating €€€, CC½.

Disney's Once Upon A Dream parade

© Disney

Chanteloup Hotel: Tucked away in the pretty little village of Chanteloup-en-Brie, just to the west of Val d'Europe, is this small, family-run hotel. With just 64 small but smart rooms, each with a double bed and 2 fold-up bunks, plus a fitness centre, jacuzzi and sauna, this is an ideal retreat after a day of frenetic theme-parking. It has a pleasant restaurant and a little foyer bar, and that's about it for the creature comforts, although there is a daily shuttle bus to Disney for €9/adult and €6/child (must be reserved at reception). To reach the hotel, turn off the A4 at Exit 13 and take the D231 past Val d'Europe for 4.5km/3mls, then turn left into Chanteloup-en-Brie. 00 33 1 64 30 00 00, **chanteloup-hotel.fr**.

Official rating **; our rating €€€, CC.

Golf Hotel: On the other side of Bussy-St-Georges is this distinctly countrified hotel, with a genuinely welcoming aspect, set on the edge of a golf course and with obvious benefits for the sporting fraternity. However, you don't need to be a golfer to stay here. The 93 light, airy rooms cater for everyone, with double, triple, twin and family rooms, the latter with a double bed and 2 fold-down or fixed bunks. Mini-bars and hairdryers are standard, as is internet access, and there is plenty of storage space.

Novotel Collégien

The large restaurant has big picture windows and an outdoor terrace, while there is a children's play area to the side and a large green for kids to expend any remaining energy on. The outdoor heated pool is open May–mid-Sept, and there are 2 private tennis courts for hotel guests. There is a small lobby bar where you can have a quiet drink.

Given the surrounding greenery you could easily think you were a million miles from the hectic Disney whirl, but you are only 10–15 minutes' walk from the RER station or 5 minutes on its free shuttle bus (on request). To get to the hotel, take exit 11 off the A4 and follow signposts to Bussy-St-Georges, cross the Place du Clos-St-Georges, then turn right at Boulevard du Golf and the hotel is on the left. 00 33 1 64 66 30 30.

Official rating ***; our rating €€€, CCC.

Novotel Collégien: Slightly off the beaten track lies this smart hotel in the business-like Novotel chain (see page 110). Just south of the A4 and the town of Collégien, it is tucked away on a mini-industrial estate. It has some surprisingly family-friendly touches, with babysitting on request and an indoor play area. There is table football in the lobby, a heated outdoor pool (mid-Apr–end Sept) and an extremely pleasant bar and lounge area (open until midnight). Le Collegien Restaurant, serving French cuisine, is open midday–3pm and 7–10.30pm. The 195 rooms (with one floor designated non-smoking) are all brightly furnished and feature a double bed and a fold-out sofa that will sleep 2 (smallish) children. Each room has a mini-bar, Wi-Fi access and TV with English channels and pay-per-view films. There are 2 pairs of connecting rooms and 6 adapted for guests with disabilities. Usefully, the toilet is separate from the bathroom.

A busy convention hotel for much of the year, it is given over completely to the tourism business in July and at

Our top 10 places to enjoy a drink at Disneyland Paris

1   The Redwood Bar – *Disney's Sequoia Lodge*
2   The Excalibur Bar – Vienna International Dream Castle
3   Fantasia Bar – *Disneyland Hotel*
4   Billy Bob's Saloon – *Disney Village*
5   The Bar at The Steakhouse restaurant – *Disney Village*
6   Captain's Quarters Bar – *Disney's Newport Bay Club*
7   Sports Bar – *Disney Village*
8   City Bar – *Disney's Hotel New York*
9   Smugglers Tavern at the Explorers Hotel
10 Pop Art bar – Hotel l'Elysée

weekends. You can find it just past the junction of the A104 and A4; heading south (to Croissy-Beaubourg), turn left off the D471, straight over at the traffic lights and it is on the right. You really do need to have a car here as it is 3km/2mls from the nearest RER station. There is a free, secure parking area. 00 33 1 64 80 53 53, **novotel.com**.

Official rating ***; our rating €€€€, CCC.

Hotel St Rémy: Finally, a hotel to suit couples. This is a touch more detached and romantic than most, set in the picturesque hamlet of Ferrières-en-Brie, but only 7km/4mls from *Disneyland Paris*. Originally built in the 19th century, but tastefully restored and reopened in 2000, it has just 25 rooms (all en suite, with satellite TV and hairdryer) with some wonderfully elegant individual touches and style, wooden floors and antique furniture. Its fabulous restaurant offers a children's menu (not Sat lunchtime or Sun evening), but there is not a lot else to keep kids amused in this quiet location. A car is

advisable, although Bussy-St-Georges is only 2km/1ml away. The hotel can be found just off Exit 11 from the A4 – follow the signs to Ferrières-en-Brie and pick up the main Rue Jean Jaurés. 00 33 1 64 66 85 48 from the UK.

Official rating ***; our rating €€€, CC1½.

Hotel Saphir: This one-off property, just to the south in Pontault-Combault, has 179 exceedingly smart rooms for 2 to 4 people, with the family rooms consisting of a double bed plus a single or a double sofa bed. While not the prettiest of hotels, it maintains a high standard of interior decor and service. The heated indoor pool is an excellent (and rare) amenity, along with a sauna and fitness centre for an additional charge. The 2 restaurants (including the art deco Le Canadel) are both family-friendly and well priced, and there is a pleasant bar, l'Ecrin. Call 00 33 1 64 43 45 47 for more info or visit **saphir-hotel.fr**. It can be found just off the N104 travelling south at Exit 15, about 20 minutes' drive from *Disneyland Paris*.

Official rating ***; our rating €€€, CCC.

The Redwood Bar at Disney's Sequoia Lodge

© Disney

Tulip Inn: Opposite the RER station in Bussy-St-Georges (2 stops from Marne-la-Vallée) is this smart hotel. It has 87 non-smoking rooms, all with high-speed Wi-Fi connection and air-conditioning. The brightly decorated rooms come with a king-size or double bed, plus 2 singles for a family of 4. The hotel's facilities include restaurant L'Olivier for breakfast daily, lunch (midday–1.30pm, not weekends) and dinner (7–9pm), with French specialities, pizza and pasta, and the Cotton Bar for drinks and snacks in a relaxed setting. There is also a variety of shops and cafés within short walking distance. There is a fee for its car park. 00 33 1 64 66 11 11, **tulipinnmarne lavallee.com.**

Official rating *; our rating €€€, CC½.**

Camping

With the ease in which you can drive down to this region of France, it makes sense to look at camping options.

Camping Les Etangs Fleuris: This campsite near the village of Touquin (13km/8mls south of the town of Coulommiers) is worth highlighting in particular. It is a wonderfully rural and secluded site with 170 pitches and a host of clean, modern facilities, including an excellent pool (with a separate pool for children), a games room, bar and take-away, plus

Parc de la Colline

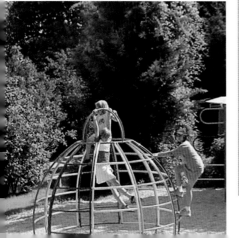

showers, toilets and a launderette. Its sporting activities include table tennis, mini-golf, petanque and fishing, plus horse-riding and nature walks nearby. The site also offers 2 types of 2-bed mobile homes, all well furnished and maintained. It is about 45 minutes from *Disneyland Paris* and an easy drive along the D231. Canvas Holidays packages the site with either a Channel crossing or flights to Beauvais or Charles de Gaulle, plus theme park tickets. 0845 268 0827, **canvasholidays.com.**

Camping Le Parc: Another site in the Seine-et-Marne region, this is 20km/12mls from *Disneyland Paris* in 10ha/25 acres of woodland just outside the town of Villevaudé to the north-east (near Meaux). With 330 tent, camper van and caravan pitches, prices start from €16.60/night for a 2-person tent without electricity but including shower use, €20 for a caravan pitch, €31 for a furnished tent and €45 for a mobile home. It has a bar-restaurant, TV room and facilities for volleyball, tennis and basketball. New in 2007 was Aquatic Park, with slides, lazy river and swimming lagoons, and there is a daily shuttle (for a fee) to Disney. 00 33 1 60 26 20 79, **campingleparc.fr.**

Parc de la Colline: Even closer, near Torcy to the west, this has a mixture of mobile homes and chalets for up to 7 people as well as campsites, all with electric hook-ups. It even has its own shuttle bus to the Torcy RER station at €7/adult and €3.50/child, and direct to *Disneyland Paris* at €16 and €8 (return). 00 33 1 60 05 42 32, **camping-de-la-colline.com.**

La Croix du Vieux Pont: For those looking to explore more of northern France, this popular and extremely well-appointed site at Berny-Rivière (near Soissons, about 80km/50mls north of *Disneyland Paris*) comes highly recommended. Set in 34ha/84 acres along the River Aisne, with 3 swimming pools, bar, restaurant and tennis court, plus a good range of

STAYING THERE

Holiday ownership

Inevitably, the explosion in hotel accommodation and tourist interest in the resort area has created the opportunity to 'buy' a piece of the holiday dream and there are several timeshare companies that would love you to sign on the dotted line. However, the only one we believe carries the right seal of approval is the extensive **Marriott's Village d'Ile de France** property, less than 2km/1ml from *Disneyland Paris* in the village of Bailly-Romainvilliers. It opened in 2003 and consists of 190 2- and 3-bed townhouses with around 117m2/1,260ft2 of living space and full air-conditioning. The Marriott Vacation Club has genuine international bona fides and strong Disney ties, so you can be sure of getting a quality product, with excellent back-up at a good price.

The Village has access to 3 nearby 18-hole golf courses, plus its own impressive array of facilities, including 2 swimming pools (one indoor lap pool and one outdoors), children's pool, whirlpool, health club (featuring a gym and aerobics room, sauna and steam room), children's facilities (games room, activity centre and outdoor playground), a bar/restaurant featuring local cuisine, a lobby lounge and a convenience store and deli (the Market Place, with a full array of fresh produce, wines and spirits, plus other essentials and even branded apparel). There is also 24-hour security and full reception services, and a regular shuttle bus to the parks.

The 2-storey townhouses offer some of the most upmarket accommodation in the region, with a king-size bed in the main bedroom, fully equipped kitchen (including microwave and dishwasher), spacious living room (with satellite colour TV, DVD player and stereo), utility room with washer/dryer, an individual terrace and TV in each bedroom.

With Marriott Vacation Club, you purchase weeks within a particular season and you are free to reserve weeks within that season. You may change dates within your purchased time period from year to year (and there are then more than 50 Vacation Club resorts worldwide you can exchange weeks for). 020 3027 3891 from the UK, 00 33 1 60 42 90 00 in France, **marriottvacationclub.co.uk**.

mobile homes and pitches, as well as facilities for the disabled, it is featured by British tour operators such as Haven, Keycamp and Canvas Holidays. 00 33 3 23 55 50 02, **la-croix-du-vieux-pont.com**.

Gîtes and Clévacances

Two other notable local forms of accommodation are the individual B&B style of the Gîtes de France, with more than 200 *gîtes* and 132 guest rooms in the Seine-et-Marne region, and the newer Clévacances, or town centre holiday homes.

Gîtes de France: Generally speaking, the village style offers charming, rural tastes of the local area and its people, with anything from 2 to 10 rooms available to guests who enjoy becoming 'part of the family'. With so many to choose from throughout France they have become a mini-industry and you can obtain a full

guide to the area's *gîtes* from the Comité Departemental du Tourisme de Seine-et-Marne at 11 Rue Royale, 77300 Fontainebleau, France, 00 33 1 60 39 60 39, **tourisme77.fr**. Log on to **gites-seine-et-marne.com** for more info about *gîtes*.

Marriott's Vacation Club

Clévacances: These are apartments, flats or suburban detached houses to let when not in use by their owners – from fully furnished weekly rentals to guest rooms. Prices are about €300–500/week and they can be found throughout the Seine-et-Marne region, many very close to *Disneyland Paris*. Reservations are usually handled directly with the owners and they are categorised for comfort by a number of 'keys' from 1 to 5. To get a free booklet or request more information, contact Clévacances Seine-et-Marne, 11 Rue Royale, 77300 Fontainebleau, France, 00 33 1 60 39 60 39, **clevacances.com/UK**.

Hotel chains

Several French hotel chains offer good, cheap, basic accommodation for those on a budget both in Paris itself and the Marne-la-Vallée area. Most are in the 1- and 2-star categories but a few offer a greater level of creature comforts.

Formule 1: This is a basic, motel-type chain that keeps things pretty much cheap and cheerful (okay, forget about the cheerful bit). Built in boxy, prefab units, they are accommodation only (apart from a basic continental breakfast,

Formule 1

€3.70/person) but they are almost invariably the cheapest in any location, with 67 in the Ile de France region. They are surprisingly high-tech, with automated check-in and clean, functional but small rooms. However, rooms do not have a shower or WC, just a washbasin. Instead, there are communal facilities on each floor. Part of the huge Accor hotel group, this is not the ideal place for families because their service is so limited (and most rooms sleep only 3) but for couples on a strict budget, they might be worth considering. 00 33 892 685 685, **hotelformule1.com**.

Our rating €, C.

Etap: Similar to Formule 1 (and with 83 hotels in the region), but better, with an in-room shower and WC. Their 'new generation' rooms are quite chic, if still fairly basic, but they include Wi-Fi and an unlimited breakfast buffet. Rooms still accommodate only 3 at most. Non-smoking rooms are also available. 0871 702 9469 in the UK, **etaphotel.com**.

Our rating €, C.

Campanile: Another motel-style group. They don't have meals or bar service, although there is usually a restaurant attached to the property. Again, they are all pretty uniform and stylised but are ideal for those on a budget, offer plenty of rooms for guests with disabilities and usually serve a great buffet breakfast. The rooms are small but clean and comfortable. Part of the Louvre Hotels group, they rate officially as 2-star in France but provide a few more thoughtful touches, such as in-room tea- and coffee-making facilities and Wi-Fi, making them a worthwhile choice. Rooms usually sleep only 3 and you need to reserve a child's fold-out bed in advance. Breakfast is around €5/person at the associated restaurant and there are children's menus, too. 0033 1 64 62 59 70, **campanile.fr**.

Our rating €, CC.

Kyriad: There are a lot more variations within this generally 2-star chain (also part of Louvre Hotels and a half-step up from Campanile) but it is still a basic family-orientated hotel. They have decent rooms that comfortably sleep 3 and some that accommodate 4 (1 double bed, 2 singles). Some hotels include mini-bars and hairdryers and provide pleasant individual touches such as a welcome snack tray and Wi-Fi. Their excellent-value restaurants all have children's menus. 00 33 1 64 62 59 70 from the UK, **kyriad.com**.

Our rating €–€€, **CC.**

The Hotel Kyriad at *Disneyland Paris* has already been noted (see page 100), but another to look out for is the **Kyriad Chelles**, a friendly 2-star property in the town of Chelles just 20 minutes' drive from the theme parks (00 33 1 60 08 54 27). The **Kyriad Prestige** version adds more upmarket touches like fitness facilities and sauna, larger, air-conditioned rooms and the signature La Rose des Vents restaurant. **kyriadprestige.com**.

Our rating €€, **CCC.**

Comfort Inn: A similar quality and style to the Kyriad and Campanile chains, the Comfort Inn hotels (part of the Choice Hotels International group) are mainly found in central Paris and offer an excellent-value selection. Their city location means there is quite a difference in the style of each property but the basic standard remains sound. 0800 44 44 44 in the UK, 0800 91 24 24 in France, **choicehotels.com**.

Our rating €€, **CC.**

There are some 36 Paris Comfort Inns, with the closest to *Disneyland Paris* being the 56-room **Comfort Inn Lagny-sur-Marne**, a good 15 minutes away. However, it is still a good choice, easily accessed via the A104 and A4. Lunch and dinner are available Mon–Fri at the on-site Casa Flavio, with drinks at the hotel bar. Babysitting, car hire service and guest laundry are available for an additional fee. There are also rooms for the disabled. 00 33 1 64 30 44 88 from the UK. The Choice Hotels group also has 38 of its more upmarket **Quality Hotel** properties in the Paris area, with an official 3-star rating and some elegant touches.

Ibis: A more upmarket 2-star choice (in the Accor group), this chain is functionally comfortable in general, with standard rooms (international satellite TV is a bonus, as is in-room internet connection) that sleep 3 (with an extra fold-out bed) and compact bathrooms. All have a restaurant, bar and snacks available 24 hours a day (part of their commitment to a more personal service), with an outstanding self-service breakfast buffet from 6.30–10am and a drinks and pastries service 4–6am and 10am–noon. The restaurant choice varies from hotel to hotel. There are 46 Ibis hotels in the Paris region, including 4 in Marne-la-Vallée (see also page 97). 0892 68 66 86 in the UK, **ibishotel.com**.

Our rating €€–€€€, **CC.**

Mercure: This member of the Accor group has a 2-tier quality system, the basic 3-star Hotel Mercure and the more distinctive MGallery, with enhanced levels of service and comfort. Most rooms accommodate 3, with some family rooms for 4, all have mini-bars and hairdryers. Non-smoking and rooms for the disabled

Mercure Marne-la-Vallée

are also available. They also specialise in weekend breaks, and most of their 41 hotels are in central Paris, with the 192-room **Mercure Noisy Le Grand** (free parking, non-smoking rooms, Wi-Fi and a nice restaurant, Les Meteors, open for dinner Mon–Fri) the nearest to D*isneyland Paris*. 0870 609 0965 in the UK, **mercure.com**.

Our rating €€€–€€€€, CCC.

Novotel: More of a business hotel in the past (and another member of the Accor group), they are increasingly looking to attract a family market, with 'Kids Eat Free' deals and other special offers from time to time, Also full of mod cons to suit tourist tastes, this modern chain offers fresh, spacious and comfortable rooms (sleeping up to 4), chic restaurants and bars, and extras like satellite TV, Wi-Fi, mini-bars and room service. Most feature outdoor swimming pools (although they close from early autumn to the end of spring) and

Sofitel Paris

conference/meeting facilities. While they can be busy during the week, they often offer great weekend breaks when they are quieter. 0870 609 0962 in the UK, **novotel.com**.

Our rating €€€€, **CCC.**

In addition to the Novotel Collégien (see page 104), look out for the large **Novotel Marne-la-Vallée Noisy**, in Noisy Le Grand, just 11km/6¾mls from *Disneyland Paris*. It features 144 rooms (112 non-smoking and 5 disable-accessible), a smart bar-restaurant, Wi-Fi and a nice heated outdoor swimming pool in the summer. 00 33 1 48 15 60 60.

Sofitel: The premium brand in the Accor group, each hotel is an individual, but all with a deluxe style in both the sumptuous rooms and the excellent restaurants, with the latter featuring some of the best cuisine in Paris. The full range of mod cons and facilities are accompanied by efficient, courteous service. However, the handful of Sofitel hotels (6 of them) in the Ile de France are either in central Paris, Versailles or by Charles de Gaulle Airport, hence their price reflects their location and upmarket nature. 0870 609 0964 in the UK, **sofitel.com**.

Our rating €€€€€, **CCCC.**

Well, that's about all the essential accommodation info you need for now. Having dealt with the preliminaries, it is finally time to … hit the theme parks!

5 **Welcome to the Parks**

or Here's Where the Fun Really Starts!

Okay, it's finally time to deal with the main business of being in *Disneyland Paris* – the theme parks themselves. There is a lot to take on board – the *Disneyland Park* alone boasts some 48 attractions on its 57 ha/ 140 acres, and there is something for all tastes and ages. The *Walt Disney Studios Park* adds even more and has also begun to fill the gap for younger visitors, adding 3 new child-friendly attractions in 2010.

In all, there is at least 3 days' worth of pure adventure-mania spread between the parks, and you need to have a pretty good idea of what's in store to get the most out of it and ensure you don't waste too much energy in the process! It is easy to get sidetracked by some of the clever details or minor attractions and miss out on some big-time thrills, while

equally, there is a genuine treasure trove of small-scale Disneyana that it would be sad to overlook. Therefore, the following chapters will provide all you need to know to draw up your own plan of campaign for visiting each one.

If you have never visited a Disney theme park before, it is probably fair to start by reminding you this is NOT a comparable experience to a day at any other European park. That is not to denigrate the likes of Alton Towers (which is pretty sizeable), Thorpe Park or Chessington World of Adventures. All possess some wonderful rides and offer good value for money. It is just that Disney builds and creates with a detail and a sense of wonder and fantasy no one else can match.

You enter a truly magical world when you pass through the gates reading 'Parc Disneyland' in 1m/3ft high lettering. For the duration of your stay, you will be beguiled by a realm

Main Street vehicles

that offers the most enchanting and thrilling range of attractions on earth.

Anyone who has already been to the parks in Orlando or California will have a good idea of what to expect. However, while the *Disneyland Park* bears a strong resemblance to both, a lot of the essential detail and many of the attractions are different. When the Walt Disney Company set out to build this new European resort experience, it wanted to update, enhance and improve, go back to the Imagineering drawing board if you like, cherry-picking the best features of its parks and re-inventing them in a dramatic new setting.

The Paris version is, to our eyes, a more refined and artistic interpretation. The Imagineers were well aware they were building for a European market and have tried to tailor their designs in a less overtly American way, even though much of the fundamental magic inherent in the parks is quintessentially American. But, there is also a greater awareness of Disney's European heritage (Walt Disney himself spent a good deal of time in France as a young man and his family traced its lineage back to French antecedents) and of the need to tell the stories in a way that makes sense to an audience consisting primarily of French,

© Disney

Peter Pan's Flight

British, Germans, Dutch, Belgians, Spanish and Italians (and they are never just plain 'rides' in a Disney park – everything has to tell a story and add to the theme).

Therefore, the multi-lingual nature of the resort is a key component to the overall feel and style of what's in store. Some of the design influences of the various nations are also evident in the theme parks themselves (the Sleeping Beauty Castle in the *Disneyland Park* is partly modelled on stunning Mont St Michel in Normandy, for example).

BRITTIP

It pays to arrive a little early for the opening time at each park to put yourself in front of the crowds for the first couple of hours and enjoy some of the rides that attract serious queues later on.

St Patrick's Day Parade

© Disney

What's new in the Parks

Disney constantly looks at new ways to engage repeat visitors and provide additional experiences, so there is a constant flow of live entertainment and other changes, updates and refurbishments. In 2009, the Resort celebrated **Mickey's Magical Party**, a year-long (to Mar 2010) festival that added an extra layer of gloss and excitement (as well as being an additional marketing 'hook' that all Disney parks seem to need these days).The annual celebration introduced several new live street entertainments to the *Disneyland Park* (notably **Minnie's Party Train**), some of which will be retained for 2010.

The *Walt Disney Studios Park* debuted the **Playhouse Disney Live on Stage!** show and the daily **Disney's Stars 'n' Cars Parade** that added even more fun and style to this rapidly evolving park. And, in 2010, there will be even more to look forward to, as it unveils the **New Generation Festival**, another annual cavalcade of character interaction and novel live entertainment (from Apr 2010 to 2011). The theme allows Disney to build the Festival around the 'New Generation' of Pixar characters like The Incredibles and Remy (from *Ratatouille*), plus Princess Tiana and Prince Naveen from the 2009 film *The Princess and the Frog*. All will be added to the daily **Disney's Once Upon A Dream Parade** at the *Disneyland Park*, while the **Disney's All Star Express** train will run along Main Street USA several times a day and a revamped *It's Party Time* show will become the new nightly finale on the Central Plaza stage (built for Mickey's Magical Party).

The big development is reserved for *Walt Disney Studios Park*, where a whole new area is being added to the Toon Studio. **Toy Story Playland** will be an interactive array of fun, games and rides aimed primarily at children, an immersive playground themed like a toy 'garden' where the likes of the Green Army Men, the Barrel of Monkeys and Slinky Dog (from the *Toy Story* films and coinciding with the summer 2010 release of *Toy Story 3)* are having some impromptu fun. There will be a junior-sized play area, with all things crawl- and climbable, and plenty of clever visuals, but the main attractions will be 3 new kiddie rides. **Slinky Dog** will be a gentle circular whirl in the company of the toy pooch; **Toy Soldiers Parachute Drop** is an exciting tower ride 25m/82ft high; and **RC Racer** adds some more thrills for older children with a 35m/114ft high back-and-forth rockin' ride. It should all add up to a major expansion for the Studios and a lot more kiddie appeal to boot!

The language challenge

The need to think in several languages provided the Imagineers with additional challenges, demanding subtitles, translations and extra soundtracks. While this adds a unique feel to familiar attractions ('it's a small world' or The Adventures of Snow White, for example), it does irk a small minority of English-speaking visitors – although we have yet to meet any children who didn't enjoy Pinocchio's Fantastic Journey simply because the commentary happened to be in French!

In our view, we always need to remember we Brits are the visitors, and it pays to try to remember those few words of French we learned at school. At the end of the day, the resort is trying to appeal to the widest possible audience and, by and large, it succeeds with extraordinarily cosmopolitan ability.

Adventureland entrance

© Disney

© Disney

Eating at Annette's Diner in Disney Village

Set menus

A point worth highlighting for anyone unfamiliar with French restaurant culture is the usual provision of a fixed-price menu (*prix fixe*) alongside the à la carte choice. Even at the standard counter-service burger-and-chips type diners, there is a set menu, usually consisting of a main course (burger, salad, pizza or pasta), a choice of dessert and a soft drink. At the full-service restaurants, the cheaper the set menu (starter, main course and dessert), the more limited the choice.

Children love meeting the characters

© Disney

BRITTIP

If you fancy a beer at one of the counter-service restaurants around the theme parks, the best value is to choose the set meal option with beer instead of soft drink and you pay just €1 extra.

For each park, we provide an At-A-Glance guide (on pages 126 and 166) that gives you some idea of what to expect to pay for food and souvenirs. Costs can quickly mount up if you buy numerous snacks – a small mineral water costs €2.50, a 25cl beer is €3.60, soft drinks variously €2, €2.60 and €3.40, 3 mini-doughnuts are €2.55 and a large portion of chips is €2.75. Kids' meals, which consist of a main course, such as chicken nuggets or pizza, chips, a small drink and a 'surprise' toy, are all €6. So you should be able to work out the kind of real cost you are looking at for a day in the theme parks (you can check the latest exchange rate at **xe.com**).

Many outlets can provide something for the veggie appetite as the full-service restaurants all offer at least one vegetarian main course and good salads are not hard to find. They will also do their best to accommodate requests from guests who have particular dietary requirements; don't

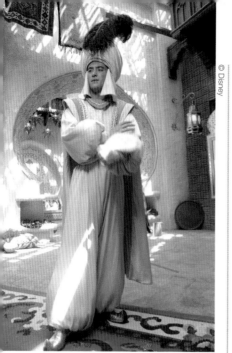

Meet Aladdin in Adventureland

Character dining

Whether you are travelling as a family, a couple or on your own, some of the most magical memories can be made when you have a meal with Mickey and Co. Meeting the characters in a more intimate setting, with no long queues to navigate, is a real treat, with one-on-one interaction that is second to none. Watching Pluto colour with the children, seeing dad's reaction when Cinderella passes by or capturing Prince Charming kissing mum's hand are moments to be treasured for a lifetime.

Characters circulate inside the restaurant, stopping at each table for play time and family photos. The amount of time available to each group is dependent upon how busy the restaurant is (so book off-hours, when things are quieter). Don't forget to bring your autograph book and a fat pen, which is easier for the characters to hold. Some children may initially be put off by the size of some characters (who appear huge to little guests!), so you may want to see how your children react to them in the parks (from a 'safe' distance) before booking a meal.

be afraid to ask. Unlike the versions of the *Magic Kingdom Park* in America, this resort does serve alcohol, but it is not cheap. A beer in one of the full-service restaurants is usually €4.50–7, while a bottle of wine can vary from €16 to €60.

Disney has also moved to make some of its food offerings – especially kids' meals – a touch healthier by introducing more vegetables and fruit. Ask for these options when you order.

Character meals can be booked as an add-on option to your package, when booking a room at a Disney resort, at City Hall or Studios Services or by

Passage Enchanté d'Aladdin

calling the Reservation Hotline (from the UK) 00 33 1 60 30 40 50.

Meals with the characters

Disneyland Park: The Lucky Nugget Saloon (usually with some characters from the following list: Chip 'n' Dale, Pluto, Goofy, Captain Hook, Tigger and Pinocchio): lunch (noon–3pm) or dinner (6.30–10pm, when park is open until 11pm, not available 31 Dec), both feature a buffet with international specialities, including starters, main courses and desserts; children have a special buffet with a drink and a surprise toy (€31 adults, €15 3–11s). Single Half Board Meal vouchers accepted as payment at this location only. At tea time (usually 3–4.30pm), Lucky Nugget hosts the *Tea Party with Disney Characters* (usually with characters selected from Robin Hood, Minnie Mouse, Chip 'n' Dale, Donald and Daisy Duck and Tigger) with a buffet selection of pastries, cakes, cookies, brownies, muffins, chocolate mousse and hot and cold drinks. Held every day, time confirmed upon booking (€14/person, under-3s free). Celebrating a special day? Add the *Happy Birthday with Disney Characters* buffet (pastries and sweets, a slice of chocolate cake, plus a surprise present, a name badge and

The Steakhouse in Disney Village

a birthday card) to your Tea Party booking for an extra €5/person. Take note, the **Plaza Gardens Restaurant** occasionally hosts the Tea Party with Disney Characters, so be sure to confirm location when you book.

Auberge de Cendrillon (with Disney Princes and Princesses, plus Suzy and Perla, Cinderella's mice) offers a set-price lunch or dinner featuring a cocktail and wine for adults (soft drinks for children), starter, main course and Cinderella Slipper dessert at €49 adult, €20 3–11s.

Disney Village: Character Breakfast at either **Café Mickey** or **The Steakhouse** (location varies; characters will include at least 4 of the following: Mickey, Minnie, Goofy, Pluto, Captain Hook, Tigger and Eeyore). Breakfast buffet of breads,

Chip 'n' Dale are regulars at Disney meals

Top 10 attractions

Here, purely for fun, is what we rate as our top 10 attractions, first for the *Disneyland Park*:

1 Pirates of the Caribbean

2 Space Mountain: Mission 2

3 Big Thunder Mountain

4 Phantom Manor

5 Indiana Jones and the Temple of Peril

6 Disney's Fantillusion Parade

7 Disney's Once Upon A Dream Parade

8 Star Tours

9 The Enchanted Fireworks (summer only)

10 Buzz Lightyear's Laser Blast

And for *Walt Disney Studios Park*:

1 The Twilight Zone Tower of Terror

2 CinéMagique

3 Moteurs…Action! Stunt Show Spectacular

4 Rock 'n' Roller Coaster starring Aerosmith

5 Crush's Coaster

6 Disney's Stars 'n' Cars Parade

7 Armageddon: Special Effects

8 Animagique

9 Studio Tram Tour

10 Stitch Live

cereals, scrambled eggs, pastries, fruit juice and hot drinks; sittings at 7.30am and 9.30am (€18 adult, €12 3–11s if you are staying at a Disney hotel – except *Disneyland Hotel*; €23 and €15 if you are staying at a non-Disney hotel – guests at Hotel l'Elysée, Pierre & Vacances Val d'Europe and Radisson SAS Hotel, second sitting only). **Café Mickey** also serves lunch and dinner continuously from noon–11pm, with the same line-up of characters present 12.15–3pm and 6–10pm. With the characters here most of the day, you will usually benefit from some of the best character interaction at Café Mickey, which the kids will love.

Disneyland Hotel: Inventions Restaurant has a character breakfast featuring selected characters from Mickey, Minnie, Goofy, Pluto, Tigger and Pinocchio – exclusively for *Disneyland Hotel* guests. But the character dinner (with some of Minnie, Mickey, Goofy, Pluto, Chip 'n' Dale and Eeyore) at the excellent Inventions buffet restaurant is open to the public. Breakfast is a buffet with breads, hot meats, scrambled eggs, baked beans, potato, fruit and yoghurts, plus hot and cold drinks. Dinner buffet includes seafood, cold meats, salads, carved roast, desserts and more (€47 adult, €24 7–11s, €18 3–6s). Arrive at Inventions early for dinner and you will benefit from some of the best character interaction, as it is seldom busy early on.

Ticket types

Moving along to more practical matters, you need to work out what type of ticket you should buy to make the most of your stay.

Park Hopper tickets: These are usually included with most packages that provide your accommodation, for the length of your stay (almost always with the Disney resorts, and with many of the non-Disney hotels

Fun awaits at Buzz Lightyear's Laser Blast

© Disney

nearby). That means you can enjoy both parks from the minute you arrive until the time you leave. It obviously provides the peace of mind and convenience of knowing you do not need to worry about the logistics of which park to visit when, as you can hop between parks at any time. However, there is a range of ticket types, including annual ones, which are worth considering if you are staying off-site or visit regularly.

1-Day Ticket: This provides admission to either the *Disneyland Park* or the *Walt Disney Studios Park* for a full day's fun (up to 11pm at peak periods). You may exit and re-enter the same park as many times as you wish throughout the day.

1/2/3-Day Park Hopper: This great-value ticket provides 1, 2 or 3 full days at the 2 parks, offering total freedom of movement between them on each day. The days do NOT need to be consecutive, which is invaluable if you are staying off-site and visiting other attractions over, say, a week. Park Hopper tickets are also valid for a year from the date of purchase (but not if they are part of a package).

Fantasy Annual Passport: This provides entry to both parks, plus some useful extras like free parking, a free annual magazine, access to the official website with special offers and invites to special occasions (like new attraction previews), plus 25% off

Café Mickey

special event tickets (such as the Halloween party), 10% off at Disney restaurants and shops and 15% off tickets for Buffalo Bill's Wild West Show. However, there ARE blackout days at both parks when the Passport is not valid for admission. In 2010 they are 22 Mar, 6–12 Apr, 1, 8, 10 May, 10–14, 29, 30 Aug, 25–30 Oct and 26–30 Dec. For 2011 dates, check out this website **http://idfoffres.disneyland paris.fr/passeport-annuel/index.xhtml** (for some reason it gives the information in French only).

✠ BRITTIP

You can save money if you are tempted to buy an Annual Passport after a visit to the theme parks, as the cost of a single day will be deducted from the cost of the Annual Passport. Visit the Annual Passport office at either theme park before you leave.

Dream Annual Passport: This version offers unlimited year-round access to both parks, access to Fantasyland in the *Disneyland Park* an hour before official opening and preferential rates on Disney hotel rooms at certain times, plus a number of exclusive advantages, discounts and events especially organised for Dream Passport holders. The bonuses include 20% off in most shops, 10% off in restaurants and bars throughout the resort, 15% off tickets for Buffalo Bill's Wild West Show, 50% off Disney's Halloween Party Night, free aperitif at table-service restaurants, free admission to

Hurricanes

© Disney

McDonald's at Disney Village

Hurricanes nightclub in *Disney Village* for the passport holder and one guest, 50% off special event tickets, free parking for the theme parks or *Disney Village*, free pushchair and wheelchair hire in the theme parks, free luggage storage, free annual magazine, priority information and reservation hotline, access to the official website with special offers and info and invitations to special occasions at the resort.

BRITTIP

If one family member buys the Dream Annual Passport, the whole party can still benefit from the many discounts at the parks' shops and restaurants.

There is a substantial difference in price between the two Annual Passports (see At-A-Glance guides on pages 126 and 166), but you can save a good deal over the course of a year if you plan on visiting more than once, and the savings against the multi-day Hoppers should also be obvious.

BRITTIP

All shareholders of Euro Disney SCA (the holding company that runs the resort) benefit from a range of hotel, park, shop and restaurant discounts similar to those of the Dream Annual Passport holders.

Where to buy tickets

So, where can you buy your tickets, apart from joining the long early-morning queues at the ticket booths at the entrance to both parks? Well, you can call the UK booking line on 08705 030303 or the 7-day-a-week French centre on 00 33 1 60 30 60 30; visit any Disney Store in Britain or on the Champs-Elysées in Paris; any FNAC store in Paris; the Virgin Megastore on the Champs-Elysées; the main RATP ticket offices on the Métro or RER; any Travelex Foreign Exchange Bureau (notably at the Eurotunnel terminal in Folkestone and at Portsmouth ferry terminal); on board P&O Ferries on Dover–Calais routes; or the Eurostar ticketing desks at the London St Pancras terminal or Ashford stations, or its Victoria station shop.

The Disney Store on the Champs-Elysées

BRITTIP

It is usually worth buying your tickets as far in advance as possible to avoid the probable annual price increase (usually in late autumn/early winter).

There are then the various official ticket brokers at travel agents and other outlets, some of whom can offer **1-, 2-, 3-, 4-** and **5-Day Hopper Tickets**. Three companies we are happy to vouch for are Attraction Tickets Direct, Keith Prowse Attraction Tickets and Theme Park Tickets Direct.

Attraction Tickets Direct: Well known for being the UK's number one ticket broker for Orlando attractions, it often runs special offers on *Disneyland Paris* 1-, 2-, 4-, and 5-Day Hopper tickets, and offers a unique price promise guarantee. It provides actual tickets, not vouchers, has free delivery within 7 days and its brochure is free on request. 0800 975 0002, **attraction-tickets-direct.co.uk**.

Keith Prowse Attraction Tickets: It runs occasional 'extras' with its tickets, plus a range of Paris city excursions, dinner shows (including the Lido de Paris, Moulin Rouge and Crazy Horse cabarets), sightseeing

Guests on Main Street USA

tours and cruises, and it is well worth getting a copy of its brochure. 08701 232425, **keith prowse.com/uk**.

Theme Park Tickets Direct: Also keenly priced. 0870 040 0210, **theme parkticketsdirect.com**.

BRITTIP

Attraction Tickets Direct has some handy discussion forums on its website and we have been known to make an appearance there from time to time, so drop in and ask us a question or tell us your *Disneyland Paris* stories!

Once you have your tickets, you can avoid the first bugbear of visiting either park – the ticket booths. These are located prominently outside both parks but, however many windows

Carrousel de Lancelot

Rides for wimps!

For those who are reluctant to hurl themselves on to the fastest rides, here (by special request!) is a guide to a walk on the 'mild side' with Disney. None of these will upset even the most sensitive of stomachs (although, with the exception of The Twilight Zone Tower of Terror, Crush's Coaster, Space Mountain, Indiana Jones, Mad Hatter's Tea Cups and the Rock 'n' Roller Coaster, there are few rides designed to be really dynamic):

1   Disneyland Railroad
2   'it's a small world'
3   Le Pays des Contes de Fées
4   Le Carrousel de Lancelot
5   Peter Pan's Flight
6   Flying Carpets Over Agrabah
7   Casey Junior
8   Autopia
9   Thunder Mesa Riverboats
10 Dumbo the Flying Elephant

Thunder Mesa Riverboat

are open, there is nearly always a slow-moving queue. If you can avoid them, you'll be ahead of the crowd.

The final thing to remember before we get to the theme parks proper is you can always escape the crowds – especially in the *Walt Disney Studios Park* – during the day by stepping out into *Disney Village* for a while. If the theme parks are heaving, the *Disney Village* and the hotels are probably a lot quieter. The great accessibility and convenience of the whole resort means it IS possible to find places without queues to enjoy a meal, have a drink or just recharge the batteries (and, at peak periods, you WILL need a breather at times) before you charge back into the hectic whirl.

Ratings

All the rides and shows are judged on a unique *Brit Guide* rating system that splits them into Thrill rides and Scenic rides. Thrill rides earn T ratings out of 5 (hence a TTTTT is as

exciting as it gets) and Scenic rides get A ratings out of 5 (an AA ride is likely to be over-cute and missable). Obviously, it is a matter of opinion to a certain extent but you can be sure

- T or A is not worth your time
- TT or AA is worth seeing only if there isn't a queue
- TTT or AAA should be seen if you have time, but you won't miss much if you don't
- TTTT or AAAA ride is a big-time attraction that should be high on your list
- TTTTT or AAAAA should not be missed!

The latter will have the longest queues, so plan your visit around these rides.

'it's a small world'

FastPass

Disney has a unique FastPass (FP) system for some of its most popular shows and rides and it is worth taking advantage of it in the *Disneyland Park* (it is not always available in the *Walt Disney Studios Park*, where queues tend to be shorter at quieter times of the year).

BRITTIP

Some rides DO run out of FastPasses before the end of the day, so it is advisable to grab one for the likes of Peter Pan's Flight and Big Thunder Mountain BEFORE early afternoon.

Here's how the FastPass works: at all attractions with the FastPass service (which is FREE – many people don't realise this), there are a series of ticket machines next to the main entrance. Insert your park entrance ticket into a machine and it immediately returns your ticket, followed by a separate slip with a time 'window' during which you should return to the separate FastPass queue (usually at least 1 hour later, occasionally 4 or more). When your 'window' is open, simply return to the FastPass queue and enjoy the attraction with only a minimal wait. You can hold only one FastPass per 2-hour period, although once you have used it you can get

Star Tours FastPass outlet

another. If your return time is more than 2 hours away, you can get a second FastPass after 2 hours have passed. For example, if you get a FastPass for Space Mountain at 9am with a return time of 1–2pm, you can get a second FastPass for, say, Big Thunder Mountain at 11am. You need FastPass tickets for EVERY member of your party.

NB: Disney was experimenting with a **paid-for version** of its FastPass system in summer 2009, whereby those who were willing to pay €80–100 could buy a special pass that gave access to the FastPass rides all day. Of course, as a special perk for Disney Hotel guests staying in suites, the **VIP FastPass** is also good for all the FastPass rides all day without having to use the ticket machines.

Big Thunder Mountain

Pin trading

In addition to collecting souvenirs, you will probably also encounter the pin-trading phenomenon. It is a particularly American idea and involves collecting – and trading – the many dozens of different enamel brooches that you can buy in almost every shop. They vary in price from €8 to €15 and serious collectors carry them on lanyards around their neck, eagerly looking to barter and swap with other members of this not-so-secret society. Various Disney Cast Members also join in by displaying lanyards with pins to swap, and they are duty-bound to swap for anything they may be displaying. Children particularly appreciate this opportunity for a sure thing, and Cast Members are usually gracious about waiting for youngsters to make a decision. Those who get hooked on it will attest to having great fun looking for potential swaps with fellow devotees (as well as spending a small fortune on their collections!). For more info, log on to the UK-orientated discussion boards of **disboards.com** or **thedibb.co.uk** and ask one of the regulars to explain how to get suitably enthused! In the *Disneyland Park*, enthusiasts will also find special pin-trading boards at a Pin Cart at the end of Main Street USA and in The Emporium shop. Cast Members will also usually give you the option to trade up to 2 from your pins with the pins already on the board (but the pin you trade cannot be on the board already).

BRITTIP

If you have young children, put a note in their pocket with details of their name, your mobile phone number, hotel, etc. Cast Members are trained to take lost children to the Meeting Place and the provision of a note makes their job easier.

Restrictions

Some rides are restricted to children over a certain height and are not advisable for people with back, neck or heart problems or for pregnant women. Where this is the case, we have noted 'Restrictions: 1.32m/4ft 3in' and so on. Height restrictions (which are strictly enforced) are based on the average 5-year-old being 1.02m/3ft 3in tall, 6s being 1.1m/3ft 6in and 9s being 1.32m/4ft 3in.

Those with neck or back problems, or mothers-to-be, are advised to avoid: Space Mountain: Mission 2, Indiana Jones and the Temple of Peril, Big Thunder Mountain Railroad and Mad Hatter's Tea Cups at the *Disneyland Park* and The Twilight Zone Tower of Terror, Crush's Coaster, RC Racer and Rock 'n' Roller Coaster starring Aerosmith at *Walt Disney Studios Park.*

The 'baby switch'

If you have small children, but don't want to leave them while you have a ride, you DON'T have to queue twice. When you get to the front of the queue, tell the operator you want to do a 'baby switch'. This means one adult can go on the ride while another adult looks after junior and, on their return, the second adult can have their turn while the first adult does the babysitting.

BRITTIP

Many children also get a big thrill from collecting autographs from the various Disney characters they meet, and nearly all the hotels and shops sell some great autograph books.

Space Mountain: Mission 2

© Disney

© Disney

Good Morning Main Street Parade

Baby Care Centre: You'll find this in the *Disneyland Park* next door to the Plaza Gardens Restaurant at the top of Main Street USA on the right, where there are nappy-changing facilities and a feeding room, with baby food (and nappies) on sale. At the *Walt Disney Studios* Park the Baby Care Centre is behind the Studio Services in the Front Lot, just inside the entrance on the right-hand side.

The Meeting Place for Lost Children: These are in the same place in both parks, with their own Disney staff.

Match the ages: If you have children of wide-ranging ages, check out the special section at the end of each park

The entrance to Discoveryland

© Disney

chapter to see which rides and attractions appeal most to which age groups. It is important in a resort of this size to concentrate on those areas that have the most appeal for YOU and, while it is not possible to be 100% accurate, the advice here is tried and tested, so you can get a pretty good idea of what is most likely to be popular with your family.

BRITTIP

Kids, try to find the thickest pen you can for collecting autographs. Most of the characters find it a struggle to write with normal-size pens in their great big hands.

Park etiquette

Some final words of warning. Picnics are NOT allowed inside the parks (although you can take bottles of water), but there is a picnic area outside at the exit of the moving walkway from the main car park.

Appropriate clothing must be worn in the parks – which means shirt and shoes – at all times. No bare chests – even for women!

Smoking, eating, drinking, flash photography and video lighting are not permitted on rides, during shows or in queues.

So what are we waiting for? First stop, the Disneyland Park

6 The Disneyland Park

or To All Who Come to this Happy Place, Welcome!

It makes sense to start by taking an in-depth look at the original development here at *Disneyland Paris*, the first Disney park in Europe, which opened in April 1992. Although it is comparable to the *Magic Kingdom* in *Walt Disney World* (America's biggest tourist attraction), be prepared for some surprises in both scale and content. The *Disneyland Park* is bigger by some 17ha/42 acres than its Orlando counterpart and, while there are fewer 'lands', the Paris version is more elaborate and involving.

The attractions range from the twee and fairly ordinary (Mad Hatter's Tea Cups and Autopia) to the wonderfully inventive (Phantom Manor and Pirates of the Caribbean) and on to the downright thrilling (Space Mountain: Mission 2 and Indiana Jones and the Temple of Peril). Disney's all-encompassing theming covers the Wild West (Frontierland), dark jungles and pirate caverns (Adventureland), film and storybook fantasy (Fantasyland) and a kind of retro future world (Discoveryland), possibly the most imaginative of all. There is at least one (depending on the time of year) unmissable daily parade and a range of other live theatrical productions that all carry the Disney hallmark of captivating family entertainment. In fact, there's plenty to make you go 'Wow!' plus a variety of attractions that will raise a big smile.

Prepare to be completely immersed in a convincing world of make-believe, where every tiny detail – from the costumes of the Cast Members to the clever signage – conforms to that land's theme. But, be aware of some fairly blatant attempts to lighten your wallet, notably at the many gift shops, especially after the rides. By Disney's own reckoning, 16,000 types of merchandise are on sale and, although 90% of it costs less than €15, it can quickly add up if you have children of the large-eyed variety!

Sleeping Beauty Castle

© Disney

BRITTIP

Take advantage of Disney's free package pick-up service if you do a lot of shopping. When you pay, ask for the items to be sent to The Disney Store in the *Disney Village* for you to collect after 6pm. If you are staying in a Disney hotel, your shopping can be delivered to your hotel's boutique for collection after 8pm.

Another slight negative to be aware of is the quality (or lack of it) in much of the counter-service dining. With only a couple of notable exceptions, the fare is neither terribly imaginative nor particularly cheap (around €10 a head, even for the most basic meal). In the course of 3 days, that can be almost €190 just in meals for a family of 4, eating twice a day at park counter-service restaurants (although the new **Half Board Meal Plan** can save as much as 15% off these costs if you are a Disney hotel guest – see page 79). Conversely, the handful of full-service restaurants DO offer some fabulous food – but at a price. Go for lunch at our favourite restaurant, the Blue Lagoon, and you could easily be €96 lighter with 4 to feed. A cheaper alternative is to stock up at breakfast, keep going with snacks from the many hot dog, popcorn, doughnut and drinks wagons around the park and have your main meal in *Disney Village* or at the hotel in the evening (where buffet options are often better value).

NB: Our Research Assistant Andy de Maertelaere reports that parts of the *Disneyland Park* shut before the official closing time in 2009, even

The Disneyland Park at a glance

Location	Off Exit 14 of the A4 autoroute, proceed to the clearly signed car park; or turn right out of the Marne-la-Vallée RER and TGV station; or through the *Disney Village* if staying at a resort hotel
Size	57 hectares/140 acres in five 'lands'
Hours	10am–6 or 7pm autumn and winter weekdays; 10am–8, 9 or 10pm spring, plus autumn and winter weekends, half-term holidays; 9 or 10am–10pm Christmas and New Year (until 1am New Year's Eve); 9am–11pm summer holidays (mid-July–August)
Admission	**Under 3** free; **3–11** €44 (1-Day Ticket), €57, €94, €117 (1-, 2- and 3-Day Park Hopper), **adults** (12+) €52 (1-Day Ticket), €65, €111, €138, €161 (1-, 2-, 3- and 4-Day Park Hopper); **Annual Passports** (per person): Fantasy €129, Dream €189. *NB: All Disney prices and hours subject to change without prior notice (see **www.disneylandparis.com**)*
Parking	€8
Pushchairs	€7.50 (Pushchair rental counter to right of main entrance, just under railway arch)
Wheelchairs	€7.50 (Also at pushchair rental counter)
Top Attractions	Space Mountain: Mission 2, Star Tours, Peter Pan's Flight, Dumbo the Flying Elephant, Big Thunder Mountain Railroad, Buzz Lightyear's Laser Blast
Don't Miss	Disney's Once Upon A Dream Parade, Fantillusion Parade and Enchanted Fireworks (summer and Christmas seasons only), 'it's a small world', La Tanière du Dragon
Hidden Costs	**Meals** Burger, chips and coke €9.95; 3-course meal at Blue Lagoon €28 (€15 for children); beer 25cl €3.60, 50cl €7.20; Kids' meal €6 (at all counter-service restaurants)
	T-shirts €10–35
	Souvenirs €2.50–37,500
	Sundries Kids' autograph book €4.90 and €9.90 Space Mountain ride photos €12, 19, 20, poster size €21

DISNEYLAND PARK

Main Street, USA
1 Disneyland Railroad – Main Street Station
2 Town Square
3 Disneyland City Hall
4 Horse-drawn streetcars and Main Street Vehicles
5 Liberty Arcade
6 Discovery Arcade
7 Central Plaza

Frontierland
8 Fort Comstock
9 Phantom Manor
10 Thunder Mesa Riverboat Landing
11 Rustler Roundup Shootin' Gallery
12 Big Thunder Mountain
13 Pocahontas Indian Village
14 River Rogue Keelboats
15 Woody's Round-Up
16 The Chaparral Theatre
17 Disneyland Railroad – Frontierland Depot

Adventureland
18 Indiana Jones and the Temple of Peril
19 Adventure Isle
20 La Cabane des Robinsons
21 Skull Rock
22 Pirates' Beach
23 Pirates of the Caribbean
24 Le Passage Enchanté d'Aladdin

Fantasyland
25 Sleeping Beauty Castle
26 Le Carrousel de Lancelot
27 Blanche Neige et Les Sept Nains
28 Les Voyages de Pinocchio
29 Dumbo the Flying Elephant
30 Peter Pan's Flight
31 Fantasy Festival Stage
32 Disneyland Railroad – Fantasyland Station
33 Alice's Curious Labyrinth
34 Le Pays des Contes de Fées
35 Casey Jr – le Petit Train du Cirque
36 Mad Hatter's Tea Cups
37 'it's a small world'
38 Le Théâtre du Chateau

Discoveryland
39 Space Mountain: Mission 2
40 Les Mystères du Nautilus
41 Orbitron – Machines Volantes
42 Star Tours
43 Disneyland Railroad – Discoveryland Station
44 Honey, I Shrunk the Audience
45 Autopia
46 Buzz Lightyear Laser Blast
47 Videopolis/Cinéma Mickey
48 Arcades Alpha & Beta

during the summer. These included Honey I Shrunk the Audience and Les Mystèrès du Nautilus (6pm some days), Phantom Manor and Indiana Jones and the Temple of Peril (10pm).

Pace yourself

The final piece of advice before we send you off on the great *Disneyland Park* adventure is to pace yourself. It is easy to try to do too much and end up a frazzled wreck by mid-afternoon! In summer, when the crowds are at their peak and the temperature can top 30ºC/86ºF, it can be a particularly tough business negotiating the rides, the long queues and the demands of tramping from one side of the park to the other in the name of entertainment. This is when you will most feel the benefit of a **solid plan**, booking your mealtimes in advance and giving yourselves a rest at strategic moments, whether it be finding a quiet corner for a drink or visiting a show that provides a welcome sit-down, preferably in the air-conditioned cool.

When it comes to eating, be aware that inclement weather quickly causes long queues to pile up in the restaurants, even in *Disney Village*. If

Disney & Co on Main Street

City Hall

you can pre-empt that sudden rain squall by getting to a café first, you will be well placed to watch the rush come in when the deluge starts. Equally, if you have brought some good **rain gear** with you, it is a great time to enjoy some of the rides while the majority seek shelter.

You will also need to **drink** a lot of water during the summer. The physical demands of the parks will quickly creep up on you unless you remember to rehydrate at regular intervals. It is, sadly, an all-too-common feature in mid-afternoon to see or hear grizzly children, often being berated by parents for not enjoying themselves (!), when all everyone needs is to just sit down for a few minutes, recharge the batteries and drink some water.

BRITTIP

Save euros by bringing a bottle of water with you and refilling it from the many drinking fountains around.

Most children (ours included) get a huge energy charge from being in the theme parks and the adrenalin keeps them going long after they should have keeled over. But that excited state can run out at a moment's notice and turn to angst if they are not regularly fed and watered – and it is easy to overlook the latter with so much going on. In summer, it is advisable to carry a good **sunscreen** and use it liberally while you are queuing to prevent an unhealthy dose of the sun, which also exacerbates the tiredness factor – your biggest enemy.

Grand entry

You actually enter 'Le Parc Disneyland' underneath the *Disneyland Hotel*, the rather fanciful conglomeration of buildings known as the Pink Palace. You pass some extremely pleasant gardens (the whimsical Fantasia Gardens, with character-shaped topiaries) and the inevitable fountains and ponds (good photo spot) before entering the main entrance plaza. The ticket booths are to the right of the entrance passage, but hopefully you already have your tickets and can head straight to the turnstiles. If you need Guest Relations or Left Luggage, bear to the right of the main hotel building and they are in front of you. Be aware there is quite a walk from the main car park to the theme parks, even with the moving walkways. You should allow at least 10 minutes to get there and pushchairs are a real boon if you have little ones.

BRITTIP

If you want a real budget option for lunch, nip out of the parks to the RER station of Marne-la-Vallée and grab a baguette, sandwich or Croque Monsieur at the station café. The beer alone is €2 cheaper!

Main Street USA

Once through the turnstiles, you enter a plaza in front of the main Disneyland Railroad station.

Town Square: Walk under the station and you are in the main entrance to *Disneyland Park* proper and the lower portion of the first 'land', Main Street USA. This is a grand, turn-of-the-century version of small-town America, with an eye-catching array of shop and office façades all built in epic detail. It is not so much a thoroughfare as a living museum to generations of genuine Americana and it offers a fabulous glimpse into an idealised past of the US.

Sleeping Beauty Castle: Here you will get your first look at the most-photographed edifice in the whole resort, Le Château de la Belle au Bois Dormant, to use its full French title.

BRITTIP

Video camera battery running down? Visit City Hall and they will recharge it for you there and then.

Disneyland City Hall: This guest relations office is to your left, where you can pick up park maps (if you haven't already got one at your hotel or in the many cubicles underneath the Railroad Station), book meals at any of the restaurants or just ask any park-related questions.

Disneyland Park entrance

© Disney

© Disney

Liberty Arcade

BRITTIP

Can't find the characters? Go to City Hall and they will tell you where they will be. City Hall is your best friend for a variety of queries – from the location of baby facilities (there are none here) to meal bookings.

Main Street Transportation Company: On your right is where several vintage and horse-drawn vehicles can take you along Main Street USA to the Central Plaza, the theme park's hub, from which radiate the other 4 'lands'. If you have time (or children), it is quite fun to take one of the horse-drawn trams or vintage cars (including a police paddy-wagon), but it's quicker to walk (especially if you use either of the covered arcades that run alongside Main Street USA).

Disneyland Railroad: One of the most eye-catching features of Main Street is the railroad station, well

Gibson Girl Ice Cream Parlour

© Disney

positioned to catch the unsuspecting visitor. (There are 4 stations; Adventureland is the only 'land' without a railroad stop.) The Victorian-style station provides an elevated view down Main Street USA, but the signature steam train ride, which circles the whole park and includes a clever 'Grand Canyon' scene en route to Frontierland (and a glimpse inside Pirates of the Caribbean), has long, slow-moving queues for much of the day. Be aware some stations may be used for offloading only during non-peak seasons. AAA.

BRITTIP

The Disneyland Railroad is a relaxing ride when there are long queues elsewhere, but DON'T join it at Main Street where few people get off. Try the stations at Frontierland or Fantasyland for the shortest wait.

Information Board: At the top of Main Street USA on the right-hand side (just after the Gibson Girl Ice Cream Parlour) is a handy board that displays the waiting times at the attractions. Late arrivals should take note of this to get an idea of where to head first (and where to avoid for a while until the queues die down).

Disney characters: Main Street USA is also one of the prime locations to meet the characters. Most days start with the official character 'opening ceremony', an early-morning

Disney's New Generation Festival

Disney loves to have a 'theme' for each year (or 2 years, as it managed to make its 15th anniversary celebrations last!), and 2010 is no different. Following hot on the heels of 2009's *Mickey's Magical Party*, this year has been declared the year of the Pixar characters, with a host of new additions honouring this 'new generation' in the great Disney animation line-up. The biggest development will be the new **Toy Story Playland** area at the *Walt Disney Studios Park*, which will bring in 3 new rides for summer 2010: a Toy Soldier Parachute Drop, the Slinky Dog ride, and a dynamic RC Racer attraction, while *Ratatouille* star **Remy** joins the daily Disney's Stars 'n' Cars parade. In the *Disneyland Park*, **Princess Tiana** and **Prince Naveen** (from *The Princess and the Frog* film that debuted in December 2009) find a place on the *Dreams of Romance* float in the Once Upon a Dream Parade, while Minnie's Party Train will transform into the Pixar-esque **Disney's All Star Express**, and **Disney Showtime Spectacular** takes over the Central Plaza stage as Disneyland's new nightly show finale.

cavalcade featuring Mickey, Pluto and others. Many of them stop to sign autographs in 3 locations: on a platform outside the Liberty Arcade (just past Casey's Corner on the left as you come up the street), in the Central Plaza and on the Royal Castle Stage to the right of Sleeping Beauty Castle.

Other entertainment: From April 2010, get ready for **Disney's All Star Express** (formerly Minnie's Party Train), which will run along Main Street USA, providing an excellent character meet 'n' greet several times a day. The mini-cavalcade chugs up from Town Square to the Central Plaza, where it stops for a host of recent Disney/Pixar film 'stars' (the characters tend to change on a regular basis) to disembark and meet guests for photos and autographs (but be ready for a bit of a scrimmage at first!). Look out also for another show

that performs periodically (although it may not feature on the daily Show Schedule). *Step In Time Mary Poppins* is a wonderful little song-and-dance act based around the Gazebo in Town Square, featuring Mary and Bert and other film characters.

BRITTIP

Main Street USA is full of clever Disney memorabilia – look for photos of Walt and his wife Lilly in Lilly's Boutique; the two murals of other Emporium shops in the Emporium; and the plates set into the street that bear the legend 'Elias Disney Contractor'. Many of the windows also bear witness to Disney Imagineers and VIPs down the years.

At **Halloween**, Main Street USA has a major pumpkin-inspired makeover and some wonderfully clever visual touches. A giant pumpkin also appears in front of the Castle, with free face-painting for children under 11.

BRITTIP

Halloween is one of the most popular periods at the *Disneyland Park*, and you can expect some of the longest queues during the school half-term break and weekends in October.

Main Street at Halloween

© Disney

Liberty and Discovery Arcades: As an alternative to walking up the middle of Main Street USA, pick one of the arcades at either side (Liberty on the left and Discovery on the right) and wander right through away from most of the crowds. The Liberty Arcade features a clever tableau about the inauguration of the Statue of Liberty (in French), while Discovery Arcade is decorated with some clever period detail, well worth a look later on.

BRITTIP

Need to stay dry? Both Liberty and Discovery Arcades are fully covered and provide back-door access to most of the shops and cafés along Main Street USA. Very popular in winter!

Shopping: Main Street USA is basically the park's principal shopping area, with a range of stores (including the gargantuan **Emporium**, which stocks just about every kind of souvenir known to mouse-kind!). In all, there are 12 cunningly arranged shops along this 100m/109yd boulevard and it is worthwhile returning in the

Main Street USA

afternoon when the rides are busiest to check out some of the amazing detail here.

You should definitely go to the **Emporium** and **Lilly's Boutique** (glass and porcelain), as well as **The Storybook Store** (books, stationery, CD and audio cassettes), **Harrington's Fine China & Porcelain** (china, crystal and glass giftware), **Disney Clothiers Ltd** (adult and children's apparel) and **Main Street Motors** (more clothing).

Main Street has plenty of shopping opportunities

Main Street characters

Character carnival

Although the Disney characters appearing change from month to month, you can be fairly sure to catch them most of the time (especially 10am–noon) at the following locations:

Town Square: In the corner by Liberty Arcade or under the Gazebo in the centre of the Square: any of Minnie, Pluto, Chip 'n' Dale, Donald Duck and Goofy; plus Mary Poppins and Friends periodically.

Main Street USA: By Casey's Corner and Liberty Arcade: Mickey Mouse.

Royal Castle Stage: In front of the Castle: Disney Princesses.

Fantasyland: By Mad Hatter's Tea Cups: some Alice in Wonderland characters, Pinocchio and Robin Hood. Outside Fantasy Festival Stage: Winnie the Pooh, and occasionally Tigger or Piglet.

Discoveryland: Between Videopolis and Space Mountain: any of Lilo & Stitch and *Toy Story* characters.

Adventureland: By Colonel Hathi's Pizza Outpost: *Jungle Book* and *Lion King* characters.

Frontierland: Outside Cowboy Cookout Barbecue: some of Goofy, Pluto, Chip 'n' Dale, Country Bears and Pocahontas characters. At Woody's Roundup Village: Mickey, Minnie and some *Toy Story* characters.

If you need any photographic equipment, **Town Square Photography** should be able to help (although beware the prices – it is cheaper to bring basics like film, batteries and flashcards with you).

BRITTIP

Looking for hard-to-find, limited edition pins? Try Town Square Photography, a less obvious location for pin-trading fans to round out their collections.

Also here is **Dapper Dan's Hair Cuts**, an atmospheric vintage barber's with the kind of furnishings you would usually find only in an antique shop

(or an apothecary's). You can stop for a haircut or shave if the mood takes you (€20 or €14; €29 for both; €18 wash and dry only; €30 cut and dry) or to get your child's hair cut (€10). Open 10.30am–6pm, reservations requested.

BRITTIP

Hunting for bargains? Stop at the Plaza East and West Boutiques before you exit the park. They stock a range of previous season's merchandise at reduced prices.

Dining: You can also find 10 different snack bars and restaurants here to provide everything from breakfast to a gourmet lunch, afternoon tea and evening dessert. Pick of the bunch is

Toy Story Meet 'n' Greet

Walt's – An American Restaurant, which offers an elegant lunch and dinner (set menu €27 for starter and main, or €37 for starter, main and dessert; €12 for children, €16 teens; Express Meal €19.90; birthday cakes available for €22). This fabulous establishment, designed like a 1900s' hotel, is a tribute to Walt Disney himself, his ideas and creations, and features a wealth of personal detail, photos and memorabilia (12–4pm daily).

☒ BRITTIP

As an example of the Imagineers' art, listen carefully outside Victoria's Home-Style Restaurant and you will catch the distinct sounds of someone using the bathroom in the 'guesthouse' above!

At the top of Main Street USA, the **Plaza Gardens Restaurant** (11.30am–10.30pm) offers an excellent series of all-you-can-eat buffets for lunch and dinner in a plush, conservatory-style setting. The buffet is €20/adult, €10/child (drinks not included) and consists of a huge cold spread – salads, meats, bread and fruit – and an array of hot dishes – casseroles, pasta, roast beef, sausages, hot dogs and several types of vegetables and rice – plus a mouth-watering selection of desserts.

Walt's – An American Restaurant

Otherwise, your eateries are mainly of the counter-snack kind, with the **Market House Deli** (sandwiches, salads and desserts), **Casey's Corner** (all manner of hot dogs, chicken nuggets, and soft drinks), **Victoria's Home-Style Restaurant** (sandwiches, pizza and salads), **The Coffee Grinder** (coffee, tea and cakes), **The Ice Cream Company** (hosted by Nestlé), **The Cookie Kitchen** and **Cable Car Bake Shop** (2 sides of the same breakfast-orientated servery, with some

Plaza Gardens Restaurant

© Disney

Once Upon a Dream Parade

delicious pastries and cookies) and the **Gibson Girl Ice Cream Parlour** (a full range of ice-cream delights). Bear in mind not all of these are likely to be open at any one time (apart from the weekends in high season).

Rope drop

If you arrive prior to the official opening time (either 9 or 10am), Main Street USA is not the place to linger as most of the crowd will flock to the **Central Plaza** in front of the Castle. This is REALLY where the action starts for a full day in the park, so don't be fooled into thinking it has opened early by letting you into Main Street USA. You need to have already planned your campaign from here to get a head start on the masses.

BRITTIP

If you are among the first to reach Central Plaza and you manage to get to the main rides first, you will enjoy the *Disneyland Park* at its best – with short or non-existent queues at the most popular attractions.

Where to wait: Depending on which of the 'lands' in front of you appeals most, head in one of the 4 directions and wait for the opening-hour 'rope drop' by the Cast Members at each entrance.

If you fancy the appeal of cowboy country and the lure of a thrill ride like Big Thunder Mountain or the scary fun of Phantom Manor, head up Liberty Arcade and, at the top, wait to turn left into Frontierland.

For the mysteries of Adventureland (including the wonderful Pirates of the Caribbean ride), move into Central Plaza and wait at its entrance on the left.

Those with children in tow, who will demand rides in the company of all their favourite characters like Dumbo, Peter Pan and the Mad Hatter, should wait in front of the Castle for the chance to get into Fantasyland first.

Or, if the appeal of big thrill rides like Space Mountain: Mission 2 (an indoor, looping roller-coaster) and Star Tours (a brilliant simulator space ride) is top of your 'To Do' list, then turn right in the middle of Central Plaza and await the rope drop for Discoveryland.

Once the ropes go down, the early-morning crowds will move (quickly!) in one of the 4 directions, so keep your wits about you. Study the park map for where you want to go and benefit from a first hour or so without lengthy queuing.

Meet Jafar in Frontierland

© Disney

BRITTIP

A perk with the Dream Annual Passport is entry to Fantasyland and Discoveryland 1–2 hours before they officially open. The Dumbo and Peter Pan rides often start half an hour early, so you can have a turn on the most popular rides without queuing.

Timing your meals: It also pays (royally so in peak periods) to avoid main meal times if you want to eat without more queues and frenzy. In *Disneyland Paris* people tend to pack out the counter-service cafés rather than the handful of full-service, sit-down restaurants. This means noon–2.30pm is a seriously bad time (unless it is an extremely quiet period of the year) to head for places like the Fuente del Oro Restaurante, Pizzeria Bella Notte, the Cowboy Cookout Barbecue or any of the other 14 counter-service diners in the park. Try to have a snack before midday or look to eat in mid-afternoon and you will benefit from slightly shorter ride queues during lunchtime.

BRITTIP

Park too busy? Don't forget it is relatively easy to head back out to *Disney Village* and grab a bite to eat at places like Planet Hollywood and Annette's Diner.

Frontierland

Phantom Manor

Alternatively, you could book lunch at the start of the day at one of the 4 full-service restaurants (Walt's, Auberge du Cendrillon, Blue Lagoon or Silver Spur Steakhouse) to guarantee a pleasant sit-down and some rest – especially with children.

Frontierland

Okay, enough of the warnings – let's get to the fun! There is masses in store, so let us take you on a full tour of the remaining 'lands' in the *Disneyland Park*. Starting immediately to your left from the Central Plaza brings you to Frontierland, a truly rootin', tootin' cowboy town that oozes child appeal and has plenty of visual creativity and stimulation for grown-ups too. It is a realm of pioneers and gold diggers, the Wild West in vivid 3-D, with a big helping of some of the epic scenery that the real-life version possesses in places like Nevada and Arizona.

BRITTIP

Go to the top of Fort Comstock and you have a great spot to take memorable photos of Frontierland.

As in virtually all other areas of the park, Frontierland rewards the casual wanderer with some great little paths leading nowhere in particular but that reveal some interesting details or amusing scenery, such as the Indian village encampment or the hot springs (complete with Old Faithful geyser).

Rustler Roundup

Fort Comstock: Once again, the loyal re-creation of the era can be seen in every building and façade, none better than the main entrance here, which is an attraction in itself, where you can see scenes from Legends of the Wild West. You can climb the wooden stairs to the ramparts, visit the US Marshall and Fort Jail, and peer into the offices (see if you can spot Buffalo Bill) and stables. Kids will want to roam the ramparts and scan other areas of the park through the telescopes provided. It is a good place to let youngsters explore on their own, too. AA.

Phantom Manor: Turn left after coming through Fort Comstock and head along the plaza past the Silver Spur Steakhouse for one of the cleverest and most amusing rides in the Disney repertoire. This elaborate haunted mansion is a variation on the theme established in Anaheim and Orlando, with a ghoulish entryway leading to an underground ride of wonderfully creepy proportions. The introductory spiel is in French (while some aspects of the commentary are alternately in English and French). However, it needs little real explanation as the gloomy entrance

BRITTIP

Queues build up at Phantom Manor from mid-morning and, although they rarely top half an hour, this ride is a good one to do early or during a parade, when it's quieter. Or wait until the last hour before park closing when it rarely has a queue and is at its spooky best!

parlour (watch for a remarkable trick here) takes you down to this spooktastic world.

BRITTIP

Research Assistant Andy de Maertelaere points out you can see a photo of Walt here. As you leave the 'stretch' room, walk the hallway, cut around the corner and you will see it on a table on the right-hand side. A real Disney heirloom!

Under-5s may find the mock-horror elements a bit too convincing but otherwise the whole experience is more fun than frightening. The story of an elaborate socialite wedding that went tragically wrong, leaving the bride as one of the 999 ghosts, is a bit hard to follow, but the ride takes you right through the manor and into a realistic haunted town in best graveyard fashion. In the queue you can study the elaborate terraces and gardens outside the manor, while you exit into Boot Hill and some more pun-laced scenery that includes various graves – such as 'Here lies Shotgun Gus, holier now than all of us'. The more attentive will also notice the sounds of knocking from the largest of the mausoleums in the graveyard. This can be a great source of amusement when people notice it for the first time on dark evenings! AAAA (TTTTT for youngsters).

Phantom Manor

Thunder Mesa Riverboat Landing:
Backtrack slightly along the plaza and you can hop on a boat offering a slow and picturesque ride around much of Frontierland on the Rivers of the Far West, including several sections that can be seen only from the water. The commentary is bilingual and it is quite a capacious ride, so there is rarely much of a queue. The 2 boats, the *Molly Brown* and *Mark Twain*, provide an enjoyably authentic experience. This is a good ride to save for later in the day when both Phantom Manor and Big Thunder Mountain are busiest, but be aware the Landing may close earlier than other attractions. AAA.

Rustler Roundup Shootin' Gallery:
Fans of the old-style arcade shooting ranges can get a quick 'fix' here, where €2 (the only additional charge for an attraction in the theme park) will give you 10 shots at various audio-animatronic targets. TT.

Big Thunder Mountain: This is one of Disney's trademark roller-coasters. While others may thrill (or terrify!) with their topsy-turvy antics, Big Thunder sticks firmly to the straight and narrow but is still as fun and inventive as most people desire, with this abandoned 'gold mine' showing it has plenty of life left in it in the shape of its runaway train. Again, you get a different version from other Disney parks; this one starts straight away with a dive into the dark under the

Thunder Mesa Riverboat

lake before whizzing around the mock sandstone monoliths and mine shafts in exhilarating fashion.

⊞ BRITTIP

If you head to Frontierland first, Big Thunder Mountain should be your opening ride, followed by Phantom Manor. Then return to the mine-train coaster and grab a FastPass for another go later!

With 3 different ascents (and plunges), the proliferation of clever scenery is never less than spectacular, so it usually needs at least 2 rides to take in all the detail (it looks great at night, too). This is one of the 5 FastPass (FP) rides, so it is well worth taking advantage of, as the queues often top an hour at peak times. Afterwards, you can buy the souvenir photo of your ride (6 package options, from €14–20; poster size €25). Restrictions: 1.02m/3ft 3in. TTTT. (FP).

River Rogue Keelboats: This river ride made a surprise return in 2007, having closed in 2001 because of operational difficulties. It features a gentle 20-minute tour of the Rivers of the Far West, following a similar path to the Thunder Mesa Riverboat but providing a more up-close experience of some of the sights and a different perspective, close to the water. Set in Smugglers Cove, the Keelboats *Racoon* and *Coyote* are piloted by 'smugglers' who tell you stories of the Old West en route (mostly in French, unfortunately). The bad news is queues build up quickly here and

River Rogue Keelboats

Mickey's Winter Wonderland

move rather slowly, hence it is often a 45-minute wait, even at quieter times. The Keelboats are usually open only 11am–6.30pm daily. AA.

Pocahontas Indian Village: If the youngsters are too short (or apprehensive!) to ride Big Thunder Mountain, head for this straightforward play area with a mixture of slides, swings and climbs geared towards under-6s. Unfortunately, this area closes when it rains but, otherwise, it is a valuable place to allow the young 'uns to let off steam. TTT (for the right age group!).

Woody's Roundup Village: The former Critter Corral petting zoo has been reborn here as a smart character meet 'n' greet area, which features the stars of the *Toy Story* films for much of the year in this cowboy-style mini-village, along with either Mickey or Minnie periodically (usually in the afternoon). Kids can enjoy more

organised character interaction here, plus extra fun at Halloween and the all-new *Father Christmas Village* for the full festive season, with the chance to meet Santa and his helpers.

BRITTIP

Brit Guide researcher Andy de Maertelaere points out that the park's elaborate Christmas decorations now stay up through the New Year period, usually coming down only after the first weekend in Jan.

The Chaparral Theater: Opposite Critter Corral, this is one of the park's 4 main live entertainment venues. The attractions here are seasonal and Disney does tend to change them at regular intervals but, at the time of writing, the main offerings were: **Goofy's Summer Camp,** a knee-slappin' live music, song and dance hoedown featuring Goofy, Donald, Daisy, Chip 'n' Dale, plus a cast of lively sidekicks. Heavy on the yee-haws and hey-howdy-heys, much of the fun is dependant upon crowd enthusiasm, so leave your inhibitions at the door and join right in! Youngsters are encouraged to participate in a rope tug competition, while adults learn a few energetic dance moves. Bilingual dialogue, with spirited hand-clapping being the main form of communication. AAA.

Mickey's Winter Wonderland takes over in the theatre from mid-Nov to

Woody's Roundup Village

early Mar, with an equally clever ice-skating show featuring Mickey and the gang (including a suitably hapless Donald Duck) that will keep youngsters enchanted for the full 25 minutes. It is a fairly straightforward song-and-dance pastiche, but once again the staging and lighting are impressive and its bilingual style ensures English speakers are not left out. AAAA.

Disneyland Railroad – Frontierland Depot: Often the best place to catch the theme park's steam train is next door, to take the slow chug all the way round.

© Disney

Silver Spur Steakhouse

🇬🇧 BRITTIP

If there isn't a queue, take the Railroad steam train for the best short cut to Fantasyland or Discoveryland. However, it is usually quicker to walk if you need the fastest way back to Main Street USA.

Shopping: Shopping is suitably cowboy orientated, with **Tobias Norton & Sons – Frontier Traders**, a leather emporium featuring hats, boots, wallets and belts; **Bonanza Outfitters**, offering the full range of Western apparel; and the **Eureka Mining Supplies**, which stocks a selection of typical cowboy-style foods and toys, including the inevitable hats and guns.

Dining: Your dining options feature 2 outstanding opportunities. The **Silver Spur Steakhouse** is a truly deluxe establishment, designed like a classic Western hotel, using rich, dark wood and plush upholstery. The subdued lighting provides an intimate dining style and there is a display kitchen at the back. Steaks are its stock-in-trade, but it also does excellent salmon, chicken, steaks and vegetarian ravioli. Set, 3-course meals are €27 and €32 adult, a 2-course Menu Pony Express for 3–11s is €12; à la carte dishes €14.50–29.90. Starters €5.90–9.50 (2-person starter €16.50) and wine €16–45/bottle. The Express Meal is €19.90 adult, €16 teen, €12 children. Superb desserts (€6.10–7.90, €12.50 2-person) add to the high quality on offer here.

Character-seekers will want to make a beeline for the **Lucky Nugget Saloon**, which offers a fabulous Tex-Mex buffet lunch noon–3pm with

Investigate the paths between Frontierland and Adventureland

© Disney

Cowboy Cookout Barbecue

characters, plus 6–10pm for dinner in high season. The restaurant is wonderfully styled like a 2-storey Western saloon, with a stage and a long bar. The food is a serve-yourself buffet (€30 adult, €15 3–11s) featuring crudités, chicken wings, nachos, salsa, fajitas, spare ribs, chilli con carne, pasta, pizza and a large choice of desserts (drinks not included). The character interaction here includes the seemingly omnipresent Chip 'n' Dale, Pluto, Gideon (from Pinocchio) and Daisy Duck. If €90 for a family of 4 (plus drinks) seems a touch expensive (as it does to us), check out the excellent daily **character tea-time** (3–4.30pm) featuring all the Disney favourites, with a tantalising spread of cakes, pastries and desserts, plus one hot and one cold drink each (€13/person). For an extra €5 a head you can enjoy the even more fun-filled character Birthday Party. Be aware the location is subject to change, with Plaza Gardens Restaurant as the alternate venue.

Otherwise, your fast-food dining choices include the **Cowboy Cookout Barbecue**, a counter-service barn of a place featuring spare ribs, burgers and smoked chicken, plus a range of meat skillets and side dishes. The lovely smoky barbecue smell, the cowboy ambience and the Country &

Western twang (with live music periodically) add up to a memorable experience, even if the food is average (€4.95–8.55; 4 set meals €9.95–11.95).

Fuente del Oro Restaurante goes down Mexico way for more counter-service, cantina style, with tacos, chilli and other Mexican specialities such as fajitas and nachos (one of the better counter-service options, but very busy noon–2pm; chilli con carne €7.55; mixed plate of chicken wings, vegetable fajita €5.95; chicken fajita €8.55; 4 set meals €9.95–12.95).

Finally, the recently revamped **Last Chance Café** (in between the Silver Spur Steakhouse and Lucky Nugget Saloon) offers more cowboy fare with typical Western al fresco decor, serving turkey legs, chips and sandwiches.

Fuente del Oro

Interconnecting paths: A unique feature of this section of the park is the latticework of paths that interconnect between Frontierland and Adventureland. This surprisingly small-scale landscaping is a notable element of the European influence behind the overall design, and the paths are almost interwoven to provide an alternative way of getting around as well as highlighting different aspects of the lands (but keep your map handy in case you get lost!).

BRITTIP

Try to get a view of the Castle from one of the small side paths between Frontierland and Adventureland, as there are a number of unusual perspectives offering good photo opportunities.

Halloweenland

If you are here in October, remember Frontierland becomes Halloweenland during Disney's Halloween Festival, with a dazzling array of spooky special effects, creepy scenery and haunted shows. A giant spider's web covers Fort Comstock, the Thunder Mesa Riverboat gets a ghoulish mummy-style makeover, pumpkins, witches and scarecrows abound, various Disney characters turn up throughout Halloweenland's pathways, and the finale show, *It's Party Time with Mickey and Friends*,

Halloween in Frontierland

A Halloween hair workshop

is taken over by Disney villains like Captain Hook, Jafar, Frollo, Gaston, Cruella De Vil, and Maleficent. Disney villains also join Tim Burton's *Nightmare Before Christmas* characters **Jack Skellington** and **Sally**, along with the Pumpkin people, in the Halloween re-themed Once Upon a Dream Parade. Children (under 12) can also get into the 'spirit' with some **Halloween Face Painting** at various points in Frontierland.

Mickey's Not So Scary Halloween Party returns on select nights in Oct, 8–11pm, with a family-friendly atmosphere even the youngest guests will enjoy. Young 'uns can dress up in their Halloween costumes for tricks and treats with Mickey, his Friends and the Disney villains, and the party offers a rare chance to capture some truly unique and memorable photos of the characters in their costumes. Some attractions remain open during the party (c.€25/person, under-3s free).

BRITTIP

A separate night-time Halloween Party event on 31 Oct is not widely publicised in the UK, so it is worth seeking out if you are visiting at that time. The party runs 8.30pm–1am (c.€32/person, under-3s free; call 00 33 1 60 30 60 53 to order tickets in advance).

© Disney

Le Pont Suspendu

The transformation of the whole 'land' – unlike anything attempted at the American parks – is hugely ambitious, but the Imagineers have pulled off quite a triumph here, making Oct a real must-visit month.

Adventureland

Africa, the Caribbean and the jungles of Asia combine to provide a host of contrasting and thrilling experiences, all with lush landscaping. This is the 'land' with the fewest attractions, but the whole area has such a wealth of detail and fine architecture (take a close look at Skull Rock and the castle façade of the Pirates ride) that it is easy to spend a good deal of time just wandering and admiring. Even if you don't eat at most of the counter-service diners, it is worth looking into places like Colonel Hathi's Pizza Outpost and Restaurant Hakuna Matata to appreciate the interior design that gives them a real storybook feel.

BRITTIP
Adventureland is the hardest 'land' to navigate, so hang on to your map to find your way from place to place.

Indiana Jones and the Temple of Peril: If you come from Frontierland, turn left by Colonel Hathi's for this 5-star thrill ride. Not content with creating a ducking and diving coaster that seems to zip along much faster when you're aboard than when you're watching, the designers added a brain-scrambling 360º loop and have reconfigured it twice to run either backwards or forwards. The theming is wonderful, with the queuing area leading you through an archaeological dig in true Indiana Jones style, before you reach the temple and your rickety mine wagon. Before you know it, you are being thrown around a tight, twisting track with its sudden loop and dramatic swoops, only to come to the end of the track all too soon once your body has got the hang of it! This is definitely not the ride if you suffer from neck or back problems as there is quite a bit of vibration but it is also quite exhilarating and much more fun than it looks. Indiana Jones is a FastPass ride, which is handy for coaster lovers as queues can be slow-moving. The first couple of hours of the day are rarely busy, and the queues often don't build up here until mid-afternoon. Restrictions: 1.40m/4ft 6in. TTTT. (FP).

Indiana Jones and the Temple of Peril

© Disney

BRITTIP

The scary aspect of the Indiana Jones ride and its position at the innermost end of Adventureland means it is often overlooked by many park visitors, hence it is a good ride to do during the morning and even the afternoon at quieter times of the year.

La Cabane des Robinson

Adventure Isle: Retracing your steps slightly and turning left brings you into this central portion of Adventureland. The Imagineers have worked overtime here to create something different from existing themes in other parks. They opted for an elaborate overgrown adventure playground. This delightful pot-pourri of attractions, mainly aimed at children, is also eye-catching and detailed enough to appeal to adults.

La Cabane des Robinson: The Swiss Family Treehouse is the first attraction you come to on the Isle. The re-creation of the treehouse of the castaway Robinson family from the 1960 Disney film is only a walk-through attraction and looks rather tired these days as the giant 'banyan tree' that was adapted to provide their shelter, food and running water is in urgent need of an overhaul. But queues are rarely a problem and there are great views from the top. AA.

BRITTIP

Adventure Isle is just about the only area of either park that is NOT accessible for guests with disabilities as it is simply not designed for the use of wheelchairs.

Spinning off the treehouse is a high-level rope suspension bridge, **Le Pont Suspendu**, which takes you on to the 4 other sections of the Isle: **Skull Rock** (a labyrinthine stone edifice that towers over one end of the lagoon), **L'Ile au Tresor** (a series of lookout towers and spooky secret caves), **Le Ventre de la Terre** (a series of galleries under the tree) and **La Plage des Pirates** (or Pirates' Beach, a clever play area of slides and climbs expressly for little shipmates). Kids will want to dash off and explore Ben Gunn's Cave, Ambush Alley and Dead Man's Bridge, and it is a good area in which to let them loose for a while. TTT/AAA.

Skull Rock

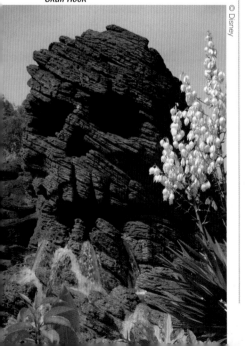

© Disney

Pirates of the Caribbean: Coming off at the top end of Adventure Isle brings you to one of Disney's trademark unmissable rides. The original version of this attraction was installed in *Disneyland California* in 1967 and

© Disney

Passage Enchanté d'Aladdin

remains an Imagineering gem to this day, highlighted by their pioneering work with audio-animatronics. These are a series of life-like figures that move, talk, gesticulate and, in this instance, lay siege to a Caribbean island! Your journey starts as you wind down inside the Spanish Fort, through secret streets and dingy dungeons, until you reach your boat for a plunge into the darkness of this pirate realm. There are 2 minor plunges (and slight splashes – front seat passengers may get a little wet), the first of which drops you into the middle of the island siege, with the clever – and distinctly amusing – action going on all around, and a second that drops into the pirate treasure caverns. Skeletons and dungeons abound, and it may be a little too intense for under-5s, but

there is little that is genuinely scary and the whole effect is so amazing you will probably want to have several turns to appreciate all the detail. While it is a popular ride, queues drop off towards the end of the day and it is often possible to ride with very little wait (it is also a welcome place to cool down during the hotter months!). AAAAA (TTTT for under 8s). NB: See if you can spot some of the elements 'borrowed' when this ride was used as the inspiration for Disney's hit film *Pirates of the Caribbean: The Curse of the Black Pearl* in 2003.

If you enter Adventureland via the main entrance off the Central Plaza, you will come straight into the **Agrabah Bazaar** area. Here you will find the **Passage Enchanté d'Aladdin**, a walk-through exhibit of the Aladdin story with some amusing tableaux and clever lighting tricks. AA.

Shopping: The shopping options tend to be rather humdrum in this area. The array includes **Indiana Jones Adventure Outpost** (safari accessories and Indy souvenirs), **Les Trésors de Shéhérazade** (magic lamps, dolls, clothes), **La Girafe Curieuse** (jungle-themed curios and wild animal toys) and **Le Coffre du Capitaine** (as you exit the Pirates ride, with a suitable range of sea-themed treasures and toys) but they are worth a look more for their décor than the merchandise.

Inside Café Agrabah

© Disney

© Disney

Colonel Hathi's Pizza Outpost

Dining: One of the real scenic highlights, though, is the magnificent indoor/outdoor shopping and dining scenario (straight out of 1,001 Nights) of the **Agrabah Café**, which offers a creative and appealing Mediterranean-oriental buffet, among the best on property. Selections include shwarma, chicken, lamb, couscous, salads and tempting desserts (€19.90 adults, €9.90 children; child's meal comes with a drink and surprise).

Adventureland is also home to one of our all-time favourite Disney restaurants, the **Blue Lagoon**, which is actually set inside the Pirates ride (so there are usually a few shouts of 'Bon Appetit!' from people setting off

Agrabah Café

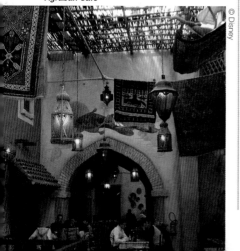

© Disney

on the ride as you dine) and is the occasional haunt of Captain Jack Sparrow himself (just outside for character meet 'n' greets and, periodically, inside as well). You enter just below and to the left of the ride entrance, and the setting alone is worth a look. You eat on a mock 'outdoor' terrace under dim lights, authentically furnished, listening to

BRITTIP

Plan a special meal, even with the kids, in the Blue Lagoon and you won't be disappointed. Book at City Hall or with your hotel concierge. A perfect pit stop in winter when it is heated to tropical temperatures!

sounds that evoke the feeling of an evening on some distant Caribbean island. The seafood-orientated menu is also a delight, with the likes of grilled swordfish with coriander, roasted prawns with basil, Jamaican pepper fillet of beef and chicken and seafood with Creole-style rice. The set Buccaneer's menu is €29 (€16 teens, €12 3–11s), while starters are €9.50–13.50 and main courses €15.60–38.90. The speciality set menu, Sea Treasures, features crab, scallops, tuna, ostrich steak, and swordfish for a princely €34. The kids' menu includes beef meatballs in a creamy tomato sauce, pasta or chicken stir-fry for €12. Desserts are €7.50–8.90.

BRITTIP

Researcher An...
surprised to see...
around the park, desp...
smoking laws in France...
smoking to specific out... areas. Cast
Members don't seem keen to ask people
to put cigarettes out.

Sleeping Beauty Castle

Recent feedback from readers
suggests standards slip here from
time to time, but our experience has
always been first class.

BRITTIP

A 'secret' route goes from the
park entrance all the way to the
heart of Fantasyland, mainly under cover.
Take Liberty Arcade up Main Street USA,
turn sharp left into Frontierland, walk
straight through Fort Comstock and
follow the covered walkway into
Adventureland. Skirt around Les Trésors
de Schéhérazade (briefly in the open),
then pick up the walkway alongside the
restaurant Au Chalet de la Marionnette
and you end up at the Peter Pan ride. It
is also a quick way OUT of Fantasyland
when the park is busy.

Counter-service options here include
Colonel Hathi's Pizza Outpost,
serving up pizzas, salads and pastas
(€6.45–7.55; set menus €9.95 and
€12.95) all in best *Jungle Book* style. A
family offering is also available at
€29.95 for a whole pizza and 150cl
drink. **Restaurant Hakuna Matata**
offers a decent safari adventure, with
rice meals and Asian finger-food,
notably spiced chicken, fish nuggets,
lamb kebab and a shrimp and tuna
salad. **Café de la Brousse** features
sandwiches, hot dogs, ice-creams
and drinks.

Fantasyland

Having arrived in the theme park's
largest 'land' via Adventureland, here
you will find the biggest selection of
rides and the most concentrated fun
for under-8s. This is the stuff of pure
fantasy and the whimsical creativity
on show is first class, from the huge
Castle down to the tiny detail of the
clock façade on 'it's a small world'.
Unfortunately, it is also the most
crowded area, with queues building
up quickly from mid-morning and
rarely abating until early evening
(when it is open until 11pm). Parts of
the back of Fantasyland also close
from 9pm to prepare for the evening
fireworks, so don't think you have the
place to yourself all of a sudden!

If you have young children,
Fantasyland should be your first port
of call as it is likely to offer the most
candidates for 'favourite ride' and it is
not unknown for families to spend
virtually all day here. If you come for
'rope drop' (highly recommended),

Sleeping Beauty Castle

should head straight through the Castle and try to do the Carrousel, Dumbo and Peter Pan Flight in quick succession. These are all terribly slow-loading rides where the queues build up almost immediately and remain painfully slow all day. Excluding Peter Pan but including the Mad Hatter's Tea Cups (another slow-loader), you might be inclined to say 'We waited ages for THAT?' at the end of the ride as they are not terribly exciting for grown-ups, being basically re-themed versions of standard fairground rides. However, children will almost certainly demand to ride Dumbo at least once and, if you have managed to get it under your belt without waiting half an hour or more (and the queue usually tops a mind-numbing hour), you will have done well!

BRITTIP

When Fantasyland is seriously busy, many people overlook the little area right at the back that is home to 2 excellent child-pleasing rides (Casey Jnr – le Petit Train du Cirque and Le Pays des Contes de Fées) where queues rarely build up but, if they do, move quite quickly. If these rides are packed out, you KNOW the park is crowded! However, during parts of 2009, these were open ONLY at weekends.

Stained glass window in Sleeping Beauty's Castle

Taking Fantasyland in a clockwise direction starting at the Castle, you have 12 main attractions from which to choose, plus 7 restaurants and 7 shops that include some of the most original gift items in the park.

Le Château de la Belle au Bois Dormant (Sleeping Beauty Castle): This is a draw in its own right, having two contrasting things to see. **La Galerie de la Belle au Bois Dormant** is easy to miss as you scamper through, but is actually upstairs in the Castle and tells the story in picture-boards and words (in French) of Sleeping Beauty. Check out the beautiful Renaissance-style tapestries that line the walls and the stunning (and highly photogenic) stained-glass

Dumbo the Flying Elephant

Blanche-Neige et Les Sept Nains

windows. You can also walk along an external balcony that provides a great view from both sides. AA.

Underneath **Le Château** and accessible via 3 different portals (including a back door of Merlin's shop, down a winding stone staircase) is the magnificent **La Tanière du Dragon**, or dragon's lair. Here, the creature that turned many a would-be saviour of Sleeping Beauty to toast lurks in steamy, underground splendour, wrapped in reptilian fashion around the stalactites and stalagmites, occasionally rearing his audio-animatronic head to threaten fire and brimstone on all those who dare disturb his slumbers. In the semi-darkness, it really is a convincing beast (watch its chest 'breathing'!) and is usually far too menacing for under-5s. TTT (for 5–8s).

Sword in the Stone: Stepping through the Castle's rear gate brings you to a courtyard and this great photo opportunity.

Le Carrousel de Lancelot: Right in front of you is this standard horsey merry-go-round that youngsters love, even if queuing can take an age and mum and dad would rather be doing something (anything!) else. AA (TTTT for under-5s).

Blanche-Neige et les Sept Nains (The Adventures of Snow White): Right next door, this is a typical Disney kiddie ride that is a fairly dark journey into the cartoon world of the classic film. The soundtrack is in French, which detracts a little if you are unfamiliar with the story (but then, how many people is that likely to be?). All kids can relate to this mildly scary trip into the realm of the Wicked Witch, her evil plans and the suitably happy ending. Under-5s may find parts of it menacing, but most soon get over their fear of the dark with parental encouragement. AAA (or TTT for under-8s).

Les Voyages de Pinocchio (Pinocchio's Fantastic Journey): Following on is another dark ride, this time in the company of Jiminy Cricket, showing his attempts to keep the wooden puppet-boy on the straight and narrow. Again, it is a touch intense for real young 'uns (especially with the surprise menace of the whale) but most find it fun rather than frightening. The special effect at the end with the Blue Fairy is well worth seeing. AAA (TTT for under-8s).

Dumbo the Flying Elephant: Needing little explanation, this is a standard fairground whirligig with elephants as the flying 'vehicles'. The front-seat passengers get to make the elephant go up and down while circling gently round and round, and that's about it. There is little to look at while you are in the queues, which move painfully

Pinocchio's Fantastic Journey

slowly, and the music is horribly repetitive, but kids seem to get a buzz out of piloting their elephant and it is a highly visible ride, thus hard for parents to ignore! Head here first thing or expect to queue for ages (the crowds do ease off a little during the parades, but there is no substitute for doing this early on). TT (TTTT for under-8s).

Peter Pan's Flight: Next door to Dumbo is Fantasyland's other serious queue-builder, which has the saving grace of being a FastPass ride (see page 122). Once you get to board your pirate ship, you rise up, up and away over the streets of London, turn right at the second star and straight on to morning, all the way to Neverland and a close encounter with Captain Hook and his inept pirates. It is another indoor dark ride (very dark as you go through the star-lit portion), but the overhead mechanism of your 'ship' and the elaborate scenery combine to create the right illusion, making it a big hit with all the family and a must-do ride for most kids. Be aware the waiting time can easily top an hour here and much of the queuing area is in the open, so your best bet is to try to take advantage of the FP. If the FPs have all gone (as often happens by 1pm in high season), leave it as late as possible or wait until a parade has just started. AAAA (TTTTT for under-8s). (FP)

The White Rabbit at Alice's Curious Labyrinth

Fantasy Festival Stage: Step out of Peter Pan, turn left and you come to where the cute **Winnie the Pooh and Friends Too** stage presentation shows 5 times daily in peak season. Join Christopher Robin, Pooh and friends on a grand adventure to the end of the rainbow, where wishes come true. There is an element of menace (courtesy of the Heffalumps), which may unnerve some children, but courage wins the day and it all ends happily ever after. The show also gets a full Christmas makeover for the festive season. AAA (AAAAA under-6s). Look out for a Pooh and Friends meet 'n' greet after the show, too.

BRITTIP

When not in use, the Fantasy Festival Stage makes a handy place to sit in peace and quiet with a drink or snack.

Le Pays des Contes de Fees

Winnie the Pooh and Friends Too

Fantasyland Railroad Station: The entrance is to the left of the Festival Stage. This will usually get you back to Main Street USA much quicker than walking, if there isn't a serious queue. Now, all the attractions so far are relatively faithful copies of Disney rides in other parks, but the next is a true *Disneyland Paris* original.

Alice's Curious Labyrinth: An interactive maze leading up to the Queen of Hearts' castle, this seems to have almost universal appeal for children up to about 12. There is a range of *Alice in Wonderland* tricks and motifs along the way, including amusing signage, squirting fountains (kids *really* gravitate towards these, trying to catch the water as it 'jumps' from bush to bush), an encounter with the hookah-smoking Caterpillar and several scrapes with the Queen of Hearts and her guards (in various audio-animatronic guises). It is gentle stuff but keeps youngsters (and their parents) amused for a good 15–20 minutes and is an ideal place to visit when waits at Peter Pan and Dumbo hit an hour. AAA. NB: This may be closed for much of the winter under new budget cutbacks.

Passing further along and under the railway bridge brings you to the little area right at the back of Fantasyland that gets overlooked by some (although it can also be closed at quieter times of the year). But, if you have young children this is somewhere you won't want to miss,

both for the instant kiddie appeal and the shorter queues. Both rides are copies from the original *Disneyland Park* in California, but they possess a timeless charm for children.

Le Pays des Contes de Fées: This is a gentle boat ride into a fairytale world, with miniature depictions of stories like *Snow White, Peter and the Wolf, The Wizard of Oz, Beauty and the Beast* and *The Little Mermaid*. For the Aladdin section, your boat is 'swallowed up' by the giant lion's-mouth cave from the story, which can be a little daunting for the youngest passengers, but the whole thing proceeds at barely walking pace, so you have plenty of time to ease any apprehensions. AAA.

BRITTIP

If you are at Le Pays des Contes de Fées out of peak periods, the boat ride is usually a walk-on attraction and has the great benefit for youngsters of being able to take them straight back on for another go. Again, be aware it may be open only on weekends.

Casey Jr – le Petit Train du Cirque: Another guaranteed hit for the under-8 brigade. In reality, it is a fairly tame, junior-sized coaster, themed in eye-catching style after the circus train in *Dumbo*. Some of the cars are designed like animal cages, others are open and, of course, 2 can sit up front

Alice's Curious Labyrinth

in the 'engine'. It glides along for some 5 minutes, encountering a couple of mild dips and gentle bends, but it gives just the right illusion of excitement to those of the requisite age (and any nervous parents!). AAA (TTTT for under-5s).

As you exit this 2-ride mini-land, you pass the disused Les Pirouettes Du Vieux Moulin, a big-wheel type ride that proved unworkable with even moderate queues and that has quietly been abandoned. It still looks good in non-working mode but sadly that is all you get from it.

Mad Hatter's Tea Cups: Another standard fairground ride, this has been given a bit of *Alice in Wonderland* top-spin to make it seem more than it actually is. Kids all seem to love the chance to ride in these manically whirling cups, which have a wheel to make them spin counter to the main rotation (Uuurgghhh! we say). We have to admit, going round in never-decreasing circles (or so it feels) was never our 'cup of tea' at all, but it remains a seriously popular ride, so it is best to do this one early in the day or later in the evening. TTT.

Continuing our clockwise tour of Fantasyland brings you next to one of Disney's signature rides.

Mad Hatter's Tea Cups

'it's a small world': Designed under the direction of Walt himself for the New York World Fair in 1964, this ride has stood the test of time amazingly well for children under 8 and remains a big hit. The exterior façade is one of the most eye-catching in the park, with all manner of moving and static elements that add up to a wonderfully artistic collage. Inside, all it really consists of is a slow-moving boat ride through a colourful series of scenes featuring audio-animatronic dolls singing and dancing in various national-themed displays, from Britain to Brazil and Africa to the Arctic. It has an insidiously catchy theme tune (we challenge you NOT to be humming it when you exit!) and an imaginative winter wonderland final scene, but otherwise it just highlights

'its a small world'

Flora in the Fantillusion Parade

the clever way in which Disney's Imagineers can take a routine ride and give it a whole new style and appeal.

Once again, it proves that if you give it the right scale and a proportionate amount of detail (with a little sprinkle of Disney 'pixie dust'), the ordinary can become quite extraordinary. Many adults are captivated by the spirit and vivacity of this attraction, and it is one that bears multiple visits. Queues rarely top 20 minutes and move quite steadily, so this is a good ride to do at most times, but especially in the afternoon (and when it's hot). AAAA.

🇬🇧 BRITTIP

Hang around outside 'it's a small world' on the hour and watch the wonderful clock (you can hear it ticking from quite a distance) come to life with a display of moving figures in best Toytown tradition.

Other entertainment: Another lively piece of 'street entertainment' is the daily *Once Upon a Time Sleeping Beauty* song and dance show in the Castle Courtyard area (by the Sword

in the Stone set-piece), which features Aurora and her Prince several times a day – ideal for young girls.

Shopping: For gift ideas, the interlinked group in and around the Castle offer worthwhile browsing. Pick from **Merlin l'Enchanteur** (a clever 'rock-carved' boutique featuring fine crystal, glassware – hand-made while you watch – and porcelain statuettes), **La Boutique du Château** (a Christmas-orientated offering), **La Confiserie des Trois Fées** (a great sweet shop in the company of good fairies Flora, Fauna and Merryweather from *Sleeping Beauty*), and the epic **Sir Mickey's** (featuring cuddly toys, jewellery, glass and ceramics, plus children's clothes, toys and games).

Dining: When it comes to mealtimes, Fantasyland has a gourmet offering in **Auberge de Cendrillon**, with an elegant ballroom-type setting. Open for lunch 11.30am–4pm and dinner 5.30–9.30pm, it features a set menu with several choices. The set meal is a hefty €55 (€20 for 3–11s), but the big attraction here is the character interaction. 'Suzy and Perla's Fantasies' features the 2 mice from *Cinderella* and a host of Disney princes and princesses, dancing and interacting with guests (reservations strongly advised, on 01 60 30 40 50 or from any Disney hotel concierge desk). There is also a pleasant

Auberge de Cendrillon

outdoor courtyard (where Cinderella's carriage stands), that offers a limited but tasty menu for dining al fresco, including soups, sandwiches and desserts.

The other 3 outlets are all counter-service and fill up quickly for lunch at even mildly busy times: **Au Chalet de la Marionnette**, which has a rear entrance opening into Adventureland, serves 5 set menus including hot dogs, burgers and salads, plus a range of desserts; **Toad Hall Restaurant**, modelled in mock English country house style, à la *Wind in the Willows*, serves fish and chips, fish burgers, chicken burgers, sandwiches, salads and cakes (set menus €9.95–11.95); and **Pizzeria Bella Notte**, an Italian-style counter-service restaurant diner modelled on *Lady and the Tramp*, offering pizza and pasta (3 set menus, €9.95–12.95; family menu €29.95 – large pizza and a litre of soda or mineral water).

BRITTIP

Of all the counter-service restaurants in busy Fantasyland, the Pizzeria Bella Notte is likely to have the shortest queues, as it is slightly off the beaten track.

More venues for a snack, ice-cream or drink include **March Hare Refreshments**, **The Old Mill** and **Fantasia Gelati**.

Au Chalet de la Marionnnette

© Disney

© Disney

Space Mountain Mission 2

Discoveryland

When the Imagineers set about designing the park's fifth and final 'land', their challenge was to come up with a new variant on a fairly well-worn theme. In both Anaheim and Orlando, this area had been developed as Tomorrowland, an unabashed attempt to predict and present the future in an amusing way. There is a mock retro styling about the previous examples, but that was felt to be an over-used idea when it came to *Disneyland Paris* and the call went out for something new. So, the Imagineers studied their European literature and came up with a new motif, that of a future world inspired by technology derived from historical luminaries such as Leonardo da Vinci and Jules Verne. This helped determine the overall look and feel of Discoveryland (a new title too, as Tomorrowland was felt to be too narrow a definition), hence the styling is a kind of 'antique' future, with much of the architecture borrowing heavily from Verne's 19th-century images of the future.

The two principal icons – Space Mountain: Mission 2 and the Café Hypérion – are magnificent re-creations of Vernian visions and help to create a visual stimulus that is both bold and exciting (can you tell we quite like this area!). The fanciful exterior of Space Mountain is one of the greatest examples of the ride designer's art because so much of it is totally superfluous to the ride itself; it is purely and simply a statement of style that epitomises the creativity inherent in a Disney theme park. And the rides are pretty good, too!

Space Mountain: Mission 2:
Completely re-themed and revamped in 2005, this breathtaking blast of a ride borrows from the Verne novel *From the Earth to the Moon* and gives it a contemporary twist. Whereas the original giant cannon Columbiad (of the Baltimore Gun Club) blasted riders to the Moon, now the over-sized gun barrel has been super-charged to send its vehicles much deeper into space, to discover the secrets of the universe! (Actually, the main ride is exactly the same, but the new theming is convincing.) You queue up through the heart of the ride itself before you reach your vehicle, which is 'loaded' into Columbiad. The dry ice flows, the music rolls, the lights pulsate and then… Pow! You are off at gravity-defying speed to explore outer space, dodging close encounters with meteorites and other cosmic phenomena, looping the loop, corkscrewing twice past thundering comets and evading an exploding supernova into 'a new dimension' as the unexpected climax to this 3-minute whiz. The high-tech light show alone is worth seeing and, if the description sounds disturbing, don't let it put you off. This is one of the smoothest coasters you will ride and it is a big-time thrill. It is also a FastPass ride, which is vital for peak periods as the crowds flock here from early on. Souvenir photos are also available. Restrictions: 1.32m/4ft 3in. TTTTT. (FP)

Les Mystères du Nautilus: As you exit Space Mountain, you encounter another *Disneyland Paris* original, a clever walk-through version of Captain Nemo's famous submarine. The realism as you go down 'underground' on a circular steel staircase is all-encompassing, bringing you into the Nautilus itself and a self-guided tour of this amazing Verne creation. Take your time to peer into all the nooks and crannies and admire the intricate detail, and sit for a moment at one of the big, circular portholes. Is that a giant squid moving in, too close…? You'll have to check it out for yourself! Under-7s must be accompanied by an adult (11.30am–5.30pm only). AAA.

Orbitron – Machines Volantes: Next door is this similarly eye-catching ride, which is really only a jazzed-up version of the Dumbo ride, spinning and climbing in regulation fashion as the front-seat 'pilot' takes the

Discoveryland

controls. The clever circulation of the accompanying 'planets' really makes this ride, however, giving it the look of something more intricate, and it is another one that is fun just to watch. TT (TTTTT for under-8s).

Star Tours: Behind Space Mountain is the impressive futuristic façade of Disney's collaboration with *Star Wars* director George Lucas. The queuing area alone is something of a masterpiece, as you are drawn into the make-believe world of squabbling 'droids C-3PO and R-2D2 as they prepare your Star Speeder for the light-speed trip to Endor. This is a faithful transplant of the ride in *Disneyland California* and *Disney's Hollywood Studios* in Orlando, with the exception that the commentary provided by your robot pilot is in French. The ride itself, though, is a 24-carat thrill, as the realistic Speeders load and lift off for outer space, where various mishaps create a series of adventures. This was the bee's knees when it made its debut in Anaheim in 1987 and is still a magical experience for Disney newcomers (although those familiar with the ride from elsewhere may feel it is a little humdrum by now; rumours of a make-over are ongoing and intriguing). Star Tours is also a FastPass ride, which is handy because you could spend 45-plus minutes queuing at peak periods. There is no height restriction, but those with bad backs or necks might want to give it a miss, and it is probably too intense for under-4s. TTTT. (FP)

Orbitron

Star Tours

The exit to Star Tours used to bring you into an amusing area of interactive games, L'Astroport Services Interstellaires, but sadly these have been scrapped in favour of some fairly standard (and rather dismal by comparison) video arcade fare, which you need to negotiate on your way out. Behind Star Tours is **Disneyland Railroad – Discoveryland Station**, but this is a good one to miss at busy times as it is second only to the Main Street station for drawing long, slow-moving queues.

> **BRITTIP**
>
> Head for Discoveryland first and you can ride either Space Mountain: Mission 2 or Star Tours without much of a queue and pick up a FastPass for the other. The new Space Mountain: Mission 2 draws heavy crowds throughout the main part of the day.

Honey, I Shrunk the Audience: Right next door to Star Tours, this 3-D film show is also a major Disney trademark attraction. Pioneered in all its American parks, it provides yet another variation on theme park thrills. Here, continuing where the hit films left off, you enter a wacky science world of the Imagination Institute (narrated by the amusing Eric Idle), where they are about to honour the inventions of a certain Professor Wayne Szalinski. An entertaining 8-minute pre-show sets

© Disney

Autopia

the scene for the main part of your adventure in the awards 'theatre' and the real fun begins once you don your 3-D glasses. The inevitable on-stage mishaps are accompanied by a sequence of special effects throughout the theatre that often have the audience in hysterics (although under-5s may find it scary). It would be a shame to spoil it by revealing anything, so just sit back and get ready to be surprised... very surprised (and beware the sneezing dog!). This is a show that requires a full English dialogue, hence headphones are provided for non-French speakers. The entire show can be in English at times in high season though. AAAA (plus TTT).

Autopia: Another attraction you need to visit early on unless you want a long wait. Rather old-fashioned, this mock Grand Prix track – a 'futuristic Formula One circuit' – is purely for kids and sits a little awkwardly among the more sci-fi laden offerings. It is often closed for maintenance (and at off-peak times) and is notoriously slow to load, so queues can touch an hour or more and move slowly. And, unless you are under 9, you're unlikely to get much of a thrill from these tame cars that run on well-defined tracks, even if they provide

the illusion of driving. Children under 1.32m/4ft 3in must be accompanied by an adult but you are not missing much if you bypass this one. T (TTT for under-9s).

Buzz Lightyear Laser Blast: This wonderful interactive family ride appeals to all ages and can be quite addictive. Riders are 'recruited' into Buzz Lightyear's Space Ranger galaxy defence force and kids in particular will not want to miss this chance to join the great *Toy Story* character in his battle against evil Emperor Zurg. You ride into action against Zurg's villainous robot army – and shoot them with laser cannons! You can spin your car from side to side and score points as you would in an arcade game, which ensures everyone

Buzz Lightyear Laser Blast

© Disney

tries it again to improve their score. Watch out for a gift shop and ride photo opportunity as you exit. It is extremely popular, though, and queues are long and slow-moving, so visit early in the day. FastPasses are often all gone by early afternoon. TTT (TTTTT for under 8s). (FP)

BRITTIP

The Buzz Lightyear robot targets have different values, with anything moving worth a higher score. Watch out for the large robot as you enter the first room. Turn your vehicle around and aim for the target on his hand – it's worth 10,000 points. Then aim for the middle of Zurg's chest and a direct hit will score 100,000 points!

Videopolis/Cinéma Mickey: Sharing the impressive Café Hypérion building, Cinéma Mickey replaced the *Legend of the Lion King* stage show in 2009, with host Mickey Mouse formally introducing himself, in animation form, on the silver screen and an hour-long festival of continuously looping Disney cartoon classics is now the main attraction. It is the stuff of wonderful nostalgia, introducing 8 cartoon shorts such as the original 1928-vintage *Steamboat Willie*, *Mickey and the Seal* (1948) and *The Lonesome Ghosts* (1937) to the younger set while engendering a sentimental smile in the over-40s. AAA.

© Disney

Discoveryland

BRITTIP

Cinéma Mickey is the perfect spot for a mid-afternoon rest with a snack or a drink. Younger children especially appreciate the gentler experience of the classic cartoons as a break from the hectic pace of the parks.

Arcades Alpha and Beta: As a final word on the attractions, the inevitable video games also make an appearance here on each side of the lower entrance to Videopolis. Older children and young teens who need a break from the family shackles for a while can head to either of these (or the arcade inside the exit to Star Tours) and shoot up a T-Rex or play football or air hockey. Be warned, the games are not cheap – one token costs €2 and there is a 1-token minimum per game. TT.

Buzz Lightyear Laser Blast

© Disney

Videopolis

Shopping: There are 2 main gift shops here, the elaborate **Constellations** (the usual range of souvenirs but with a ceiling twinkling with a 'universe' of stars) and **Star Traders** (for all your *Star Wars*-related merchandise, other space toys and sports gear).

Dining: When it comes to eating, the **Café Hypérion** is worth investigating even if you don't visit the counter-service diner, which serves very average cheeseburgers, chicken burgers and chicken nuggets. **Buzz Lightyear's Pizza Planet** (easy to miss, but it's just to the right of Honey, I Shrunk the Audience) is a disappointing offering if you expect something out of the *Toy Story* film. The interior is very plain and the €7.95 (€4.95 for children) pizza is not dissimilar to cardboard. Alternatives are the chicken sandwich (€5.95), vegetarian sandwich (€6.15) or pizza burger (€6.45), plus 3 salad selections (€6.95). The **Rocket Café** at the back of Space Mountain offers some additional snacks and drinks that you can eat in relative peace and quiet at the tables outside Pizza Planet.

BRITTIP

To prove Disney also thinks on a small scale as well as the large, check out the audio-animatronic pigeons (!) attached to the Hypérion airship at the entrance to Café Hypérion.

Parades, shows and tours

As if 5 'lands' weren't enough, you have several other sources of great entertainment along the way. Chief among these is the daily parade (or parades if you are here in high season or for a special event like Halloween or Christmas). **Disney's Once Upon a Dream Parade** was new for the park's 15th Anniversary in 2007 and continues to be the daily highlight (except for Oct when it takes on a Halloween theme and the festive period from mid-Nov to early Jan when it becomes the **Christmas Parade** – see page 24). If you have never seen a Disney parade, this is a genuine must-see experience. Yes, the queues at many attractions do tend to shorten while the parade is running, but it is a shame to miss something as creative and dynamic as this. Each one starts in the Discovery Arcade corner of Town Square and continues up Main Street USA to the Central Plaza, where it turns right in front of the Royal Castle Stage and moves into Fantasyland before finally exiting next to 'it's a small world'.

Belle on parade

BRITTIP

Be aware people start staking out the best spots to watch the parades – along Main Street USA and around the Central Plaza – up to an hour in advance. There can also be a bit of push-and-shove as late-comers try to squeeze in.

Children are truly captivated by the scale and elaboration of the huge floats, as well as the chance to see a multitude of their favourite characters at fairly close quarters. The music is memorable, the dancing amazingly energetic (especially given the heat in summer) and the splendour of floats themed to a variety of 'dreams that really can come true' is truly enchanting. The 8 floats feature a series of Disney characters bringing their dreams of Imagination, Fantasy, Laughter and Fun, Friendship, Power, Adventure and Romance to life, and the whole spectacle takes a good 25–30 minutes to pass by. You will take a LOT of photos – if you don't end up being sidetracked by watching children's faces around you. AAAAA.

Disney's Once Upon A Dream Parade

BRITTIP

For the main daily parades, the route through Fantasyland is less crowded than elsewhere, while the corner of the Town Square in front of City Hall is also a good place to wait as it is often overlooked and offers some shade when it's hot.

Disney's Fantillusion parade adds to the picture for the high summer and winter season evenings (usually around 10pm), and is equally stunning. It features an eye-popping

Disney's Fantillusion Parade

The Disneyland Park with children

Here is a rough guide to the rides that appeal to different age groups. Obviously, children vary enormously in their likes and dislikes but, as a general rule, you can be fairly sure the following will have most appeal to the ages concerned (also taking into account the height restrictions):

Under-5s

Disneyland Railroad, Main Street Vehicles, Thunder Mesa Riverboats, Pocahontas Indian Village, Pirates' Beach play area, La Cabane des Robinson, Goofy's Summer Camp, Winnie the Pooh and Friends Too, Blanche-Neige et les Sept Nains (Snow White), Les Voyages de Pinocchio (Pinocchio's Fantastic Journey), Le Carrousel de Lancelot, Peter Pan's Flight, Dumbo, 'it's a small world', Le Pays des Contes de Fées, Casey Jr – Le Petit Train du Cirque, Alice's Curious Labyrinth, Buzz Lightyear Laser Blast, Orbitron (not recommended for babies), Autopia, Les Mystères du Nautilus, Cinéma Mickey, Disney's Once Upon A Dream Parade.

6–8s

All the above, plus Phantom Manor (with parental discretion), Fort Comstock, River Rogue Keelboats, Rustler Roundup Shootin' Gallery, Big Thunder Mountain, Adventure Isle, Pirates of the Caribbean, Le Passage Enchanté d'Aladdin, La Tanière du Dragon, Mad Hatter's Tea Cups, Star Tours, Honey, I Shrunk the Audience.

9–12s

Phantom Manor, Fort Comstock, Rustler Roundup Shootin' Gallery, Big Thunder Mountain, The Tarzan Encounter, Pirates of the Caribbean, Adventure Isle, Indiana Jones and the Temple of Peril, Peter Pan's Flight, Mad Hatter's Tea Cups, Alice's Curious Labyrinth, Arcades Alpha and Beta, Buzz Lightyear's Laser Blast, Orbitron, Space Mountain: Mission 2, Les Mystères du Nautilus, Honey, I Shrunk the Audience, Star Tours.

Over-12s

Phantom Manor, Big Thunder Mountain, Rustler Roundup Shootin' Gallery, Pirates of the Caribbean, Adventure Isle, Indiana Jones and the Temple of Peril, Mad Hatter's Tea Cups, Arcades Alpha and Beta, Buzz Lightyear's Laser Blast, Orbitron, Space Mountain: Mission 2, Honey, I Shrunk the Audience, Star Tours.

cavalcade of Disney favourites in a high-tech setting of glittering lights and dazzling floats. The parade comes in 3 parts and unfolds with an almost balletic grace, first as Mickey himself brings the Gift of Light, then a darker section as the Disney villains threaten to take over (with some spectacular special effects as Jafar transforms into a serpent, Maleficent becomes the wicked dragon and the winged Chernabog commands fire) and finally a joyful conclusion as the glittering heroes and heroines,

princes and princesses get together with Minnie to save the day.

It features a fabulous soundtrack by Bruce Healy and a seemingly endless fairytale pageant of shimmering, twinkling lights. The overall effect is

Disney's Once Upon A Dream Parade

© Disney

BRITTIP

Stake out a spot in front of the Castle. It is the only location where you can see all 3 stops during the Fantillusion Parade.

© Disney

Halloween Parade

so thrilling, even by Disney standards, that it is worth keeping the kids up to see it. The whole parade stops at various points for a few well-rehearsed routines from the costumed dancers, and it can take a good 30 minutes to pass by. But, whatever you do, don't miss this one! AAAAA+.

The **Halloween Opening Parade** adds to the daily fun throughout Oct (check your park map for timings) and is another visual riot of creepy costumed capers, song and dance,

The Pumpkin Men on Main Street

© Disney

BRITTIP

You can watch the Fantillusion parade from the steps of the Disneyland Railroad Main Street Station on Town Square, then, once it has passed, take one of the Arcades up to Central Plaza to be ready for the fireworks while people are still watching the parade on Main Street!

with various characters joining the extravaganza. Here, the Disney villains have usurped the stage for a darker (but still fun) cavalcade of ghosts, goblins and witches, with some inventive, skeleton-inspired touches. Jack Skellington and Sally from Tim Burton's *Nightmare Before Christmas* take a leading role, and watch out for the Pumpkin Men and Ladies creating havoc along the way! AAAA.

It is worth taking a mental step back from all the clever artistry of the floats to appreciate the non-stop energy and quality of the many dancers in the parades, who keep up their efforts for every second of every performance, day in, day out. It takes immense dedication, but they also have a lot of fun and get a real kick out of the reaction they get from their audience – especially the kids. So don't hesitate

© Disney

Disney's Showtime Spectacular

scenes, priority seating at shows and parades and assistance with dining reservations at the restaurant of your choice. At €500 (regardless of party size) this isn't a budget option, but the chance to spend 4 hours getting tips, enjoying priority access to some rides, and asking any questions you have about the parks and attractions could prove a magical experience indeed!

BRITTIP

Research assistant Andy de Maertelaere points out that the VIP Tour goes inside the Star Tours building for a rare view of the simulator with the lights on – a real treat for Disney die-hards.

And that, folks, is *Disneyland Park* in all its detailed splendour. Hopefully, after a day here (even when crowds are at their heaviest), you will agree with us in judging this to be a work of art in the business of having fun. Take time to acquaint yourself in advance with all that's here and you should be well prepared to get the most out of these immensely diverse attractions. As we advise for visiting any Disney

BRITTIP

Unless you are particularly speedy in leaving the theme park at closing time, you might be better off taking the 15- to 20-minute walk back to the big hotels such as *Disney's Hotel Santa Fe*, *Disney's Cheyenne Hotel* and *Disney's Newport Bay Club*, as the crowds at the shuttle bus stop can mean another lengthy wait.

park, try to take some time along the way to slow down and appreciate all the intricate detail that's involved.

There is just so much packed into this theme park in particular, it would be a shame if you went home without seeing the history of Dapper Dan's barber shop, the nostalgia of the 2 arcades and the whimsy of restaurants like Pizzeria Bella Notte and the Blue Lagoon. It is a wonderfully complete and immersive environment that really does transport you a million miles from everyday life, so make sure you get the most out of it. But we can't stop here. There is a whole new park to explore yet. It's on to the *Walt Disney Studios…!*

Once Upon a Time Sleeping Beauty Show

© Disney

Walt Disney Studios Park

or Lights, Cameras, Action!

While the original park is the grande dame of *Disneyland Paris*, the *Walt Disney Studios Park* is more the brash teenager – fun, lively, a bit raucous and not yet fully polished or refined.

It is certainly a smaller development and a completely different entity to its older sibling, something that complements the first park but doesn't attempt to copy its formula of non-stop rides and 'pixie dust' magic. There are far fewer attractions, but what there are tend to be much bigger in scope and offer a contrasting experience. There's more emphasis on shows, plus the iconic Twilight Zone™ Tower of Terror, while the movie theming is extensive.

There is also a major difference in the geography and topography between them, as well as the newer park being almost half the size (although with scope to continue to grow). It consists of just 4 main areas and, aside from the imposing Tower, there are no great distinguishing features once you have passed through the entrance complex known as the Front Lot. It is an easy park to negotiate, though, and getting from one area to another for the various shows is a lot less problematic than it can be at the older park. You can walk from one end to the other in little more than 5 minutes and it positively invites you to step outside for lunch in *Disney Village* as it's all so simple.

Another notable difference is in the sound of the 2 parks. In the *Disneyland Park*, the accompanying music provides a background to all the fun and rides. In the *Walt Disney Studios Park*, the music is right up front, setting the scene and providing a soundtrack almost everywhere you go, most notably in the Backlot area. This dramatic musical accompaniment underscores the film-orientated nature of the Studios and adds an important extra layer to the overall theming.

Get with the theme

There are only 13 out-and-out main attractions (plus the forthcoming new trio of rides with the opening of Toy Story Playland in summer 2010) as well as the daily parade on which to concentrate. Of course, being Disney,

Simon and friends

© Disney

there are always some delightful extras along the way and here you have several other live elements, and a lot of character meet 'n' greets, adding to the fun factor.

The depth and elaboration of the theming, both architecturally and in the landscaping, is not on the same scale as the *Disneyland Park* either. Some say the *Studios* environment is actually lacking imagination. But, as one Cast Member explained, 'Well, our theme is a movie studio. What do you expect a movie studio to look like, apart from a collection of big, fairly bland buildings?' Of course, there is more to it than that, but it is a pertinent point.

The whole idea is to surround you with the magic of the movies and, to that end, the collection of large studio soundstages that house most of the

Walt Disney Studios

attractions can look vey functional by comparison with the neighbouring park. However, Disney's Imagineers are adding extra embellishments all the time and the internal effects are rarely short of spectacular (just wait until you see the lobby inside The Twilight Zone™ Tower of Terror!).

Walt Disney Studios Park at a glance

Location	Off Exit 14 of the A4 autoroute, proceed to the clearly signed car park; or turn right out of the Marne-la-Vallée RER and TGV station; or through the *Disney Village* if staying at a resort hotel
Size	25 hectares/62 acres in 4 areas
Hours	10am–7pm winter and spring off-peak weekdays; 9 or 10am–7pm all summer (Extra Magic Hours from 7 or 8am for Disney Hotel guests on select days)
Admission	**Under 3** free; **3–11** €44 (1-Day Ticket), €57, €94, €117, €137 (1-, 2-, 3- and 4-Day Park Hopper), **adults** (12+) €52 (1-Day Ticket), €65, €111, €138 (1-, 2-, 3- and 4-Day Park Hopper); **Annual Passports** (per person): Fantasy €129, Dream €189. *NB: All Disney prices and hours subject to change without prior notice (see www.disneylandparis.com)*
Parking	€8
Pushchairs	€7.50 (Pushchair rental counter to left of Studio Photo, on right side of entrance courtyard)
Wheelchairs	€7.50 (also at pushchair rental counter)
Top Attractions	The Twilight Zone™ Tower of Terror, Rock 'n' Roller Coaster starring Aerosmith, Moteurs… Action! Stunt Show Spectacular, Crush's Coaster, Studio Tram Tour, CinéMagique
Don't Miss	Disney's Stars 'n' Cars parade, Disney Studio 1

Hidden Costs		
	Meals	Burger, chips and coke €9.95; Buffet dining €21 for adults and €9.90 for kids (Restaurant des Stars); beer €4.90 33cl; wine €4.20–4.50; Kids' meal €6
	T-shirts	€15–35
	Souvenirs	€2.50–6.95
	Sundries	Face-painting €8–12

WALT DISNEY STUDIOS

Front Lot
1 Walt Disney Studios Store
2 Studio Photo
3 Disney Studio 1
4 Les Légendes d'Hollywood
5 Restaurant en Coulisse

Toon Studio
6 Art of Disney Animation
7 Animagique
8 Flying Carpets Over Agrabah
9 The Disney Animation Gallery
10 Crush's Coaster
11 Cars Quatre Roues Rallye (Cars Race Rally)

Toy Story Playland
12 Slinky Dog Zigzag Spin
13 RC Racer
14 Toy Soldier Parachute Drop

Production Courtyard
15 CinéMagique
16 The Studio Tram Tour
17 Catastrophe Canyon
18 Stitch Live!
19 Playhouse Disney Live on Stage!
20 The Twilight Zone™ Tower of Terror
21 Restaurant des Stars
22 La Terrasse
23 Place des Stars

Backlot
24 Armageddon: Les Effets Spéciaux (Special Effects)
25 Rock 'n' Roller Coaster starring Aerosmith
26 Moteurs…Action! Stunt Show Spectacular
27 Café des Cascadeurs
28 Disney Blockbuster Café
29 Rock Around The Shop

The one possible concern for parents with younger children is there isn't as much for them to do here as next door. There are 6 main kiddie rides (including those in the new area) and 3 shows that are primarily for them, while several attractions are not ideal for young eyes and ears (too loud, fast or scary). The daily parade, however, is a genuine source of family fun, and the high level of character interaction helps round out the experience. You should certainly find it easier to meet Mickey and Co here as there are several regular set-piece meeting points, plus frequent appearances throughout the park.

BRITTIP

As with the *Disneyland Park*, you can take advantage of the Disney Shopping Service for purchases you make here. Instead of having to carry them around, they can be sent to *Disney Village* for you to pick up at the Disney Store from 6pm.

Staying dry

The other clever element of the Studios is that nearly all of the attractions are under cover, which is vital in winter and quite welcome in summer, too. With the exception of the Flying Carpets Over Agrabah, Cars Quatre Roues Rallye and the new Toy Story Playland area, the attractions provide a much longer and more

Monsters Inc. photo opportunity

Flying Carpets Over Agrabah

involving experience. Several of the shows last half an hour or more, which means you can spend longer doing fewer things than in the *Disneyland Park* (with less time spent queuing) but there should still be enough to keep you occupied for a full day (with the option to move between parks with the multi-day Park Hopper tickets – see page 117).

Another difference between the theme parks is the eating opportunities. While the *Disneyland Park* has a comprehensive mix of restaurants, cafés and snack bars, the *Walt Disney Studios Park* is limited to just 4 counter-service options, plus a series of snack wagons. With *Disney Village* just 5 minutes' walk from the front gates, it is easy to argue you have plenty of choice (plus a chance to escape the hubbub), but we look forward to seeing some development in future. At least one full-service restaurant is needed to provide a bit of breadth to the studio style (anyone who has eaten in the Sci Fi Dine-In Theater or the 50s Prime Time Diner at *Disney's Hollywood Studios* in Orlando will know what we mean!). However, there are also fewer shopping opportunities in this park and you don't feel quite so much a target for the hard sell.

© Disney

Susan at Walt Disney Studios

Right on queue

One lingering concern about the park is its ability to handle the queues, especially around its big-draw attractions of The Twilight Zone™ Tower of Terror and Crush's Coaster. With fewer attractions but some hugely popular rides and shows, the park struggles at times to manage the crowds, especially first thing in the morning (for the initial door-opening rush) and with the capacity of some of the rides. There are only 4 FastPass attractions and, while they are not always needed at quieter times of year, this can also add to the congestion at peak times as FastPass distribution is not always predictable.

The initial crowd heading to The Twilight Zone™ Tower of Terror is controlled (stay in the orderly queue on the way rather than rushing ahead!), but our observations have showed an ongoing problem with Crush's Coaster. The mad rush to be first here in the morning can be disconcerting, with the Cast Members unable to channel the initial charge into an orderly queue.

Rides that continue to draw big queues – like the Studio Tram Tour and Flying Carpets Over Agrabah – are less pressured and the shows continue to have the ability to soak up large numbers at one time. Queuing for the big Stunt Show Spectacular has improved in recent years and the big arena also helps to manage the crowd flow.

Towards the end of the day you should still be able to enjoy rides such as Rock 'n' Roller Coaster starring Aerosmith and the Flying Carpets over Agrabah almost unhindered (Simon's record is 5 goes on Rock 'n' Roller in the final hour!), even if the queues remain long at Tower of Terror and Crush's Coaster. Many people leave the park after the daily parade and, when this is at 4pm (occasionally in high season), that can still leave a good 2 hours in which to do most of the rides.

Enter, stage centre!

Okay, without any further preamble, let us introduce you to the *Walt Disney Studios Park…*

If you approach from the main car park, the Studios will be straight ahead of you as you come through the moving walkways. From *Disney Village*, bear left past the Gaumont Cinemas and, from the bus or train station, continue straight on, passing *Disney Village* on your left. The park is subdivided into 4 main areas, although there is little visual distinction between them, and your adventure starts as soon as you walk through the imposing gates.

The grand layout in front of you makes it clear what's in store – film adventure and lots of fun in the inimitable Mickey style. The 33m/

Character Meet 'n' Greet in Production Courtyard

© Disney

108ft water tower edifice (based on the same structure at Burbank, California), topped by a large pair of mouse ears (we kid you not), is called … wait for it … the Earffel Tower (!), and sets out the visual style in no uncertain terms, as well as providing a handy marker for the front of the park.

Talking tactics

Unlike the *Disneyland Park*, this is not somewhere you need to be right on opening time (unless you have youngsters who are keen to try out the new Toy Story Playland rides). With much of the entertainment centred on the big show times, such as the Moteurs … Action Stunt Show and CinéMagique, you can arrive in more leisurely style, head for the shows first and be reasonably sure you can get into most of them with only minimal queuing. With that said, if the lure of the Tower or Crush's Coaster calls strongly to you, plan to be ready for the opening rush or risk standing in long queues!

BRITTIP

Although the shows have large capacities, it is still advisable to arrive 10–15 minutes early to benefit from being the first to be seated.

If you are after the thrills, your best plan is to start by going to either The Twilight Zone™ Tower of Terror or Crush's Coaster immediately upon park opening. If you have young children with you, visit Toy Story Playland or Cars Quatre Roues Rallye first, as the various kiddie rides are slow loading and draw long queues for much of the day. If you prefer a gentler start, make the Studio Tram Tour your first stop. Waiting times can build up to half an hour or more later on. If you then take in Armageddon and Rock 'n' Roller Coaster, you will have 3 (or 4) of the biggest crowd-pullers under your belt early on. Alternatively, if you have younger children, they will certainly want to ride the Flying Carpets Over Agrabah after visiting Cars, as this is another ride where slow-moving queues can build up.

Front Lot

Once through the turnstiles, you come into a lovely Spanish-style courtyard that marks the entrance to the first main area, the Front Lot

Place de Frères Lumières: This is the 'office' part of the theme park and houses the more functional elements such as pushchair and wheelchair hire, lost property, lost children centre, baby-care centre, first aid station, cash dispenser and currency exchange. You will also find the **Studio Services** here, for any queries about the park (like when and where to find the characters). Visitors with disabilities can also pick up a *Guide for Guests with Special Needs* if they haven't done so already and the

Place de Frères Lumières

© Disney

The Front Lot

Assisted Access Card, if required, which allows guests with a disability incompatible with waiting in the regular queue to wait in an alternate area (see page 31).

This area is an extremely elegant piece of design, with the central **Fantasia fountain**, flanked by palm trees, providing a great photo opportunity. The left-hand side of the courtyard is taken up by the **Walt Disney Studios Store**, the theme park's biggest shop, while on the right is **Studio Photo** for all your photographic requirements (although it is better to bring your own).

BRITTIP

The Front Lot courtyard, **Place des Frères Lumières**, makes a good place to visit in early afternoon if the park is busy. Grab a drink or snack inside Disney Studio 1 and head out to enjoy the relaxing surroundings.

In the early morning, you can meet several **Disney characters** here (usually Goofy, Pluto, Minnie, Donald, Daisy and Chip 'n' Dale), and it is worth pausing to enjoy the classic 1930s-style architecture as the theme park transports you into the world of movies, Hollywood style.

This is also where you'll find the **Toon Train** arriving 5 times daily. Chip 'n' Dale dance and frolic to live music against a backdrop of 3 mobile sets, encouraging children to participate in the fun. When Clarice, their

glamorous cohort, makes her appearance, a swinging jazz-fest ensues, which is sure to get you clapping and your toes tapping.

Disney Studio 1: You really get the full effect as you walk through these doors (remember to pick up a park map as you enter). It is almost an attraction in its own right, even if it is in many ways just a covered version of Main Street USA in the *Disneyland Park*. It is 70m/230ft long, 35m/115ft wide and 20m/66ft high, making it the second-largest 'soundstage' in Europe (okay, it isn't actually a working facility, but the impression is pretty good). The overall effect is as if you have walked into the middle of a Hollywood film shoot, with all the paraphernalia of movie-making.

Shutterbugs at Studio 1

Partner's statue in Animation Courtyard

BRITTIP

You can get films processed in 2 hours at the Studio Photo in the Front Lot courtyard. It's not cheap, but you can check your prints while you still have a chance to retake them!

The film 'sets' are all unfinished and provide almost a kaleidoscopic montage of scenery in each direction, with a series of façades and hoardings, which change the perspective in a multitude of ways with the aid of some brilliant lighting effects. Down the left side is **Les Légendes d'Hollywood** store, while on the right flank is **Restaurant en Coulisse**.

BRITTIP

Restaurant en Coulisse gets pretty busy midday–2pm but is ideal 3–4pm for a late lunch or early tea.

The shop is cleverly disguised behind no fewer than 6 different façades, giving the impression of a whole movie 'street' modelled on various Hollywood stores – both real and imagined – from the 1920s to 60s. Designs that stand out include Last Chance Gas (a mock Route 66 petrol

Les Legendes d'Hollywood

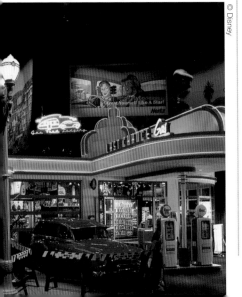

station), The Alexandria Theater (a classic Los Angeles 'movie palace') and The Gossip Column (a news and magazine stand) and, of course, you can buy a range of film-related souvenirs as well as the usual Disney souvenirs. Also here is **Shutterbugs**, a fun photo studio that can put YOU in the Disney picture with various well-known characters (€16.50–25).

BRITTIP

One of our favourite 'hidden gems' in the Studios park is playing with the lighting effects inside Disney Studio 1. Look for the 2 big lighting consoles, one in front of Club Swankadero (marked 'Illuminazione Produzione'), which changes the lighting on the Hollywood & Vine façade, and the other inside the Liki Tiki, which lights the jungle roof and starts a thunderstorm!

On the other side, the restaurant is a combination of another 6 imaginary 'sets', with the counter-service diner concealed behind such legendary establishments as **Schwab's Pharmacy** (a classic 1940s' American drugstore), the **Brown Derby** (the famous Hollywood restaurant in the shape of a bowler hat), **Club Swankadero** (an imaginary nightclub), the **Gunga Den** (a well-known bar) and the **Liki Tiki** (a wonderful thatched South Seas-themed bar).

© Disney

Art of Disney Animation

![BRITTIP logo] **BRITTIP**

The Studio 1 area has a handy Restaurant Reservations kiosk, where you can book meals for later in the day at the full-service restaurants in *Disney Village* and the *Disneyland Park*.

Here, the fare is French continental for breakfast and standard burger-style the rest of the day, with pizza, lasagne and salads as your alternatives. If you arrive before breakfast, stop here for a set meal of orange juice, a hot drink and a croissant (€5.50; 8–11am). For lunch or dinner, choose from 5 set menus (€9.95–11.95) including a burger with chips and a soft drink or double chicken burger or bacon cheeseburger with chips, cake and drink. Upgrade your soft drink to a beer for an additional €1.

There are actually 670 seats for dining here, so it absorbs a lot of people, and the upstairs terracing – 'Carmen's Veranda' (ouch!) – also provides a great view over the whole of Studio 1, as well as the best seats in the house for watching the hustle-bustle below.

![BRITTIP logo] **BRITTIP**

Check the Information Board as you exit Studio 1 to find out the waiting times at the attractions and which queues to avoid.

Toon Studio

Turn right as you exit the doors of Disney Studio 1 and you are immediately in the area of the park that caters mostly for younger children (it was Animation Courtyard until Crush's Coaster and the Cars Quatre Roues Rallye opened in 2007). As well as more chances to meet, photo and get autographs from the characters, you have 2 genuine kiddie rides here, the most enchanting of the park's shows and the wildly popular thrill of Crush's Coaster plus, from summer 2010, Toy Story Playland.

Art of Disney Animation: The first big set-piece attraction, located under the giant Sorcerer's Apprentice hat, this is a 4-part adventure into the history, creation and magic of animated film. The first section concentrates on the history and is the least interesting for younger children. It is basically a pre-show area, with a series of exhibits around the room, showing how animation developed from its most basic into the art form that Walt Disney helped to pioneer. The highlight, amid several hands-on opportunities (like a Zoetrope and a Magic Lantern), is one of only 2 surviving multi-plane cameras, a tool developed by Walt Disney himself in the 1930s.

![BRITTIP logo] **BRITTIP**

Check out the carpet in the post-show area of the Art of Disney Animation. Can you pick out a certain set of Mouse ears in the pattern…?!

Toon Studio

© Disney

As the doors close behind you, a large video screen comes to life and Walt pays tribute to the European pioneers of animation, along with former Walt Disney Co chairman Roy Disney (Walt's nephew). Annoyingly for us, it is all dubbed in French (you would have thought one of the showings would be kept in English) with English subtitles, but it sets the stage for the 225-seat Disney Classics Theatre next. The doors underneath the screen open and you pass into the mini-cinema for 8 minutes of highlights from the Disney classics (including some recent Pixar hits) that are sure to keep everyone happy.

Stage 3 is another theatre-like auditorium, set up like an animator's office, where a part live and part film show brings Mushu from Mulan to life and explains how this dragon-character came into being (with an amusing voice-over from Eddie Murphy). The interaction between the live 'artist' and Mushu is wonderfully scripted and, although the on-stage part is in French, there are headphones to provide a full translation (watch out for the finale as the Murphy-dragon imagines himself as The Mushu of Nôtre Dame!).

You exit the theatre into a final room of 6 'animation stations', which give you the chance to try your hand at drawing, colouring or providing a

Animagique

voice or sound effects for various characters. It is great fun for children of 6 upwards, and the Animation Academy with a real artist is presented in both French and English. In all, it is a fascinating and thoroughly enjoyable look at the artistry of feature animation and the queues move steadily here, so you are rarely waiting long. AAAA.

Animagique: Opposite the Sorcerer's Apprentice hat, this is a unique live show featuring the innovative Czech art of 'Black Light' stagecraft and Japanese 'Bunraku' puppet manipulation. If that sounds a bit dry, prepare yourself for 25 minutes of pure Disney fun in the company of Mickey, Donald Duck and the cast of *Dumbo, Pinocchio, The Jungle Book* and *The Lion King*.

The Art of Disney Animation

Waiting for opening

If you arrive half an hour before the official opening time, you will still be admitted through the main turnstiles of the *Walt Disney Studios Park*. This brings you into the Place de Frères Lumières courtyard in the Front Lot, where you are likely to meet Goofy or Pluto as they welcome you to the park. Children can stop for a photo and an autograph, and you can then pass into Disney Studio 1 and either have a bite to eat or browse the shops. Finally, at the appointed opening hour (either 9 or 10am), the crowd starts to gather at the doors at the far end and, with a final countdown – 'Lights, Cameras, Action! – the Cast Members open all the doors simultaneously and let in the eager throng.

If you are looking for the thrills first, the highlight of The Twilight Zone™ Tower of Terror is straight ahead of you (it's hard to miss!), and Cast Members will direct the flock of early birds into the queuing area. Turn left for the Backlot area and Rock 'n' Roller Coaster while, for Crush's Coaster, go sharp right into Toon Studio and Toy Story Playland. If you have young children, you should concentrate on this area and head first for Cars Quatre Roues Rallye, which quickly builds up some long, slow-moving queues, and the 3 newest kiddie rides.

BRITTIP

Try to arrive a few minutes early for the Animagique show as the 1,100-seat theatre comes to life with a series of clever sound effects that ring and echo in delightful style around the auditorium before it begins.

The story (partly in French and Donald Duck-ese!) sees Donald stuck for inspiration at the drawing board. Ignoring Mickey's warnings, he opens the Disney vault and unwittingly lets loose a host of animated characters who run riot on stage, with a big song-and-dance finale that will have you humming the catchy theme tune as you leave. Some excellent effects surprise you along the way (which we won't reveal) but be prepared for some extra fun, especially if you are in the first dozen or so rows. The high-tech show (involving digitally synchronised lighting, audio and machinery effects, in addition to the puppetry) is presented 6 to 7 times a day and show times are posted both outside and on the park maps. AAAA.

BRITTIP

If you have children, try to sit in the central section of the theatre, no more than 10–12 rows back and you will enjoy one of the best special effects of Animagique.

As you exit Animagique, watch out for the New Stars, characters from the latest Disney films, as they often appear in the Courtyard in front of the Art of Animation and in the specially designed scenery of Toon Plaza to the left of Crush's Coaster. Buzz Lightyear (or Buzz L'Eclair, as is he known in France) is often to be found here.

Cars Quatre Roues Rallye (Cars Race Rally): Located opposite Animagique, this attraction borrows from the 2006 Disney-Pixar film *Cars*. It visits Radiator Springs, where Lightning McQueen is starring in a movie being filmed down in the canyon, and you're invited to co-star. But be warned: you'll be doing your own stunts and spin-outs as they are all part of the action! In all honesty, this is just another variation on the basic spinning tea cups ride and it is a fairly short experience (barely 90 seconds),

Cars Road Rally

© Disney

Crush's Coaster

but it has great kiddie appeal, so you should head here early if your children are likely to want to do it. The ride has that swing-'em-around motion (3 revolving platforms that then add an extra spin with each car) that pre-schoolers seem to love. The crowds do build up quickly here and it is a slow-loading ride, hence the queue is pretty slow moving. TT (TTTT under-7s).

Flying Carpets Over Agrabah: At the innermost end of Toon Studio is the second main children's ride, which is another variation on the Dumbo/ Orbitron attractions of the *Disneyland Park*. This has been transported with a slightly different theme from the ride in Orlando's *Magic Kingdom*. Here you line up (in a loosely themed area like a film 'green room', where actors prepare for their next scene) to

take part in a 'casting' for a role in a movie, with the Genie (from the 1992 Disney film *Aladdin*) as the director (in French and English). Once aboard your 4-person 'flying carpet', there are controls in the front seats to make it go up and down and in the rear seats to add a bit of tilt 'n' turn. In all honesty it is a fairly tame ride, but children under 10 always seem to get a thrill from it. However, the queues can build here through the middle of the day, so it is best to visit early on or wait until the last hour of the day. TT (TTTT for under-10s). (FP)

Crush's Coaster: This is a breathtaking, high-speed journey along the 'East Australia Current' (or EAC), riding on Crush's back as he plunges and swirls through a mock undersea world, full of inventive lighting and special effects, with a brief plunge outdoors before diving back inside again. You board your 'turtle shell' alongside a Sydney harbour fishing village (each shell holds 4 riders sitting in back-to-back pairs), where guests facing forward at the start soon find themselves spinning backwards (and the back seats become the front seats), dipping and swirling through the great bubbly blue. The ride includes a slower-paced dark section where you meet Nemo and Squirt in their undersea habitat (courtesy of some high-tech visual effects) before you are bumped into the main part of the ride, a wild

Flying Carpets Over Agrabah

Toy Story Playland

and twisting spin both up and down the EAC before Crush guides you back to safer waters. Dude, it's just too cool!

The attraction will probably appeal to most of the family, although it may be too dynamic for under-6s (top speed is only 37mph/57kph but it feels faster with all the tight twists and turns). It is also something of a slow-loader, hence queues build up quickly and often remain at an hour-plus for much of the day. Try to do this early on, especially as it is NOT a FastPass ride. (Restrictions: 107cm/3ft 5in). TTTT.

Toy Story Playland

This 'land within a land' is due to open in summer 2010 and will add a considerable amount of new fun and excitement for children. The setting is Andy's back garden (the owner of Woody and Buzz Lightyear), where the visitors have been 'shrunk' to the same size as the toys. As well as the 3 new rides, the clever over-sized theming will include an interactive, climb-crawl-and-slide play area (full details unknown as we went to press) for the under-6 age group. The down side? None of these rides is a fast loader or high capacity, so they may draw quite long queues at peak periods. If this kind of thing will appeal to your youngsters, definitely try to do these early in the day.

Toy Soldier Parachute Drop: Joining a 'mission' with the Army Men from

Andy's bedroom, young guests will get the chance to be lifted up the 25m/82ft tower and then 'parachute' down again. This tower ride (on 6 lines for 2 riders each) will offer quite an exhilarating drop and bounce for 6–12s and provide a good view over the park at the same time! TTT (expected; TTTTT, under-12s).

Slinky Dog Zigzag Spin: Taking another leaf from standard fairground rides and giving them a heavy Disney overlay is this circular spinning ride. While Woody's classic slinky toy friend chases his tail (around a huge fire hydrant!), riders will revolve around and up and down on a fairly lively round track. Like the Mad Hatter's Tea Party in the *Disneyland Park*, don't

Slinky Dog Zigzag Spin

expect anything startling, but children are sure to enjoy this pooch-with-attitude. TT (expected; TTTT under-12s).

RC Racer: This is the one new element that may scare a few young 'uns – and thrill their teenage siblings! Riders will board a version of the Remote Control Racing Car (again from Andy's bedroom) and zoom backwards and forwards on a big U-shaped track, which eventually takes them up the full 35m/114ft height for 2 minutes of high-speed hither and thither. The technical terminology for this kind of ride is a 'half-pipe', apparently – and we can't wait to ride it! TTTT (expected; TTTTT+ under-12s). Expect a height limit for this ride, but that was unknown as we went to press.

The Tower of Terror

© Disney

Other entertainment: For a great photo opportunity, visit the **Monsters Inc** display between Studio 1 and Animagique – and see how loud you can be on the Scream Monitors. Mike and Sulley, from the *Monsters, Inc* film, also appear here for photo opportunities periodically.

Shopping: There is only one main shopping option, but it is a good one, **The Disney Animation Gallery** at the exit of the Art of Disney Animation (inside the giant Sorcerer's Apprentice hat), plus a smaller kiosk in the Courtyard area. The Gallery offers a rather upmarket range of souvenirs and serious collectables – figurines, statues, books and genuine Disney film cels – for those with a fascination for the true art of Disney.

Dining: For a snack in this area, the **Studio Catering Co** has 2 outlets, themed like truck trailers, offering hot dogs, burgers, fish and chips, club sandwiches, popcorn, ice-cream, doughnuts, muffins and cookies, as well as drinks.

Production Courtyard

Retracing your steps brings you into the Production Courtyard area. This middle section offers 5 main attractions, including the new Playhouse Disney – Live on Stage.

The Twilight Zone™ Tower of Terror: Enter a new dimension of sight, sound and high-speed, hair-raising fear! The Hollywood Tower Hotel's glamorous heyday lies dormant beneath layers of dust and abandonment, hinting at the tragedy that befell its last 'visitors' – and now awaits you! Pass through the lobby into a dimly lit library, where Rod Serling (the original TV programme host) warns of the Tower's terrible past and then invites you to step aboard a maintenance service elevator heading directly to ... The Twilight Zone. Sounds from the boiler room prompt you forward through grim and grimy surroundings until you finally reach the elevator and, once inside, your fate is sealed.

A Towering achievement

The original art deco-style Tower of Terror opened in Orlando in 1994, themed as an episode of the popular television show, *The Twilight Zone* (1959–64). The show's host, Rod Serling, recounts that fateful night when a bolt of lightning struck the Hollywood Tower Hotel – a glamorous Hollywood Hills retreat catering to the brightest stars of the late 1930s – propelling 5 unsuspecting guests into the Fifth Dimension, never to be heard from again. But their ghostly figures haunt the hallways, and the door they passed through into the unknown has opened again. This time, you will step through it…!

California's Tower opened in 2004, based on the same storyline, although the façade is pueblo-deco and the setting is downtown Hollywood. The ride is essentially the same, but Orlando's ride vehicles utilise a continuous circular loop technology, with vehicles moving horizontally into a separate drop shaft, and guests loading and unloading in separate locations, while the versions in California, Tokyo and now Paris all feature independent drop shafts, with ride vehicles that horizontally back into the shaft before making their hair-raising journey.

The *Disneyland Paris* Tower, opened in early 2008, continues the Twilight Zone theme, again in a late 1930s *pueblo*-deco style setting. Orlando's Fifth Dimension element (ghostly apparitions appearing before the vehicle enters the drop shaft) is replaced by a mysterious looking-glass effect, in which riders see their own reflections before their image morphs into ghostly figures.

The version in the *Tokyo DisneySeas Park* changes the storyline completely. This gothic-style edifice is known as Hotel Hightower and the setting is New York City in the late 1890s. The hotel's owner, Harrison Hightower III, collector of rare artefacts, has unwittingly transported Shiriki Utundy, protector spirit of the tribal Mtundu village, into the hotel, where the idol takes its revenge, plunging Harrison to his death inside an elevator. But his body has never been found. Years later, in an effort to save the abandoned hotel, guided tours are being offered, but the curse – and the mystery – persists.

The Tower of Terror is arguably Disney's most recognisable ride worldwide. The artistry that went into creating a totally convincing environment, from Rod Serling's seamless delivery (Serling himself died in 1975, at the age of 50, and his 'presentation' was achieved by the laborious process of splicing together segments from the TV show, then adding a voice-over where needed) to the placement of props from famous episodes, the Tower's eerie silence, broken only by screams coming from the elevator shaft, will convince you to … Fear Every Drop!

> **BRITTIP**
>
> The queue is so spectacular even non-riders should do it just to enjoy the theming. They are then free to duck out of the ride without boarding.

The remainder of the ride is a thrill-seeker's dream, with astonishing special effects and moments of sensory deprivation that will leave you shaking – and eager for a second ride! And do ride again. With a drop-and-rise sequence that leaves you breathless, you may well miss some of the clever details en route, so you will need several visits to take it all in. Unmissable both visually and as an attraction, the Tower represents Disney Imagineering at its finest. Most importantly, it is also a FastPass ride, but with the ride's popularity it is not unusual for FastPasses to run out by early afternoon. Restrictions: 102cm/3ft 4in. TTTTT. (FP)

Lights across the Studios

© Disney

CinéMagique: One of the park's undoubted highlights and a real *tour de force* of imagination, this award-winning half-hour film show, exclusive to *Disneyland Paris*, starts out as a tribute to the history of both European and American cinema, but soon takes an unexpected dramatic turn. It ends up as a hilarious series of scenes featuring comedian Martin Short as a hapless 'time traveller' moving through a range of cinematic genres linked by a wonderful love-interest storyline.

CinéMagique

� BRITTIP

Waiting in the holding pens for CinéMagique is fairly dull, but the large capacity of the theatre ensures everyone usually gets in, while you can often wait until the last minute and still find a seat. There are up to 6 shows a day in high season, and it is possible you'll want to see this twice in one day.

The show includes numerous funny scene shifts (the 'cowboy shoot-out' scenario is inspired) and a couple of eye-popping special effects, which we won't reveal but that add hugely to the fun (hint: an umbrella might be a good idea!). French actress Julie Delpy is the co-star and the show takes place inside a beautiful 1,100-seat theatre with an art deco theme harking back to classic 1930s' Hollywood movie palaces.

It probably won't hold the attention of younger children (say, under-4s) for the full 30 minutes, but there is enough amusing on-screen action to keep older children entertained. Adults will enjoy the clever interweaving of scenes, with Short popping up in all manner of unlikely but well-known film scenarios. AAAAA.

Film set on the Studio Tram Tour

Props on the Studio Tram Tour

The tram takes you on a behind-the-scenes look at a movie studio, learning some tricks of the film trade, such as location sets, props, costumes and special effects. Each tram has a video screen with a full commentary (the English version supplied by a wonderfully laconic Jeremy Irons) that points out the key areas along the way. You pass a whole array of film props and scenery (notably the imposing Waterfall City façade from the *Dinotopia* mini-series) before entering the tour highlight, Catastrophe Canyon.

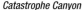 **BRITTIP**

In CinéMagique, the 'Western' sequence involving different snippets from films *The Magnificent Seven*, *Once Upon a Time in the West*, *The Wild Bunch*, *Tombstone* and *The Good, The Bad and The Ugly* is an absolute *tour de force* and worth going in to see on its own.

Studio Tram Tour: Behind the Magic: This large-scale, 15-minute ride has been adapted from *Disney's Hollywood Studios* in Orlando and enhanced with several new elements, making it a must-see attraction. Cleverly arranged with an English-French soundtrack, it is a tour of heavyweight proportions.

BRITTIP

Young children may be scared by the loud and dramatic special effects in the Studio Tram Tour. An explanation and reassurance that it's safe and just a film trick is a good idea. The left-hand side of the tram may also get a little (?!) wet.

Catastrophe Canyon: Here, you are supposed to get a dry-run version of an elaborate special effects set-up but the 'director' mistakes the tram for his film 'extras' and starts the action sequence with you in the middle! Before you know it, the tram has been

Catastrophe Canyon

hit by earthquake, fire and flood, and the culmination, when 265,000l/ 58,300g of water are dumped on the flaming set, is quite breathtaking. Having 'survived' the canyon, you continue on past some more film props before passing the **Star Cars** garage exhibit of well-known movie vehicles (like Cruella de Vil's car from *101 Dalmatians*, the Humvee from *The Rock* and the sports car from *Runaway Bride*). Finally, you enter the smoking ruins of London, circa 2022 (or at least a remarkable film-set facsimile). Here, for anyone familiar with the summer 2002 blockbuster film *Reign of Fire*, you get a close encounter with one of its 'stars'. Well, not actually one of the dragons, but a fairly 'hot' close-up of its fiery breath, which blasts out twice on the right side of the tram.

The shock effect, the noise of the fire and the feel of the heat will definitely scare young children (and some adults!), so think carefully before taking your youngster on this tour. However, the encounter is over pretty quickly and the rest of the set is something to marvel at. Avoid this just after a Stunt Show has finished in the Backlot area, as many of that 3,000-strong crowd head straight here (and there's not much to see while waiting). AAA/TTTT. (FP)

Stitch Live!: This is your chance to interact with the mischievous blue alien when Disney Studios sends a satellite beam directly into outer

Stitch Live

space for a live audio and visual connection between Stitch and the studio audience. Children can ask questions and Stitch responds directly to each child – and may even ask a few questions of his own! Each encounter is personalised, unpredictable, hilarious and filled with the sort of gentle irreverence that makes Stitch a family favourite. The 20-minute theatre-style show, located inside the former Walt Disney Television Studios, runs up to 3 times per hour, with shows alternating in French and English (check the times schedule posted outside the attraction). Although the attraction is geared toward youngsters, the technology is so convincing (if you have seen Turtle Talk With Crush at the *Epcot* park in *Walt Disney World*, you will have some idea of what to expect), even older children and adults will be enchanted. AAAA.

Look out for Cruella de Vil's car in the Star Cars garage

Playhouse Disney – Live on Stage:
New in 2009 (and also occupying part
of the old Disney Channel TV Studios
building) was this show performance
– a mix of live actors, costumed
characters and puppetry – based on
various characters from Disney's TV
Playhouse programmes but centred
on the Mickey Mouse Clubhouse. The
likes of Handy Manny, Winnie the
Pooh and The Little Einsteins also
appear, providing plenty of lively fun,
sing-alongs and audience
participation for the pre-school
brigade, and the show is performed
up to 10 times daily, alternately in
English, French and Spanish (check
the board outside for details of which
language the next show will be in).
Everyone sits on the floor but the
theatre takes up to 480 at a time, so
there is rarely a long wait to get in,
and it is a guaranteed hit with
younger children. AAAA (under-6s).

Other entertainment: Most days, the
Place des Stars Stage (in front of
CineMagique and Stitch Live!) is home
to the **Good Morning Walt Disney
Studios** parade and character
greeting, with a cavalcade of vehicles
arriving to disgorge the likes of
Minnie, Pluto, Goofy and Chip 'n' Dale
for a musical welcome to the park
(usually at 10.30am). Great fun for
kids, so have those autograph books
handy! Mickey and Friends appear
here periodically (usually 11am–1pm)
for more character meet 'n' greets,
while this is also the stage for other
small-scale street shows from time to
time, so keep an eye on your Show
Schedule with the park map.

Shopping: Amazingly, there is not a
single stand-alone gift shop in this
area (although the Tower of Terror
does have its own range of souvenirs
as you exit the ride).

Dining: When it comes to grabbing a
bite to eat, the Production Courtyard
has the best of the theme park's
dining in the shape of the **Restaurant
des Stars**, a 300-seat café-type diner
in full art deco style, which now offers
a set-price buffet meal. The speciality
is a meat carvery but the range of
food is extremely broad (similar to the
Plaza Gardens Restaurant in the
Disneyland Park), from baked fish to
penne pasta Bolognese, roast
chicken, vegetable lasagne and a wide
variety of salads (€20 adults, €10

The Backlot

© Disney

© Disney

Armageddon: Special Effects

3–11s). The walls display a fine array of authentic Hollywood photos and film memorabilia. **Remy**, from the popular Pixar movie *Ratatouille*, also makes periodic daily appearances both inside and outside the restaurant. It's a charming encounter, worth seeking out when you are in the area.

✠ BRITTIP

For that extra special occasion, you can order a birthday cake at the Restaurant des Stars at the beginning of your meal. It costs €22 and serves 4–8. But be warned: don't come here when the Stunt Show has just finished and 3,000 people are in the vicinity!

Backlot

This area is past the Restaurant des Stars and features some more action-packed offerings, with 3 contrasting thrill elements.

Moteurs … Action! Stunt Show

© Disney

Armageddon: Les Effets Spéciaux (Special Effects): This unique, elaborate show that puts YOU at the heart of the action (although it's not one for young children) is the first of the thrills. You enter a pre-show area, full of models, exhibits and diagrams from the blockbuster film starring Bruce Willis (there are 2 studios, 7A and 7B, and the array of models does vary), where a Cast Member greets you and acts as the show's 'director'.

✠ BRITTIP

The props on display in the pre-show area of Armageddon: Special Effects include the spacesuit worn by actor Ben Affleck in the film.

With the help of your director and a video that explains the eye-popping scenario of the film, your role as 'extras' in a special effects scene is explained in amusing detail (in English and French). The screen is then turned over to a tribute to Frenchman Georges Méliès, who is credited with inventing film special effects. It shows how the movie world has taken his ideas and developed them with astonishing creativity in the last 100 years. The video continues with the explosive arrival of Michael Clarke Duncan, another of the *Armageddon* stars, who explains how the film's technical wizardry was carried out. You are then invited to see for real how it is done, under 'directorial' guidance, in an amazing mock-up of the movie's Russian space station – just as it comes under threat from a meteor shower! The ensuing chaos, as the station almost literally blows up all around you, is brilliantly scripted and the array of effects incredibly realistic, with smoke, sparks, bursting pipes, buckling doors and a huge central fireball that adds some real heat to proceedings.

In our opinion, the sights and sounds (it is pretty loud) are much too intense for under-7s, but there are no real warnings of this outside. However, the space station itself is a work of art and the hectic action is suitably breathtaking. They could do with adding a bit of interest to the plain waiting area outside, though. TTTT.

BRITTIP

It is a good idea for an adult to experience an attraction first to check on its suitability, if you are worried that certain elements might be too scary for your children.

Rock 'n' Roller Coaster starring Aerosmith

© Disney

Rock 'n' Roller Coaster starring Aerosmith: This next attraction is a real blast of a ride, rocketing from 0 to 100kph/62mph in just 2.8 seconds! It is a revised version of the Orlando ride, making it a different experience.

BRITTIP

Listen out for Aerosmith lead singer, Steve Tyler, completing a clever 'sound check' as you board the Rock 'n' Roller Coaster – it adds considerably to the fun.

Here, you enter the rock 'n' roll world of the American supergroup Aerosmith, as they discuss the creation of this unique rockin' ride, described as a 'revolutionary musical experience' produced by Tour De Force Records. As the record company's VIP guests, Aerosmith invites you to enter the 'research and development' area to try it out at first hand and you pass into the launch area, complete with 'sound engineers' and computer models of the ride systems, which feature 'Soundtracker'

cars. These are fitted with 5 state-of-the-art speakers per seat so you literally 'ride the music'. Once you are harnessed into your seat, the countdown begins and you blast off into a topsy-turvy 'rock video' that features 2 loops and a corkscrew as well as some eye-popping lighting effects. There are 5 music tracks to accompany the ride, hence 5 variations on the ride experience. Aerosmith has even re-recorded a couple of their tracks, so see if you can notice the new lyrics (hint: the 'adapted' songs are 'Love In An Elevator' and 'What Kind of Love Are You On?'). Waiting time can hit an hour at peak periods but there is rarely much of a queue for the first few hours or in late afternoon. It is not recommended for anyone with back or neck problems or for pregnant women. Restrictions: 1.2m/3ft 9in. TTTTT. (FP).

BRITTIP

The queue for Rock 'n' Roller Coaster drops off during a performance of the Stunt Show next door but it should be avoided just after the show finishes as many people make a beeline for it.

Moteurs … Action!

Moteurs…Action! Stunt Show Spectacular: Next door to the Rock 'n' Roller Coaster, this is one of Disney's most remarkable shows. Full of genuine high-risk stunts and hugely skilful car and motorbike action, it will have you shaking your head in amazement for a while afterwards.

BRITTIP

People start queuing for the Stunt Show a good half-hour before a performance at peak times (3 to 4 a day) and the middle shows of the day are always packed. It is better to head for the first one or stay until the last to minimise your wait.

Seating starts a good 20 minutes prior to show-time, and there is some amusing pre-show chat (in English and French) and freestyle show-boating by one of the bike riders to keep people amused before the serious stuff starts. An audience member is also recruited to help in one of the scenes and a roving cameraman picks out people from the crowd to highlight on the big video screen in the centre of the 'square'. The huge set is based on a typical Mediterranean village and is

© Disney

Walt Disney Studios Park with children

Here is a rough guide to the attractions in this park that are most likely to appeal to the different age groups (taking into account any height restrictions):

Under-5s
Art of Disney Animation, Playhouse Disney Live on Stage, Animagique, Toy Story Playland, Slinky Dog Zigzag Spin, Flying Carpets Over Agrabah, Meet Mickey, Cars Quatre Roues Rallye, Stitch Live, Moteurs…Action! Stunt Show Spectacular (with parental discretion), Disney Stars and Cars Parade, Toon Train.

6–8s
All the above (except Playhouse Disney Live on Stage), plus Toy Soldier Parachute Drop, Studio Tram Tour (with parental discretion), Crush's Coaster, High School Musical Party, Disney Studio 1, CinéMagique, Armageddon (with parental discretion).

9–12s
All the above (except Cars Roues Rally), plus RC Racer, Rock 'n' Roller Coaster starring Aerosmith, The Twilight Zone™ Tower of Terror.

Over-12s
Crush's Coaster, Disney Studio 1, Art of Disney Animation, Studio Tram Tour, CinéMagique, Armageddon, Rock 'n' Roller Coaster starring Aerosmith, The Twilight Zone™ Tower of Terror, Moteurs…Action!, High School Musical Party.

magnificently crafted to have an 'aged' appearance. Once the preliminaries are completed, you are treated to a 45-minute extravaganza of daredevil stunts, with a Car Ballet sequence, a Motorbike Chase and a Grand Finale that features some surprise pyrotechnics to complete a truly awesome presentation (keep your eyes on the windows below the video screen at the end). Each scene – featuring a secret agent 'goody' and various black-car 'baddies' – is set up and fully explained by a movie 'director' (and the need for bilingual commentary is handled skilfully). The results of each 'shoot' are then played back on the video screen to show how each effect was created and how it is all spliced together to create the desired end product.

All the cars were specially created for the show by Vauxhall and there are some extra tricks (including an amusing appearance by Herbie from *The Love Bug* film) in between the main scenes. The whole thing was designed by Frenchman Rémy Julienne, the doyen of cinematic car stunt sequences, who worked on the James Bond films *Goldeneye* and *Licence to Kill* and other epics such as *The Rock, Ronin, Gone in 60 Seconds*

Moteurs … Action! Stunt Show Spectacular

© Disney

⚡🇬🇧 BRITTIP

Be aware there is some loud mock gunfire during the Stunt Show, which can upset young children, while the motorbike scene includes a rider catching fire, which can be quite frightening for them.

and *Enemy of the State*. It all adds up to a breathtaking show, and kids are sure to want to come back, another good reason to see it early on. There is nothing like it in any other theme park in the world (except for the copycat version in *Disney's Hollywood Studios* in Orlando), and the fact so much of it involves genuine, live co-ordination makes it truly thrilling.

However, the exit is quite a scrum as 3,000 people have to leave through 2 fairly narrow thoroughfares and it can take 10–15 minutes to get clear of the auditorium. So, if you can sit towards the front either on the right or left of the grandstand, you will be out quicker. TTTTT.

High School Musical Party: This seasonal roving stage show is a big hit with teenagers. Join the students from East High in a high-energy pep rally, Wildcat style. All the biggest hits from the popular Disney Channel TV films send an unstoppable beat through the Backlot as it moves in stages to Production Courtyard and Place des Stars, before exiting by Disney Studio 1, up to 5 times daily. Get into the swing as East High's cheerleaders, athletes and students coax guests into the action, and fans of the film won't want to miss the action-packed 15-minute performance. AAA.

High School Musical Party

Shopping: The only shop around here is Rock Around The Shop, at the exit to Rock 'n' Roller Coaster starring Aerosmith, offering rock-related goods, plus the chance to buy your ride photo (€15–25).

Dining: When you need something to eat, **Café des Cascadeurs** is an imaginative little diner (themed as an art deco studio café for the stuntmen and women) around the corner from Armageddon, serving a fairly simple selection of salads, sandwiches, hot dogs and crisps, but the train carriage setting is good fun.

High School Musical Party

Pirates of the Caribbean

The newly re-themed **Disney Blockbuster Café** (formerly The Backlot Express) is a counter-service café with the interior split in 2 parts, one for High School Musical (with a full array of banners, posters and film props and actual costumes worn by the film's stars) and the other in *Pirates of the Caribbean* movie style (with props and decorations straight from Davy Jones' Locker, or somewhere nearby!). In truth, the new theming is less extensive and interesting than the prop-intensive Backlot Express version, but HSM and Pirates fans will probably enjoy the atmosphere. The food is fairly ordinary – Mickey pizza (€4.95), toasted sandwiches, baguettes and salads (€4.95–8.90) and a set

sandwich, crisps, dessert and drink meal (€11.95) – but it holds up to 500, plus there is outdoor seating in summer.

BRITTIP

In Café des Cascadeurs, help yourself to a selection on the classic 1950s-style jukebox.

Here comes the parade

In best Disney park fashion, no visit is complete without the daily procession. **Disney's Stars 'n' Cars** left *Disney's Hollywood Studios* park in Orlando in 2009 and found a new home here. This is themed like a 1930s Hollywood film premiere, with a series of genuine vintage cars and clever replicas being used to mount a cavalcade of Disney showbiz favourites. It provides the likes of *Aladdin, Mary Poppins, Mulan*, the *Muppets* and *Monsters, Inc.* with a chance to show off in larger-than-life fashion. Watch out for the *Star Wars*™ 'Land Speeder' with a radio-controlled R-2D2, while the lead car also features any special guests at the Studios that day – or a visiting family instead. If you haven't seen your favourite characters yet, this is a good chance to get a wave and a photo of

Disney's Stars 'n' Cars Parade

several in a relatively short time. Wait in the Production Courtyard and you should get a great view as the parade stops for a character display at Place des Stars before retracing its steps. AAAA (usually at either 2.45 or 4pm).

Other entertainment: The park has additional fun provided periodically by alternating performing acts, which pop up here and there to give impromptu shows that have a central theme but include some improvisation. Special acts perform at Christmas (including an *a capella* carol group), which vary from day to day, so you never know who's going to appear. Look out also for **Push, The Talking Trashcan**, a remarkable interactive 'performing rubbish bin' that moves, rattles and even talks to visitors (often in the Backlot area)!

For those keen to learn more about the park, there is a 1-hour **Guided Tour** (€12 adults; children 11 and under free), which gives an in-depth view of the park's history and architecture. Book at Studio Services when you first arrive (subject to availability).

As with the *Disneyland Park*, the *Walt Disney Studios Park* looks even better in early evening, when all the clever (and hidden) lighting effects come into play. There is definitely room for

Disney's Stars and Cars

improvement, but the high quality of the attractions here (The Twilight Zone™ Tower of Terror, CinéMagique and Moteurs…Action! Stunt Show are all true works of art) still provides a rich and rewarding experience. You will also leave with an improved knowledge of the movie business and a heightened respect for those who work in it. The essence of a theme park is that it envelops you with its sense of design and purpose and we feel the *Walt Disney Studios Park* does this, ensuring you believe you have truly had a movie-world adventure.

Right, that should be enough theme parks for now. But the fun doesn't stop here. Oh no! There is still plenty to do and see when we visit the *Disney Village*, Val d'Europe and more. It's time to go beyond the parks…

Twilight Zone Tower of Terror

8 Beyond the Theme Parks

or Let's Shop Till We Drop and Other Fun Pursuits

Having led you, quite literally, up the theme park path, it is now time we took you beyond those confines and explored some more of what makes this resort – and this whole area of the Ile de France region – so enticing.

To backtrack slightly and put things in context, the Ile de France is the central region of France, the 'island' around which lie the other great regions of Normandy, Picardie, Champagne-Ardennes and Burgundy. The Ile itself is made up of eight *départements*, namely **Yvelines**, **Essonne**, **Seine-et-Marne** and **Val d'Oise** (these form a large outer ring) and then **Hauts-de-Seine** (immediately to the west of the city), **Seine-St-Deni**s (to the north-east), **Val-de-Marne** (to the south-east) and **Paris** itself. The *département* of Val-de-Marne should not be confused with Marne-la-Vallée, where *Disneyland Paris* is situated, in the *département* of Seine-et-Marne.

Before 1989, when construction began, there was little here apart from sugar beet fields, but the development since has been swift and dramatic. There is, in fact, no real town or village of Marne-la-Vallée, it is a made-up name given to the RER/TGV station here, which acts as the terminus for the RER's Line A. The nearest sizeable village is Chessy,

hence the RER station is properly known as Marne-la-Vallée Chessy. However, to all intents and purposes, Marne-la-Vallée IS the site of *Disneyland Paris*, hence this is how the majority refer to it.

Marne-la-Vallée is also (confusingly) a sub-district of the Seine-et-Marne *département* closer to Paris (between the towns of Noisy-le-Grand and Lognes). When driving, therefore, you should always aim for 'Les Parcs Disneyland'.

Circus performers at Disney Village

© Disney

More to see and do

When it comes to the associated attractions 'beyond the theme parks', there are 5 distinct topics to cover. First and most obvious is all the fun, fine shopping and dining of **Disney Village**. Second, Disney has also developed its own sporting connections – at **Disneyland Golf**, plus the novel challenge of **Davy Crockett's Adventure** nearby. Next, the neighbouring development of **Val d'Europe** offers another scintillating array of great shops and restaurants, including the Auchan hypermarket and the outlet shopping village of La Vallée. Finally, the highly family-friendly **Sea Life** aquarium centre is situated inside the Val d'Europe shopping centre and is another good reason to go beyond the parks.

The golfing opportunity is obviously primarily for devotees of the sport but the others should all be on your must-see list if you are here for 4 days or more (or if you are on a repeat visit). The **Panoramagique** balloon flights over *Disney Village* are quite breathtaking and especially worthy of note.

As this is primarily a new-town area (the great Disney trail-blazing has given rise to a flurry of modern suburban development), there are not many other out-and-out tourist attractions here, but it does make a

© Disney

Entrance to Disney Village

great base from which to explore Paris and some of the more genuinely historic points of interest in the region (notably the towns of Provins and Meaux, see Chapter 9).

Disney Village

Starting at the top, it is almost impossible to miss this hugely colourful and imaginative entertainment centre situated between Disney's hotels and the theme parks. This impressive complex was designed by American architect Frank Gehry, who was also responsible for the Guggenheim museum in Bilbao, Spain, and it originally featured a host of complex, almost abstract ideas designed to link the Village to the railway station. However, some of these were removed in 2005–06 (notably a series of large towers), giving the Village a more open look.

Panoramagique

© Disney

Disney Village

1 Planet Hollywood
2 Annette's Diner
3 King Ludwig's Castle
4 Sports Bar
5 New York Style Sandwiches
6 Billy Bob's Country Western
  Saloon and La Grange restaurant
7 The Steakhouse
8 Rainforest Café
9 Café Mickey
10 McDonald's
11 The Disney Store
12 Starbucks
13 The Disney Gallery
14 Disney Fashion
15 Hollywood Pictures
16 World of Toys
17 Gaumont Cinema
18 Buffalo Bill's Wild West Show
19 Hurricanes
20 Marina Del Ray/Panoramagique
21 IMAX Cinema

DISNEY VILLAGE

If you come straight in by car or train, you just might not notice *Disney Village* on your left as you scamper headlong for the *Disneyland Park*, but otherwise it is fairly obvious. From one end (nearest the theme parks), it is dominated by a massive gateway topped by a huge red banner with 'Disney Village' emblazoned across it. From the hotels end, you enter via the Lake Disney entrance, with a spread of restaurants – Café Mickey, Rainforest Café and McDonald's – before you.

In a way, it is easy to see the Village as one big merchandising opportunity. There are a dozen different ways to spend money here – from the shops to video games – and even some of the restaurants have their own gift store. But, ultimately, this has the hallmark of the Imagineers once again (even if the Rainforest Café, Planet Hollywood, McDonald's and Starbucks all have their own internationally recognisable stamp). It has a wonderful outdoor café style, especially in the evening, and the brilliant lighting is well worth stopping to see. The main concourse provides periodic live entertainment (weather permitting) and there are other stalls, vendors and games from time to time, which all help to create a carnival atmosphere (as well as set-piece seasonal events, such as St Patrick's Day in March and the Christmas festivities). When you add in the entertainment possibilities of Buffalo Bill's Wild West show, the

Inside the Sports Bar

© Disney

© Disney

Disney Village from Lakeside

cinema complex, the live music of Billy Bob's Country Western Saloon and the late-night disco, Hurricanes, you have a serious array of choice as to how to spend your time.

What's there

Roughly speaking, you can divide the offerings of *Disney Village* into **restaurants and bars**, **shopping** and **entertainment**. But, to get maximum enjoyment, you need to be aware of a couple of things. First, the restaurants normally start to fill up from 6–7pm. In high summer, when the theme parks are open until late, the peak period for the restaurants and shops is more likely to be 9pm. Unless you've made a booking (and only 4 of the restaurants actually accept reservations), you are likely to find queues of half an hour or more for places such as The Steakhouse, Planet Hollywood and even Annette's Diner.

BRITTIP

The restaurants at the theme parks end of *Disney Village* fill up the quickest, with Planet Hollywood being the most popular venue.

The other factor is the weather. On a fine evening, it will be easier to get a table; but, when it is wet, everywhere fills up extremely quickly, so you need to anticipate the rain to avoid being left out in it! It is also worth pointing out the Village is relatively quiet during the day, so it is the ideal spot for a more relaxed lunch away from

The rumour mill

The basic form of *Disney Village* has changed little since the early days of the resort. King Ludwig's Castle was added in 2003 and a new Starbucks Coffee in 2009 (replacing the Buffalo Trading Co shop). The NEX Game Arcade and bowling alley opened in 2007 only to close again little more than a year later following a serious flood, finally re-opening in summer 2009 after a heavy refurbishment.

But that doesn't represent a lot of change in the past 6 years, hence the rumour mill has been in overdrive. Various ideas have been suggested, the most likely of which sees a dramatic, 2-storey **World of Disney** store arriving to anchor one end of the Village in 2010–11. This would be the start of a whole new 'street' behind the existing one, expanding from the IMAX cinema all the way back to the old car park area (behind McDonald's on the lake side of the Village). It would also mean the existing Disney Store closing, which would free up that space for more dining and retail options, with a Jules Verne-themed pub among the ideas being discussed.

Almost certain to join the line-up in 2010, though, is an **Earl of Sandwich** café, which has proved highly popular in *Walt Disney World* in Orlando, offering a range of hot and cold sandwiches, salads, cakes and snacks. Well worth trying.

the parks and some leisurely afternoon shopping. You have free pick of all the restaurants (apart from La Grange at Billy Bob's Country Western Saloon, where the buffet is evenings only) and it is particularly convenient if you are in the *Walt Disney Studios Park*, where there is no table-service dining. If you just need a quick snack, there are plenty of fast-food carts dotted throughout the Village.

Restaurants and bars

Planet Hollywood: Taking *Disney Village* from the theme parks end, as soon as you come through the gateway you face the immediately recognisable 2-storey edifice of this popular international chain. Planet Hollywood is a huge draw from early evening until late, and reservations can be made for early evening only, which takes care of most of the queues. But, if there is a queue, there

Imax Gaumont

© Disney

is a great bar area and some snazzy bar staff to make the wait more fun. An unhurried lunch is also available at any time. If the queue can be seen outside, you'll be looking at a good 30-minute wait for a table.

BRITTIP

When the *Disneyland Park* is open until 11pm, head to Planet Hollywood for dinner at about 6pm and you should have your pick of its best tables.

The huge variety of movie models, costumes, portraits and other memorabilia in this 500-seat restaurant are subdivided into differently themed areas, each with its own video screen that shows well-known film clips, music videos and (worth looking out for) special trailers for forthcoming movies. The memorabilia, which will certainly get film buffs wandering around to study it, varies from James Cagney to Wesley Snipes, Arnold Schwarzenegger and Sylvester Stallone. The upstairs section includes a sci-fi dining area and an adventure area, as well as the lively bar, while downstairs there is a *Raiders of the Lost Ark* section and the

Zebra Room (for obvious, stripy reasons). In the inevitable gift store, also downstairs, you will probably find the Planet Hollywood merchandise a bit cheaper here than in London.

Different nationalities seem to dine at different times of the day. The Brits tend to eat earlier, hence there will be a UK predominance in the restaurants 5–7pm, while the Spanish are almost invariably the last ones out! The menu has also been adapted for the more European mix of customer, so several dishes have been tweaked (spinach dip replaces the more usual nachos, and lasagne is a house speciality). Several regional specialities have been added (such as the typically French Croque Monsieur, a ham and cheese toastie).

BRITTIP

Can't decide what to pick at Planet Hollywood? Look for the VIP Platter for starters (€18.50), which comprises 4 of its best offerings, and the Dessert Sampler (€10.40), which features a taste of several of its best menu items. Enough for 4 to share!

Planet Hollywood

© Disney

Night-time at Planet Hollywood

The full range offers starters (€8.50–11.75), salads (€14.50–14.90), sandwiches and burgers (€15.50–16.50), steak, chicken, ribs, salmon, boeuf bourguignon and fajitas (€19.50–24.50), pasta dishes (€15.50–16.90); while desserts include double chocolate brownie, strawberry cheesecake, crème brûlée, ice-cream and an excellent white chocolate bread pudding (€6.50–9.40). Vegetarian options (4 starters, 6 main courses, €7.90–21.90) and a kid's menu (up to 11, €12.50) are available.

Of all the Planet Hollywood restaurants we have visited, the food here is usually the best, which we ascribe to that extra bit of French flair. It also freshens the menu from time to time (new dishes in 2009 included manicotti, chicken or shrimp Alfredo and a delicious rump steak) and have some tempting cocktails, including an exclusive Summer Specials menu. TVs in the bar show all the major sports events, and the latest football results are usually available (in English).

BRITTIP

If you have visited the cinema, save money at Planet Hollywood by showing your cinema ticket stub for a €5 discount.

If you haven't been to a Planet Hollywood before, you will probably be wowed by its lively entertainment mix (even its soundtrack is carefully balanced so you can talk at the table without having to shout), so you should make a beeline for this one. If you are already familiar with their style, head here anyway and try the LA Lasagne (a layered pasta that is rolled, cut in half, deep fried and then smothered in their tomato sauce), which will make your taste buds quiver with delight and your waistline shudder!

We will admit to being slightly biased in our liking for the brash cinema-style motif of Planet Hollywood, but we reckon it is one of the most fun dining experiences in the whole resort. Hours 11.30am–11.30pm, but it stays open until the last person leaves!

Annette's Diner: Opposite PH stands this classic 1950s' rock 'n' roll-style restaurant. Straight out of *Grease* and *Happy Days*, the bright, vivid decor provides a suitably fun, family atmosphere, with waiters and waitresses who dance on the bar top at various moments. The large icons are all typical Americana from this period, and the menu is equally in keeping with the theme, with a line-up of burgers, hot dogs, chilli, fajitas, salads and sandwiches. The restaurant has 2 (rather noisy!) levels, the mezzanine floor offering the best views of the restaurant, which also features a classic Cadillac and Corvette by the entrance.

Open from 10am for its American-style breakfast (until 2pm, €12.90), there is also a featured set Kids' Meal for lunch/dinner (for under-12s) at

Annette's Diner

© Disney

€12.50, while the burgers are €12.95–17.95 (for the humongous 'Big One' at €25.95 – finish it all and qualify for a free milkshake!). The desserts are possibly its best feature, with a range of ice-creams, sundaes and shakes to appeal strongly to those with a sweet tooth. When the queues get long (as they often do), there is a handy take-away window at the side, and Annette's is open 10am–midnight.

BRITTIP

To book any of the restaurants in *Disney Village*, up to 8 months in advance, call (from the UK) 00 33 1 60 30 40 50 or make a reservation through the concierge at your hotel.

King Ludwig's Castle: Continuing along the main *Disney Village* thoroughfare brings you next to this hugely elaborate establishment, which opened in June 2003, with a 2009 expansion adding a bar area. Inspired by Neuschwanstein Castle in Bavaria (built by 'mad' King Ludwig II), King Ludwig's has been designed primarily for German visitors but will, we think, appeal to anyone who enjoys good beer, Bavarian food and castles in general. With more than 300 seats on 2 floors, the interior of the restaurant is redolent with castle theming, including wooden panelling, flags and ornate carvings.

The menu is designed to appeal to international tastes, with starters (€5.90–8.90) such as *weisswurst*

Inside King Ludwig's Castle

© Disney

© Disney

King Ludwig's Castle

(sausages with mustard), soup, and morteau sausage and onion salad; 3 starters to share (€8.90), and main courses (€16.50–27.80) such as Oktoberfest chicken, *wiener schnitzel*, pork shank and Royal Sauerkraut (smoked pork loin, bacon, sausage and potato on a dome of sauerkraut); while desserts (€6.90–8.20) include various strudels and a delicious chocolate cake. There are also more straightforward salads and pastas, plus burgers and even a tandoori chicken dish, as well as a simple kids' menu (€12.50), but the feature dishes are all well worth trying.

This can all be washed down with a good choice of beer and schnapps, plus a generous Happy Hour 7–10pm with various beer specials. There is also a set menu at €17.90 (a starter and main course, or main course and dessert, including a 1l beer). A magnificent design inside and out, the castle has a fantasy-orientated and whimsical touch rather than the usual more formal approach. The set lunch menu (main course, dessert and drink) is €15 (11.30am–4.30pm), dinner €17.90, and the gift shop sells branded merchandise – glass, porcelain and the inevitable swords – under the mark of Prince Luipold of Bavaria (a direct descendant of King Ludwig II and the owner of the Kaltenberg brewery). It is open 11.30am–11pm (Sun–Fri) and 11.30am– midnight (Fri and Sat).

© Disney

Sports Bar

BRITTIP

Arguably the best value food in *Disney Village* comes from the rather plain New York Style Sandwiches, with its range of hot dogs, sandwiches, salads, soups and all-day breakfast. However, look out for the **Earl of Sandwich** in future, as this café chain usually offers some delicious and well-priced alternatives.

Sports Bar: Diagonally opposite the Castle, this regular haunt for many Brits is the nearest the Village gets to a proper pub. With an outdoor terrace, indoor seating and a cinema-style video screen at one end (plus a dozen TV screens sprinkled through the bar), this is the place to come for a British-style beer, a quick snack and, more importantly, the footy on telly at weekends and midweek! It shows a great variety of European action and keeps all the latest scores and tables on big blackboards behind the bar.

Popular with Disney Cast Members, the Sports Bar can be a lively place most evenings, but especially at weekends when the locals come out to play. The draught beers are usually Kronenbourg 1664, Fosters, Beamish (stout) and Carlsberg, while there is a good choice of bottled beers, including Heineken, Guinness, Budweiser, and Strongbow. Open

2pm–1am Mon–Fri, midday–2am Sat and midday–1am Sun (with food until 11pm), it serves hot dogs, pizza, nachos and chicken nuggets; chips and crisps are also available (with a set meal of a hot dog and fries, or chicken nuggets, plus a brownie and a soft drink for €11, or a beer instead of a soft drink for €12). It is usually packed for the big European football games and can be a bit rowdy, so it is not an ideal atmosphere for children, although they are always welcome.

New York Style Sandwiches: Next door to the Sports Bar (and sharing the outdoor terrace), this rather nondescript deli-style, diner/take-away offers baguettes, hot and cold sandwiches, soups, salads and paninis, plus ice-cream, hot dogs, crisps and drinks. The set children's menu (choice of cheese sandwich, hot

New York Style Sandwiches

© Disney

dog or chicken nuggets and chips, plus yoghurt and a drink) costs €7, while main menu items are €6.50–8.75. The deli is open from 9am– midnight (Mon–Thurs), 9am–11pm (Fri and Sat) or 9am–midnight (Sun).

Billy Bob's Country Western Saloon: Just down from King Ludwig's Castle, you come to this wonderful mock cowboy saloon, with a large bar and a stage for live music every evening. There are periodic guest performers, while excellent house band Big Joe and the Space Cowboys are usually on stage Sun–Thurs at 9.30 and 11pm. The 3-storey Grand Opry-style building (copied from an original in Austin, Texas) is superbly designed inside (anyone who has been in the old Cheyenne Saloon in Orlando will know the idea), with tiered balconies all providing a good view of the stage. You can learn to line dance here (8pm Thurs), take in some rock 'n' roll (every Wed), try its salsa classes (one Fri every month) or just sit back with a drink and enjoy the Space Cowboys, who are genuine American exponents of the Country & Western genre (even if it's not your usual cup of tea, their live style is worth checking out).

Billy Bob's

BRITTIP

If the other restaurants are heaving in the evening, try Billy Bob's buffet upstairs in La Grange restaurant. Not many people notice it and it is usually possible to get a table without much of a wait.

Bar snacks include chicken wings, spare ribs and nachos, or try out the excellent buffet at La Grange restaurant, which is at the top of the bar at the back (take the stairs to your left and keep going up!). **La Grange** is open 6–11pm, and offers a great value spread (€25/adult and €15/child)

La Grange

The Steakhouse

featuring salads, roast pork and beef, fajitas, chilli con carne, rice, pasta and vegetables, chicken wings, spare ribs, cheese tray and a huge choice of desserts. Billy Bob's can be booked in advance through your hotel concierge. It is open 6pm–1am (Sun–Fri) 6pm–2am (Sat), with snacks (€3.50–13.50) served 6–10.30pm. Early evening usually sees a kids' dance session, when the saloon is given over to a more youthful, energetic vibe, ideal for the 8–14 brigade. To book before you go, call 00 33 1 60 30 40 50 from the UK.

Starbucks Coffee: Okay, we moaned long and loud about there being no decent coffee bar in *Disney Village*, and the powers-that-be must have listened because this finally opened in summer 2009. And, while it is not in the best European traditions (of Lavazza and Illy), it definitely increases the quality of the dreadful counter offerings in the parks. Be prepared for a surprisingly low-key and whimsical atmosphere in keeping with its Disney location. There is also an obvious commitment to 'going green', from countertops made of recycled mobile phones to entry mats created from recycled French aeroplane tyres. Be ready for some higher-than-average prices, though: €3.90 for a grande latte or cappuccino, and €5.60 for a venti frappuccino. Open 8am–midnight (Sun–Thurs) and 8am–1am (Fri and Sat).

The Steakhouse: Right next door, this offers the real fine-dining opportunity in *Disney Village*. In fact, only the California Grill in the *Disneyland Hotel* and Hunter's Grill in *Disney's Sequoia Lodge* can rival this for quality. It is a spectacular venue, with a Chicago-style warehouse interior in 3 sections – the main warehouse, the smart bar and the conservatory-like annexe. It is all decorated in 1930s' Americana, with lots of dark woods, rich upholstery, wood panelling and elaborate candelabra lighting effects. The bar area is straight out of the TV programme *Cheers*, but it is also extremely elegant for such a large restaurant and provides a great backdrop for a special-occasion meal (although it is also popular with families early in the evening and you will find a lot of children here).

The mouth-watering menu is pretty broad-based, too, although the obvious speciality is steak (fillet, entrecôte, rump steak, sirloin, Brazilian strip, rib-eye and steak tartare) along with spare ribs, a couple of excellent fish dishes (try the grilled bass fillet), a chicken curry and a vegetarian lasagne. The à la carte prices are not too outrageous (steaks are €21.90–26.50, while starters are €8.50–14.90) and there is a set menu for €33 that offers a choice of 4 starters, main courses and desserts. Arrive before 7pm for its Early Bird Specials.

Starbucks

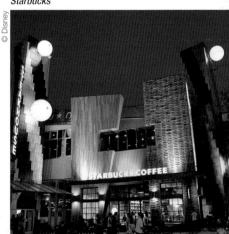

For children, the Scrooge McDuck Menu (€11.90) is also a cut above usual kiddie fare (although they can still get the ubiquitous chicken nuggets). Reservations are highly recommended at most times and the restaurant is open daily midday–midnight. This is also the place to come for a superb **Sunday Brunch** with Disney characters, midday–3pm. It's a tad pricey at €35/adult and €10/child (no Half Board on Sun) but it does make a memorable meal and is rarely crowded, so the kids have plenty of time with the characters. Call 00 33 1 60 30 40 50 (from the UK) to book.

Rainforest Café: This unmistakable, international chain restaurant, providing a larger-than-life jungle adventure and whose decor owes a lot to the artistry of the Imagineers, is next up on the Village restaurant tour. Here you will find tropical aquaria, waterfalls, streams and a host of (animatronic) animals to accompany your meal, all in a realistic rainforest setting punctuated by thunderstorms and rainfall. You don't just go to eat here you go 'on expedition' and it is as much the decor and atmosphere as the food that creates the experience.

In truth, the food is fairly regular diner fare given a bit of a twist and a few fancy names (Rasta Pasta is

Inside the Rainforest Café

penne pasta with chicken, broccoli, peppers and spinach tossed in a cream sauce, while Mojo Bones is BBQ ribs with coleslaw and chips), but the portions are huge and usually good value. Salads, pasta, burgers and grills (try the Awesome Appetiser Adventure for 2, Caribbean Coconut Shrimp or Paradise Pot Roast) range for €15.90–25.90, while the starters are €6.00–18.50. Cocktails and desserts are both specialities of the house, and the Chocolate Diablo Cake alone is worth coming in for (along with the delicious Gorilla in the Mist Cheesecake and Bambas Pancake).

Children in particular love the rainforest style and pick up on the many environmental messages, while the kids' menu (€14.90) is one of the best. The café doesn't accept reservations, so you just have to turn up and wait, but there is a huge gift shop to inspect before you eat and plenty of audio-animatronics to keep the kids happy (the big 'alligator' outside seems to provide an almost endless source of amusement). Open 11.30am–midnight every day, with the gift shop open from 9.30am.

Café Mickey: This is another fun and lively venue that stages character meals throughout the day. Once again, the decor is both bright without being garish and amusing without being obvious. The upstairs dining area has a magnificent view over Lake Disney from the terrace. TV

Café Mickey

screens showing classic Disney cartoons help to keep children happy if the food doesn't (and the food is way above average), but it is more likely to be the excellent character visits that make their day. A big breakfast buffet runs 7.30am–9.30am (with separate seatings at 8 and 9.30am), while lunch is available noon–5pm and dinner 5–11pm (Sun–Fri) or 5pm–midnight (Sat). The dinner menu is an extended version of the lunch fare. Hotel Supplement €17 adult, €12 child, full price €25 and €17.

BRITTIP

Tigger, Pluto and Co appear in front of Café Mickey (weather permitting) in the early evening to strut their stuff and amuse the younger crowd. This is also one of the best character dining experiences in the whole resort.

You can perhaps see the European influence at work here most, with a wide-ranging choice and a highly thoughtful and appetising selection (from pizza and pasta standards to seafood, vegetarian dishes and salads), way above usual diner fare. Try the Fantasia Mushrooms starter (garlic mushrooms beautifully roasted with pesto and parmesan), then progress to Pinocchio Pasta (creamy wok-cooked penne pasta with chicken and broccoli) or King Triton's Favourite (pan-sautéed fish medley), or give its wood-fired oven pizzas a try. Then follow up with a wonderfully tempting array of desserts (of which Mickey's Chocolate Fondant Cake is quite dreamy!). The 3-course set meal is €21.90 for adults. Under-12s get their own menu (€17.90) and a special Mickey surprise at the end. The characters circulate fairly constantly to keep everyone happy and the smart decor ensures adult sensibilities are not forgotten. Booking is highly advisable (with the possible exception of lunchtime). In France, call 01 60 30 40 50.

Earl of Sandwich: Strongly rumoured to be arriving in 2010, this chain started at *Downtown Disney* in Orlando and is now an international franchise. It features a terrific range of hot sandwiches (14 at the last count), plus wraps, salads and desserts, as well as a good kids' option. Some venues also offer breakfast and smoothies, hence there is a good chance this will be a valuable addition to the *Disney Village* line-up in more ways than one.

BRITTIP

If *Disney Village* is too crowded for your tastes or you can't get a table for dinner, try going to *Disney's Hotel New York* (see page 85) for its Parkside Diner, where you can usually get a table at any time, or the upmarket Hunter's Grill at *Disney's Sequoia Lodge* (see page 88). Both have great bars, too.

McDonald's: Completing the impressive spread of restaurants is the inevitable (and huge) McDonald's, albeit quite a smart, almost high-tech version of the ubiquitous American burger chain. Open 8am–midnight (8am–1am Fri and Sat), it is a major draw in the evenings as it is obviously one of the relatively cheaper options (with a Big Mac costing €3 and 4 kids set meals at €7.80), but it also has a high capacity with an outdoor terrace, providing a pleasant place to sit in the

Rainforest Café

© Disney

right weather. The original architecture is based on Italian theatre and the split-level arrangement also offers a games area for the kids.

Hand-carts: Finally, if you're after a late-night snack, there are various hand-carts throughout the Village where you can grab a hot dog, popcorn, crêpes or toffee apples. There is also an **Ice Cream Kiosk** beyond McDonald's overlooking the lake.

Shopping

Okay, if that sums up your eating opportunities in the Village, the retail therapy offerings aren't quite so wide ranging, as you will find much of the merchandise recurring in different shops. However, there is still an imaginative array of interior styling and it is worth wandering through the likes of The Disney Store and the Rainforest Café shop just to have a look at the splendid decor.

Disney Store: This is first on your left when you enter *Disney Village* from the theme parks end. It's the biggest in the resort, and a huge character emporium that offers a seemingly infinite variety of souvenir goods and brilliant ways of displaying them. It sells the widest selection of character and souvenir wares of any of the stores, from books and cuddly toys to DVDs, watches and jewellery, plus an extensive clothing selection and, nearer the festive season, an array of Christmas decorations, too. Kids will love browsing (if they can be prevented from trying to buy everything in sight!), while above them are a host of wonderful things to watch – large-scale moving models, mobiles and Mickey Mouse flying a spaceship.

Planet Hollywood: This gift store is almost opposite, for restaurant souvenirs and other movie memorabilia. You can also check out the movie and TV star hand prints on the wall outside.

King Ludwig's Castle: Next door, this fun restaurant also has a specialist shop, with various Bavarian souvenirs as well as a selection of toys and the all-important swords and shields for kids to re-enact the Battle of Waterloo!

Disney Gallery: This is opposite the new Starbucks Coffee, offering a more upmarket selection of gift items for cinema and art fans. Disney collectors will want to make a beeline here to check out the range of limited series lithographs and original animated film cels. There are some great books (here's where you might still get a copy of Didier Ghez's superb book *Disneyland – From Sketch to Reality*) and photographs, and it also has the latest collections of china figurines

The smart exterior of The Disney Store

Shopping savvy

and snow globes, plus novelties like a Mickey telephone (every home should have one!).

Disney Fashion, Hollywood Pictures and World of Toys: Immediately next door, you enter these 3 interconnected shops (handy in the rain) and, while you will probably have seen some of the merchandise already, there is more novel stuff, too. Disney Fashion is a rather ordinary clothing store (everything from hats to shoes), Hollywood Pictures offers an array of film-themed clothing, photo albums and gifts (and the inevitable cuddly toys), and World of Toys is almost a reprise of The Disney Store, with yet more kids' playthings (beware the pirate paraphernalia and swords!), costumes and a big sweet counter. You will also find a Pin-Trading Super Station here.

Rainforest Café: Finally, inside the main entrance to this café lurks an animal-themed gift shop just waiting to ensnare the unwary with another line-up of soft toys, games, clothing and environmentally aware souvenirs. Its audio-animatronics make it fun for children and should keep the kids amused while the grown-ups browse the merchandise.

Others: Essential services are provided by a **currency exchange** next to The Disney Store, 2 regular **cash dispensers**, an **Information & Ticket** kiosk in front of Hurricanes nightclub and **baby change** facilities (between The Disney Store and Sports Bar), while there is also a big **tourist information office** just outside the *Disney Village* gates in front of the train station. There used to be a **post office** in the Village but that is now just inside the RER station, facing the tourist office.

Village entertainment

If all that isn't enough to keep you occupied, Disney has a third array of opportunities to entertain and amuse. Foremost of these is **Buffalo Bill's Wild West Show**, plus **Hurricanes** nightclub, but there is also live music and other periodic street entertainment throughout the Village. When you consider the big seasonal events, like Christmas, St David's Day, St Patrick's Day, Halloween and Fireworks Night, which are all either based or have a significant presence here, this can be an exceptionally lively scene at times.

Gaumont and IMAX Cinemas: One of the most eye-catching features of the theme parks end of the Village, however, is the fully modern 15-screen Gaumont Cinema complex, which is largely a French-language operation, and the neighbouring IMAX Cinema. However, Monday night is often Original Language night

World of Toys

© Disney

(usually at 7.45 and 10.30pm) when one major current release is shown in English (with French subtitles). The IMAX can offer both the signature giant-screen films and 3-D movies, as well as DMR productions – digitally re-mastered versions of normal-screen films (like the *Spiderman* series), which can be shown in clear, sharp pictures on the IMAX screen. The plush interior was designed by French design guru Christian Lacroix and features some of the most comfortable cinema seats anywhere, plus the kind of sound system to make audio fans salivate.

Buffalo Bill's Wild West Show

Next door to the Gaumont – and arguably the most prominent feature of the village – is Buffalo Bill's Wild West Show…With Mickey and Friends, a 90-minute sit-down dinner spectacular that relives the myths and legends of America's cowboy country. The huge indoor arena, some eye-catching stunts and the full Western style ensure this is a hit with all the family (but especially children in the 4–12 age range).

BRITTIP

Buffalo Bill's is not advisable for anyone who suffers from asthma or other respiratory complaints as the animals kick up a fair bit of dust in the indoor arena.

The food is unremarkable, but there is always plenty of it – chilli con carne, chicken, ribs, sausage, vegetables and potatoes, plus apple cobbler, ice-cream and either tea or coffee – and there is a separate children's platter (roast leg of chicken, sausage, potatoes and chocolate mousse, plus a soft drink or mineral water), which always seems to go down well. There is a constant supply of either beer or Coca-Cola (with the meal only – you pay for your drinks in the pre-show Colonel Cody's Saloon) as part of the entrance price. Everyone gets a straw cowboy hat, and you sit in one of 4 colour-coded sections

BRITTIP

In summer, watch out for Buffalo Bill's Wild West parade in the *Disney Village* at 6pm as a prelude to the day's first show (weather permitting).

Buffalo Bill's Wild West Show

© Disney

Buffalo Bill's Wild West Show

corresponding to the different cowboys in the show, who go through a series of games and competitions to decide the 'numero uno' for the evening.

You need to be in best audience participation and hat-waving mood as you cheer and clap for your cowboy and hiss and boo the others, and it all adds up to good raucous fun. After a revamp in 2009, Mickey, Minnie, Goofy, Chip 'n' Dale all now play a special role in the show, adding guaranteed child appeal at regular intervals, while Annie Oakley, the 'Queen of the Winchester', also puts in an appearance, literally shooting the lights out. There are some magnificent horse-riding tricks and skills, too, and much of the narration is in English as the 60 performers are nearly all American. A Native American element also features and, at one point, the curtain at one end of the auditorium rises to reveal a majestic rocky outcrop, which complements the superb lighting and sound effects. There are wagon trains and cattle drives, cavalry charges and rodeo games, along with a big finale with the inevitable stagecoach – and it is all performed with great gusto and zest by the large cast.

BRITTIP

A vegetarian or pork-free menu is available upon request at Buffalo Bill's. You can also order wine or champagne (at additional cost).

The degree of authenticity is remarkable, with the Native Americans from a variety of tribes (including Blackfoot, Sioux and Cherokee), the buffalo from Canada and longhorn cattle from Texas, while the horses are all original Pintos and Appaloosas (for the Native Americans) or quarterhorses (for the cowboys). It is staged twice a night at 6.30 and 9.30pm. Guests can arrive up to 45 minutes before and enjoy the saloon bar atmosphere and live music, and, at €70/adult for Category 1 seating, €58 Category 2 seating and €56/3–11s Category 1, €44 Category 2, it provides an excellent mix of entertainment, spectacle and fun. You can book your tickets in advance by calling (from the UK) 00 33 1 60 45 71 00, but it is usually possible to book when you arrive, either at your hotel or at the ticket office in *Disney Village.*

Hurricanes

If the Wild West is not your scene, then Caribbean-themed dance club Hurricanes may be (especially if you can arrange child-minding or babysitting for the evening through your hotel concierge). Here, upstairs and to one side of the Rainforest Café, the late-night crowd can really

Annie Oakley at Buffalo Bill's

© Disney

expend some energy as Hurricanes only gets going at 11pm and keeps bopping until 4am (Mon–Sat). The weekdays are usually quieter (especially out of season), but Fri and Sat can be extremely lively when the locals flood in. The dance floor is large, the sound system excellent and, if the bar service is a little slow when busy, that is only a minor quibble.

Hurricanes offers free entry for all Disney hotel guests (with hotel ID) and Annual Passport holders, otherwise it costs €15/person. The evening line-up varies from week to week, but there are regular special events and themed nights, like its Foam Parties (Sun in summer) and 1980s Night.

Of course, you can also check out the live music (and dancing) at **Billy Bob's Country Western Saloon** (see page 200), with 2 or 3 sessions a night (highly recommended if Big Joe and The Space Cowboys are playing) or the soccer on the big TV screens in the **Sports Bar** (page 199).

Fun, games – and Panoramagique

Disney Village is sprinkled with various types of fun games (all of which require a few extra euros), such as mechanical bull-riding and Ring the Bell (the typical fairground attraction). There are also – strictly for kids – 3 variations on the remote-

Billy Bob's

control driving games, with boats and trucks. The more energetic might also like to try their hand (and feet) on the bungee trampolines at each end of the Village, plus a rock-climbing wall, which adds another – extra cost – element to the entertainment line-up.

BRITTIP

The Village's main toilets are located between the Sports Bar and The Disney Store. However, their cleanliness often leaves something to be desired, so a dash across the plaza to The Steakhouse is usually better.

La Marina: From here on Lake Disney, you can hire pedaloes (€10 for 20 minutes), Hydrobikes (€5 for 20 minutes) or electric boats (€30 for 20 minutes). Or try something a bit more active, onboard a fun **Segway** 2-wheeled electrical transporter (€20 for 20 minutes). All can be hired 3–9pm at weekends and public holidays. Or take a gentle pedal round the whole of Lake Disney on a **quadricycle**. These multi-seat bikes are available 5–10pm Mon–Fri, 4.30–10.30pm Sat, and 11am–1pm and 3pm–10pm Sun (€10 per 20 minutes 2–4 seat, €20 per 20 minutes 6–seat). On a summer evening, it is a great way to while away some time.

Street performers: At peak times and for seasonal events, the Village comes alive with a series of performers such as jugglers, stilt-walkers and diabolo throwers, which all help to enhance

Village Circus

Imax cinema

the carnival nature and intent of this long entertainment thoroughfare. There is also a summer season **Village Circus**, with a clown, juggler and acrobat performing along the main street. It is a lively, and occasionally even raucous, affair (not a big hit with seniors usually), although the atmosphere is decidedly different in the cold and/or wet.

NEX Games Arcade: Underneath the IMAX cinema is the newly renovated high-energy video and games arcade, which features a host of high-tech amusements, many offering the very latest gaming technology. Downstairs you will find a unique car and motorbike racing set-up, along with flight simulators, shoot-'em-ups, basketball and dancing. Upstairs is a clever mini bowling alley (a scaled – down version of 10-pin, with light-weight balls and no need for special shoes), plus online games, table football and pool tables. There is also a dedicated area just for younger children, mostly operated by tokens (€2 each, or 3 for €5, 7 for €10 and 15 for $20). Open 3pm–1am Mon–Fri, to 3am on Sat, and 11pm on Sun.

Panoramagique: This is a magnificent tethered balloon that takes flight over Lake Disney up to 6 times an hour, soaring to 100m/328ft (dependent on the wind) over the Village, with a superb view in all directions. The flights last around 6 minutes and can carry up to 30 passengers at a time. It is one of the largest balloons of its kind in the world, taking off and landing from its own purpose-built platform on the water, and is styled in best Jules Verne Victorian fashion. It can fly in most weathers (although you wouldn't want to go up when visibility isn't good) but winds of more than 35kph/22mph will see the balloon grounded for a while. It costs €12/adult and €6/3–11s and, on a clear day, it is possible to see all the way to Paris and the Eiffel Tower.

However, the real fascination is getting a true perspective on *Disneyland Paris* itself, seeing how all the elements fit together, including the hotels of Val de France, getting a bird's-eye view of the parks and looking at all the areas of possible future development. It is amazing just how much you can take in and its smooth take-off, ascent and landing – plus the huge size of the cage-like metal basket – mean you feel totally safe. We would certainly rate it a must-do attraction for the resort. However, those who have a fear of heights or suffer from vertigo may not agree.

BRITTIP

Susan – not the happiest of people with heights – found she could ride Panoramagique quite comfortably as long as she looked out to the sides and not down the middle at the balloon's cable system!

Panoramagique

If you are staying at a Disney hotel or one nearby, you are very conveniently placed for *Disney Village*, and the new multi-storey Vinci car park, which brings you out by the new IMAX cinema. Once on site, everything is within a short walking distance and it is so easy just to wander around, sample a variety of different establishments and then wend your way 'home' again in this safe, well-organised and thoroughly entertaining environment.

Of course, for those without a car or a Disney hotel booking, the usefulness of the **RER station** is paramount. Here, you can enjoy the convenience of a public transport system that runs on schedule 99 times out of 100 and keeps working until a little after midnight each day, ensuring you can get back to the many hotels linked to the Line A (and within walking distance of the stations along the way). It is efficient, user-friendly and good value. Miss out on a night in *Disney Village* at your peril!

BRITTIP

The Vinci car park, which costs €2/hour, is free to Disney hotel guests. Just take your ticket and show your hotel ID to the office on the ground floor when you are ready to leave.

Disneyland Golf

Disney Village at night

Disneyland golf

Golf aficionados will be keen to indulge in their favourite sport at the **Golf Disneyland** course in the neighbouring village of Magny-le-Hongre, which is barely 10 minutes' drive from the resort itself. Although quite a modern set-up, it has all the characteristics of something a lot more mature and its 3 9-hole courses should provide a good test for all standards of golfer, as well as offering what amounts to 3 different 18-hole rounds. All the courses start and finish in front of the clubhouse so they can easily be combined.

Open year-round, 7 days a week, the facilities are second to none in the Paris area (there is another good course at nearby Bussy-St-Georges, but the variety and challenge at **Golf Disneyland** are far superior).

A driving range and practice green (complete with a well-known Mouse head silhouette!) are situated each side of the clubhouse, which has an extremely pleasant bar and restaurant, and an outdoor terrace where you can enjoy the best of the summer weather.

From the striking circular restaurant building, the view over the green of what is, effectively, the 18th hole, the driving range and the practice green is superb and highly conducive to a satisfying lunch. There is also a well-equipped pro shop that hires electric and manual carts, full sets of clubs

Everyone will enjoy Davy Crockett's Adventure

and golf shoes, as well as offering the usual range of equipment and clothing to buy. A TV lounge, changing rooms and showers complete the clubhouse set-up and there is a large car park.

Green fees start at €30 for a winter weekday 18-hole round and go up to €60 for a summer round on a weekend or bank holiday. For a 9-hole round, prices are €25–42, with reduced rates for under-18s. Club hire is €5 per club or €25 for a full set, while hand-carts are €6 and electric ones €25 for an 18-hole round. A bucket of 30 balls for the driving range costs €4, 5 buckets is €14 and 11 buckets €30. Tuition is available from one of the 2 fully qualified instructors from €25 for a half-hour lesson to €75 for an accompanied round. For more details about playing there, visit the website **disneylandparis.co.uk** and click on the 'Golf' section.

Davy Crockett's Adventure

Thrill-seekers with a love for the outdoors will surely enjoy this unique forest adventure next to *Disney's Davy Crockett Ranch*. The **Davy Crockett Adventure** comprises 5 trails with more than 80 activities in 5 levels of difficulty, from green – the easiest, accessible to children at least 1.10m/3ft 7in tall – to black, for real daredevils. The activities are linked by platforms and ropes that blend in with the environment. Each course

features suspended stations (Tyrolean traverses, monkey bridges and swings) linked by platforms and cables, and adventurers move from tree to tree using special harnesses, tethers, karabiners and pulleys. The course includes creeper-swinging, suspended bridges, wobbly tree trunks and monkey bridges, as well as a dizzying 200m/656ft suspended footbridge and its trademark 16m/52ft Tarzan leap.

Davy Crockett's Adventure covers 5ha/12 acres of the Grains national forest full of 100-year-old oak trees. The entrance is just to the right of *Disney's Davy Crockett Ranch* (see pages 92–95), just after the reception (off Exit 13 of the A4). Access, parking and reception are all located at the Ranch (and you will have to drive here as no transport is laid on). There is a 30-minute initiation on the equipment and safety rules, but then participants are on their own to tackle the course progressively, under the close watch of the course supervisors. It should provide around 3 hours of physical challenges in the great outdoors and costs €25 for those over 1.40m/4ft 7in tall and €15 for those shorter (or €3 just to watch). It is

Davy Crockett's Adventure

open from 9am in high season (first departure at 10am, last departure at 4pm) and from 1pm in low season (last departure at 3pm). However, you MUST book in advance, on 0825 150 280 (in France) or online at **aventure-aventure.com**.

Val d'Europe

Leaving the immediate environs of *Disneyland Paris* behind, the nearby **Val d'Europe** shopping, leisure and business complex is well worth taking at least half a day to explore. Opened in October 2000, it has its own RER and bus stations and has given rise to a sprawling but smart new-town development. Covering some 24.5ha/60 acres, the central portion is basically a glorified (but very attractive) mall, with 2 additional elements (the Sea Life Centre and a big health and fitness centre called Moving), plus the associated development of **La Vallée Village** (outlet shopping) in an outdoor pedestrianised area at one end.

As well as the mall and associated development, the main street through

> **BRITTIP**
>
> If you find it too expensive to feed your brood at *Disney Village*, head for Val d'Europe where prices are lower and you can stock up on snacks etc. at the Auchan hypermarket.

La Place de Toscane

the town (outside the RER station) also boasts a number of pleasant restaurants, cafés and hotels, notably the pub/brasserie of **L'Agape Café**, the **Asian Wok** and the **Pizza Di Roma**.

> **BRITTIP**
>
> Need fuel? The Shell service station in the Val d'Europe car park is rated the cheapest in the Ile de France, so it is the ideal place to fill up for the journey home. However, you CANNOT use the ground-level pumps (they accept only French credit cards), so you must use the services in the underground car park.

For anyone who enjoys retail therapy, this should definitely be high on their list of priorities. The 2-level mall has a huge number of high-quality shops (around 130 stores, restaurants and cafés), many of which are internationally recognisable (Sephora, Etam, Quiksilver, Esprit, Levi's, Naf Naf, Gap, Zara, Benetton, Swatch, Swarovski and H&M) or uniquely French and wonderfully chic. Choose from the likes of L'Occitane en Provence (candles, perfumes and cosmetics, made with plants and flowers from southern France), Yves Rocher (make-up and beauty products with the accent on health), Carnet de Vol and Brice (men's fashion and sportswear), Carré Blanc (household items such as towels and carpets, all with that essential French style), Maisons du Monde (some fabulous interior decor items from around the world), Petit Bateau (the must-have women's T-shirts), Armand Thierry (men's and women's fashions), Le Tanneur (leather handbags, luggage and wallets) and – women take note – Orcanta lingerie.

> **BRITTIP**
>
> July usually means *Sales!* in French shops, so don't forget to check out the mall and La Vallée for some bargains if you're here in the summer.

The mall at Val d'Europe

There are 5 shoe shops (check out Beryl and San Marina for the latest fashions), 9 jewellery outlets (including Claire's and Swatch), 4 children's clothing shops (with Sergent Major offering a range from 1 month to 14 years) and 3 sports stores, plus one of our favourites, the Belgian chocolates and ice-cream of Jeff de Bruges. There is even a high-quality Paris souvenir shop, Articles de Paris, where you can get that essential mini Eiffel Tower; and another Disney store, Rendez-vous Disney, which is worth checking out for periodic sales.

Services

The clean, airy, uncluttered confines of the mall, some wonderful architecture (inspired by the great Parisian styles of the late 19th century) and the user-friendly way of doing things all add up to a true 21st-century shopping experience, enhanced by an array of tempting cafés and rest areas (around 250 armchairs are dotted throughout the mall). If you avoid the weekend, you will also find it free of crowds and easy to negotiate – no queues here!

There are 5 'welcome points' (including 2 in the huge car park) to assist with finding what you need, along with baby-care centres for

nursing mothers where hostesses can even provide jars of baby food. Four free play areas are available for children, with a variety of slides and climbs (excellent for 3–8s). Other services include valet parking, shoe repairs, photo printing, hairdressers (3) and opticians (3).

Tired of walking? Take **Le Petit Train** that goes from one end of the mall to the other and back again at regular intervals (for a small fee). It also stops at each of the main 4 entrances to the mall.

BRITTIP

There are 2 pharmacies in Val d'Europe, located between the RER station and the mall entrance.

Hypermarket

Also here, and on both levels, is the **Auchan hypermarket**. If you have brought the car, this is where you can fill up with essentials such as wine, beer, spirits and a host of other items. The lower level features all the food (a huge choice in serious quantities, with a magnificent wine selection at very reasonable prices!) while the upper (ground floor) level stocks a massive range of domestic goods, clothes, books, CDs, toys, Disney merchandise and even furniture. The levels are linked by a sloping moving walkway, which means you can take your trolley around the whole store with ease.

Paul Café at Les Terrasses

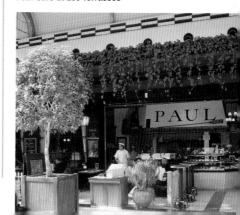

BRITTIP

If you regularly take the car to Calais to stock up at the many hypermarkets, Val d'Europe offers a much more civilised and user-friendly way to do your shopping.

The Auchan chain is well known all over France and offers considerable savings on comparable goods in the UK, so it is worth having a good look round. The whole store covers some 21,000m² (more than 5 acres!) and is open 8.30am–10pm, independent of the rest of the mall. Look up more on **auchan.fr**.

Les Terrasses

The Val d'Europe RER station is only 5 minutes from Marne-la-Vallée, and the mall is only a couple of minutes' walk from the station (turn right as you exit and it is straight ahead). Walk right through the mall and you come to the main café area, **Les Terrasses**, a monumental conservatory-style annex, with luxurious vegetation filling the iron and glass construction. Here, your choice of dining options is both wide and mouth-watering – from a fine tea-house and crêperie (just called Paul) to a proper Italian pizzeria, a fine seafood restaurant (the boat-themed La Criée), an elegant Chinese (Le Dragon d'Europe,

Les Terrasses

with set menus at €19.40, €14.20 and €13.20, plus a kids' menu at €8.20 and a 2-person set menu at €48), a wonderfully fresh and inviting café La Croissanterie, the eclectic Hippopotamus (beef, lamb, steaks and kebabs) and the inevitable McDonald's (although even that has a much smarter appearance than usual). Other highlights include Le Paradis du Fruit restaurant for natural drinks, salads and desserts, the new Kyoto Japanese restaurant and the Lebanese cuisine of Noura, with sandwiches, salads and meze. You will also find live entertainment, with shows for the children and music in the evenings for an older audience.

The shopping part of the mall is open 10am–9pm Mon–Sat (closed Sun) but Les Terrasses is open 9am–midnight

Les Terrasses Café

Pirate Exhibition at the Sea Life Centre

every day. Visit **valdeurope.fr** (then click on English version and 'Vos magasins') for more information.

BRITTIP
For an excellent cup of tea and the chance to sample some exquisite crêpes, give yourself a break at **Paul** and just sit and admire the wonderful architecture of Les Terrasses.

Sea Life Centre

On the lower level of Les Terrasses (down the escalators) is the Moving health and leisure centre and the excellent **Sea Life Centre**. If you have children aged 2–12, this interactive aquarium (belonging to UK-based Merlin Entertainments Group, which has 6 similar Sea Life Centres in Britain and another 23 in Europe and beyond) will keep them amused for a good couple of hours, and provide a welcome diversion from all the hectic theme-parking.

BRITTIP
The Sea Life Centre is fully accessible to the disabled.

Many hotels offer a free daily shuttle to Val d'Europe, so you can usually come straight here or you can just get a bus to the Marne-la-Vallée RER station and take the 5-minute train ride. Seasonal special offers for Sea Life – such as 'free child entry with every full-paying adult' – are worth looking out for.

Opened in April 2001, this 'aquatic park' offers a marine journey through 55 contrasting displays, exhibits and shows that trace an underwater journey from the source of the Seine river out into the Atlantic and on to the Caribbean. From tiny shrimps to menacing sharks and moray eels, from small tanks to the gigantic main aquarium holding 600,000l/132,000g of water, there is plenty to amuse, entertain and educate young minds.

The journey starts with a gentle introduction to the sea through a mesmerising exhibit, Jellyfish, Keepers of the Dark, then into the world of predators and a trip along the Amazon. Children can pick up a scratch card at the entrance, which invites them to visit the 10 question panels throughout the centre and choose the right answer on their card. Get more than 8 correct and they win a prize! All the explanations are bilingual and staff can give talks and answer questions in English.

Each fish tank and aquarium is presented in a different way. The highlights are the walk-through underwater tunnel (a 360° experience with sharks, rays and other fish

The stingray tank at the Sea Life Centre

swimming all around you), the 'Pirates – The Legend of Blackbeard' challenge, the Stingray Pool (where patient and gentle children can actually touch these fascinating creatures), a film presentation on the Atlantic Ocean (and how deep-sea exploration developed), the jellyfish exhibit and the Coral Reef tank.

BRITTIP

The Sea Life Centre is a good alternative when the weather turns cold and wet. It is also worth a visit when the temperature outside goes sky high, as it is air-conditioned and blissfully cool on hot days.

The interactive theming, with different walkways, passageways and alcoves, invites you to explore every nook and

Sea Life Centre walkway

cranny – and learn quite a bit along the way. Talks and demonstrations with the sharks, stingrays and touch-pool are given at regular intervals, while various feeding times add still further to the experience. At the end, there is a handy little seating area, with vending machines, where parents can grab a drink and sit while they unleash their offspring in the play area, which has a ball pool, climbing structure, nets and slides, and kiddie rides – a very thoughtful addition. Sea Life is open daily (but not Christmas Day and 1 January) 10am–5.30pm and costs €15/adult and €11/3–11s (under-3s free; under-14s must be with an adult). For more details, call 00 33 1 60 42 33 66 (from the UK) or visit its website, where you can purchase tickets online **sealifeeurope.com.**

BRITTIP

You can come and go as you please once you have bought your Sea Life Centre admission. That means you can go shopping and come back later in the day if there is a particular show or demonstration you want to see.

La Vallée Village

Now, step through the doors of Les Terrasses and you enter **La Vallée Village**, right outside the Val d'Europe complex. This outlet shopping village will appeal most to dedicated shoppers as all prices are guaranteed to be reduced by at least 33% on high street stores and you can often save much more. The 90 shops vary from homeware, luggage, shoes and accessories to high fashion, but most are clothing stores, with the accent on designer names and famous labels. Luxury goods feature strongly, too, but, at prices like these, they are more akin to regular high street offerings. The shopping options are exceptional, including **Paul Smith, Dolce and Gabbana, Jimmy Choo, Guess, Polo Ralph Lauren, M Missoni** (part of the Valentino fashion group), top French linens, bedding and soft

La Vallée

furnishings name **Descamps**, the French fashions of **Sandro** and the Italian women's style of **Pinko**.

There is a **Starbucks** coffee shop and chic little French café, Bert's, when you need a drink or a bite to eat, plus the delicious kiosk offerings of **Amorino**, for hot chocolate and ice-cream!

The Village design, with its winding streets, encourages you to stroll the length of the complex and all the shops are unfailingly inviting, with courteous staff seeming light years away from the more usual high street surliness and disdain. There is a useful **Welcome Centre** to get you started, a well-designed children's play area and clean, well-maintained toilets and baby-changing facilities. Start by visiting the Welcome Centre for the latest news and store promotions, and you can also use its pushchairs and umbrellas, if necessary.

For decoration and homeware you have the choice of Bodum, Villeroy & Boch (a famous glass and china store), Anne de Solène (household linens), Lalique and Baccarat (two of the leading French brands), while the Samsonite store, the French Lancel and Lamarthe and the Italian Furla and Mandarina Duck offer a wide range of luggage, handbags and accessories. For outlet children's wear, you have fashionable Bonpoint and K.I.D.S. Teenagers can choose from well-known names such as Miss

Sixty/Energie, Guess and Cerruti Jeans. If you are hunting for designer shoes, check out Robert Clergerie, and Heschung (French), Salvatore Ferragamo (Italian) or Manfield-Bowen (international).

Women's high fashion is represented by Anne Fontaine, Façonnable, Kenzo, Gerard Darel, Celine, MaxMara, Christian Lacroix, Givenchy, Furla, Zadig & Voltaire, Nitya and Ventilo, plus the Lingerie Shop, Chantal Thomass, Wolford, Calvin Klein and Chantelle for lingerie; while the men can choose from Café Coton, Porsche design, Charles Tyrwhitt, Feraud Homme, Kenzo and the American westernwear brand MCS.

BRITTIP

Book a session with La Vallée Village's Personal Shopper for an expert look at your perfect wardrobe. Two-hour sessions include style tips and individualised guidance in selecting your optimum styles.

International brands positively abound and you will find tempting outlet stores for all of the following: Longchamp, Diesel, Salvatore Ferragamo, Molton Brown and Tommy Hilfiger, plus other well-known names such as Reebok, Puma, Timberland, Dunhill and Burberry. And there is plenty more besides.

La Vallée

For serious shoppers it is a veritable Aladdin's cave of desirable items, all with some major mark-downs, which makes you wonder why we ever bother paying the usual high street rip-off prices (you can tell we enjoy shopping here!). There is so much packed in, you can't fail to come away with a major bargain or three.

BRITTIP

Unlike Val D'Europe, which closes on Sun, La Vallée is open 7 days.

La Vallée is open 362 days a year (closed on Christmas Day, New Year's Day and 1 May) 10am–7pm Mon–Fri, 10am–8pm Sat and public holidays, and 10am–7pm Sun. A useful daily shuttle bus service also operates from the Disney and Val de France hotels. Check with your hotel concierge for details and visit **lavalleevillage.com** for all the latest news, as it is still adding shops to its line-up.

And there's more

Wander outside the immediate confines of the Val D'Europe mall and La Vallée and you will encounter some charming (and usually traffic-free) streets and pedestrian areas where there are several other notable shops and restaurants. La Place de Toscane (at the north end of Les Terrasses) is a delightful circular plaza of restaurants and apartments, with a central monument and fountain.

Koreana Restaurant

La Vallée

Here you will find the likes of **Le Menhir** crêperie and **Cañas y Tapas** Spanish-style café, both with lovely outdoor terraces for al fresco dining (or just watching the world go by). You can also try **Epices & Chocolat** for some tempting chocolate treats, drinks, spices and ice-cream. Our favourite, though, is **Koreana** barbecue grill, featuring Korean cuisine where you grill your food at the table and it serves up some mouth-watering combinations of meats, vegetables, sauces and spices. The **Place D'Ariane** is the other notable thoroughfare, with more cafés, brasseries, shops and the Hotel Elysée, with its award-winning **Pop Art** restaurant and the Japanese **Sakura**. More outlets are opening all the time, though, as this busy town develops (in partnership with Disney), hence it rewards a casual meander anywhere in the vicinity of the mall. Try it – you never know what little treasure you will discover!

And that sums up all the various alternative fun and entertainment on offer away from the theme parks. A meal in Les Terrasses is highly recommended at any time, while the general opportunity to travel easily thanks to the great convenience of the RER line (and the good road system) comes as a major bonus for those who like to explore. But let's not stop here. There is much more to be seen in the city itself – and beyond – so we'll conclude with a closer look at the main attractions of Paris and the Ile de France.

9 The Attractions of Paris

or Getting an Eiffel of the City

Okay, we will admit to a bias here but Paris is a wonderful city and we reckon you'd be crazy to spend several days nearby and not consider paying a visit. Even with children to keep amused, there is a huge amount of family-friendly fare on offer, while the Eiffel Tower itself remains one of the greatest sources of child fascination and wonderment in the world.

Given that it is so easy to get into the city centre from Marne-la-Vallée on the RER (and even easier from some of the off-site hotels in the vicinity of Line A), visiting some of the great monuments, parks and museums of Paris is a natural adjunct to all the theme park frolics. Public transport in the city is plentiful and reliable, and is far and away the best, cheapest and most hassle-free way to see the sights (driving – with the eternal bugbear of parking – is not recommended, even if you are comfortable with using your own car in France).

It takes just 35–40 minutes to go from Marne-la-Vallée into the city centre, which means you can have almost a full day in one of the Disney parks and then head off for an evening in Montmartre, the Latin Quarter or for a stroll along the Champs-Elysées.

Getting around

Thanks to the comprehensive and integrated public transport system, involving the trains (RER, or Réseau Express Régional), underground (the Métro) and buses, getting to the sights is a doddle. Sign-posting is usually clear, the modern buses each have a route map and a board indicating each stop, and reliability is outstanding. The Métro system will get you to every tourist site in the city with only the minimum of walking and it runs until around 1am every day, while the last RER service back to Marne-la-Vallée is around midnight (check **ratp.fr** for public transport details – in English as well as French).

The **Paris Visite** card is almost an essential adjunct to sightseeing and can be purchased at any Métro ticket office, RER and SNCF railway station,

Sacré Coeur

✦ BRITTIP

Arguably the best ticket in town is the Paris Visite, a travel card enabling you to use all the public transport services. The all-day, go-anywhere pass covers the RER, Métro and bus systems.

bus terminal counter, airports and Paris tourist offices. The card provides unlimited travel on the whole Paris public transport system, including the SNCF (suburban) trains and the Montmartre funicular. The system is divided into 8 regional zones, with *Disneyland Paris* in zone 5.

BRITTIP

The Paris Visite card also comes with an array of discounts and special offers with a host of tourism partners in the city, including the Cité des Sciences (the excellent Museum of Science), Bateaux Parisiens river cruises, the Wine Museum and Crazy Horse dinner show.

Do it all with Disney

With all these possibilities on the doorstep, it stands to reason Disney would see a way to give guests even more value and purpose to staying on-site. So it has teamed up with **Cityrama** bus tours, offering a daily sightseeing excursion into and around the city on one of their big, modern double-decker coaches. Because we believe it is the ideal way to visit the key experiences in Paris with minimal effort and maximum use of time, we highlight Cityrama in this chapter.

Tours run daily at 9.45am from *Disney's Hotel New York* and are usually very popular, so it is advisable

The Louvre

to book early – with your tour operator in advance or at the hotel concierge desk when you check in. The tour returns at about 6pm, so you still have some park time left at the end of the day. The Cityrama buses are extremely comfortable and well equipped, with air-conditioning, toilets, drinks service and audio commentary on multi-lingual headphones.

The basic route takes you first into the heart of the city and provides a well-narrated overview of the geography, architecture, art, history and culture. The history is graphically illustrated with sites such as **La Bastille** (one of the city's oldest districts, now transformed into a more upmarket and happening area, with nightclubs, restaurants, piano bars and cafés) and **Le Marais** district, a mini-city in its own right, full of little streets, markets and several substantial mansions, now occupied by chic art galleries, cafés, health food shops and piano bars.

BRITTIP

The key word to look for in shop window displays is 'Soldes'. This means 'Sales' for all keen bargain hunters!

At the heart of Paris is the **Ile de la Cité**, the original settlement site, dating back to the 3rd century BC. The tour continues through the Quartier Latin (Latin Quarter), the famous Left Bank district that has been the centre of the city's university life for more than 700 years, and offers a cheaper selection of cafés and shops for more student-like budgets. You then pass the magnificent **Palais du Luxembourg**, with its 20ha/50-acre gardens, and travel along **Rue Bonaparte**, Paris's version of Bond Street, for exclusive shopping.

The Louvre

Across the **Pont Neuf**, one of the 12 main bridges that link the 2 halves of the city, you drive past the **Louvre**, the massive repository of just about

The Louvre from the Musée d'Orsay

every example of artwork known to mankind. Its principal claims to fame are the exhibits of the Venus de Milo, Mona Lisa and Van Gogh's Sunflowers, but you could easily spend a day or more investigating the wealth of art on display. It is divided into 7 departments: Oriental Antiquities (including Islamic Art); Egyptian Antiquities; Greek, Etruscan and Roman Antiquities; and, for the modern period, Paintings, Sculptures, Art items, Prints and Drawings. For more details, visit **louvre.fr**.

BRITTIP

Many Paris museums are free on the first Sunday of the month (though queues will be longer). The museums owned by the Ville de Paris (except the Catacombs) are free every Sunday. See **www.parisinfo.com/museum_monuments** for details.

Continuing your coach tour, you head back along the Left Bank and through the St Germain area, passing the **Musée d'Orsay**, another of the great repositories of French artwork. A conversion of the Orsay Railway Station inaugurated in 1900, it houses an art gallery of the finest order, featuring works from 1848 to 1914. Visit **musee-orsay.fr**.

Champs-Elysées

A drive around the vast octagonal expanse of the **Place de la Concorde** reveals more of Baron Haussmann's outstanding design, especially as you continue along the **Champs-Elysées** and into the **Place Charles de Gaulle** (aka Etoile), at the centre of which stands Napoleon's magnificent **Arc de Triomphe**.

BRITTIP

If you are going into central Paris on public transport, the main Métro stops to look for are Concorde, Charles de Gaulle–Etoile, Trocadéro, Palais Royal–Musée du Louvre and Cité.

Along Avenue Kleber you can marvel at more monumental architecture, especially as you enter **Place du Trocadéro et du 11 Novembre**, where a statue of the First World War military leader Marshall Foch stands in front of a grand vista representing 3 centuries of architecture. The view across the Seine to the Eiffel Tower is breathtaking and on a par with the great landmarks of the world such as the Sydney Opera House, the Acropolis and the Statue of Liberty.

The **Hôtel des Invalides** is another significant 17th-century landmark and its Musée de l'Armée showcases 2,000 years of military history, from antiquity to the end of the Second World War, in an opulent setting. The Dôme within contains the tomb of Napoleon Bonaparte.

River trips

After all this coach-bound sightseeing, it is time to step on to a

Hôtel des Invalides

different mode of transport (all part of the Cityrama tour) and view the city from the River Seine on the Bateaux Parisiens. Here, either under a glass roof or out on deck soaking up the sun, the English commentary (on a hand-held audio device) continues to cover just about every angle of the city, ensuring you get a well-rounded experience and an in-depth view of the history and accomplishments of Paris and its people (or just a fabulous view if you choose to put your feet up and watch the vistas as you sail by).

Nôtre Dame

Your boat drops you off back in the Ile de la Cité for lunch, and an opportunity to visit the stunning cathedral of **Nôtre Dame**. This masterpiece of Gothic architecture was built from 1163 to 1345, and is free to enter to view the awe-inspiring serenity of its vast interior. There are some serious queues here at most times of the day (you'll be used to that at Disney!) but they move steadily. There is a small fee to visit the belfry and you may have to wait 30 minutes or so for your turn. You have a good 90-minute break here, so you can

> ### BRITTIP
> There are 2 handy, quiet restaurants on the Quai de Montebello, on the west bank of the river flanking Nôtre Dame. Stroll to the rear of the cathedral, turn right across the bridge and the crowds quickly disappear.

Nôtre Dame

Eiffel Tower

divide your time between the cathedral and lunch.

Up the Eiffel Tower

You get back on the boat at the Ile de la Cité pier and continue your hour's cruise, finally returning to the marina at the Port de la Bourdonnais in front of the **Eiffel Tower**. Your city tour then finishes in style with an organised visit to the tower itself. Your tour guide will lead you up the steps and across the Quai Branly to one of the lifts and a trip to the first floor (the second and third floors are extra, but you usually have time if you wish to go the extra distance yourself). This 324m/1,063ft, 10,100-ton steel edifice is a breathtaking sight close up, and the trip up by lift or stairs is a rewarding one, both for the view and the story of the tower told along the way. The perspective on the city is quite startling (especially from the glass-sided lifts between the first and second floors!) and totally unequalled. There is even a high-quality restaurant on the second floor – the Jules Verne – that you can book separately. If the price tag (in excess of €100) puts you off, try the first floor 58 Tour Eiffel, a chic Parisian

> ### BRITTIP
> At peak times in summer (midday to around 5pm), the Eiffel Tower often stops selling tickets for the top deck, and the second floor becomes extremely crowded, too.

Les Bateaux Mouches

Paris is famous for its river tours along the Seine, providing both a great view of many well-known monuments as well as a relaxing and highly enjoyable form of transport. The collective name for the half a dozen or so companies that run these tourist boats is Les Bateaux Mouches. They ply their trade along the central section, from the Eiffel Tower to the Ile de la Cité and back, with plenty of history during the day and a generous helping of romance in the evening, when you can choose just an alternative view of Paris by night or a more elaborate dinner cruise. Tours must be booked in advance. Call 00 33 1 76 64 14 45 (from the UK) or visit **bateauxparisiens.com**.

brasserie (book from the UK on 00 33 1 72 76 18 46 for 58 Tour Eiffel and 00 33 1 45 55 61 44 for Jules Verne).

The Eiffel Tower has 3 lifts (at the north, east and west legs) and 3 staircases (south, east and west), and ticket office queues reach up to an hour in high summer. However, if you are travelling independently, arrive early and you will enjoy this amazing attraction at its very best, while the evening sees it in truly sparkling mode, with a magical lighting presentation. From dusk to 2am (1am in winter), the Tower's 20,000 special light bulbs (requiring 40km/25mls of electrical cable and 120kw of power)

come to life in a glittering display each hour on the hour for 10 minutes. Once you have been up this modern marvel, you can walk the gardens of Le Champ de Mars for the full ground-level perspective.

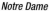

BRITTIP

The Eiffel Tower draws some sizeable crowds during the day, attracting the inevitable vendors (selling bottled water and trinkets) who are a constant nuisance. Take extra care with your belongings.

At the north leg you can check out the memorial to Gustave Eiffel, while ticket-holders have access to the clever lift machinery that he designed under the east and west pillars. A bureau de change can be found in the concourse under the Tower, plus a Paris Tourist Office (not to be confused with the ticket office) and souvenir shops (as well as those on the Tower itself), plus a cafeteria-style snack bar. For more info, visit **tour-eiffel.fr**.

All in all, the Cityrama day tour provides a pretty comprehensive beginner's guide to the city and the perfect way to get an overall appreciation of all the main sites in just a few hours. Tickets can be purchased at any of the Disney hotels or those in the Val de France area and it costs £53 for adults and £28 for 3–11s.

Notre Dame

Paris by night

If that is the story by day, Cityrama's **Illuminations** tour, also available on site at *Disneyland Paris*, is the city by night. Paris fully deserves its alternative title of 'The City of Light' and the tour portrays this to the full. The English commentary, via individual earphones, is specially adapted to the ambience of Paris by night, bringing its history to life with amusing stories, accompanied by background music and French songs that celebrate the city. The Cityrama coach departs every Mon–Sat at 9pm from the front of *Disney's Hotel New York* and returns to the hotel at around midnight (depending on traffic). It costs £38 for adults and £12 for 3–11s.

Paris information

Of course, there are dozens of other museums, churches, monuments, gardens, memorials and parks, not to mention the shops, restaurants and nightclubs and other modern city paraphernalia that make Paris such a deliciously heady place. Here are your contacts for essential information.

- **France Information Line:** 090 68 244 123 (60p per minute), **info.uk@franceguide.com**, **http://uk.franceguide.com**.

- **Ile de France Tourist Office:** l 00 33 1 60 43 33 33 (from the UK), **http://english.pidf.com**.

- **Maison de la France:** 300 High Holborn, London WC1V 7JH.

- **Paris Tourist Office:** 08 92 68 30 00 (in France), **en.paris info.com**.

The magic of Paris by night

View from the Eiffel Tower

⊞ BRITTIP

The **Paris Museum Pass** costs just €28.50 for a 2-Day pass, €42 for a 4-Day and €57 for a 6-Day. It gives no queuing, no-limit access to 70 museums and monuments in Paris. It is on sale at the tourist office, FNAC shops and online at **parismuseumpass.com**.

Further afield

If you would prefer to escape from the hubbub for a while, the **Seine-et-Marne** region can offer some more down-to-earth but equally enchanting sources of fascination. With a car, there are some wonderful possibilities a little more than an hour's drive from *Disneyland Paris*, where you can get a feel for rural France, untouched by the hectic rush and modernity of the city.

⊞ BRITTIP

The Seine-et-Marne region has an excellent tourist office in Fontainebleau (00 33 1 60 39 60 39 from the UK, **tourisme77.net**). It also has a tourist office next to the Marne-la-Vallée RER station open 9am–8.45pm every day.

Vaux-le-Vicomte

Barely half an hour from the Disney resort is the magnificent 17th-century masterpiece of **Vaux-le-Vicomte**, a historic château and gardens some 24km/15mls to the south down the D471. In the rich land of Brie, this pinnacle of period architecture – created by some of France's greatest artists, including Le Vau, Le Brun and André Le Nôtre – was the inspiration for Versailles. Here you will discover the full château splendour, from the kitchens to the magnificently decorated reception rooms (that have featured in many films).

BRITTIP

If you can visit Vaux-le-Vicomte on a Sat in May–Oct or Fri in Jul and Aug, you can enjoy the amazing Festival of Light, when some 2,000 candles are lit throughout the château and gardens.

Your visit should include a full tour of the château (complete with audio-guide), the extensive French gardens, designed by Le Nôtre, who was also responsible for the Jardins des Tuileries in Paris, plus the Carriage Museum and the Le Nôtre exhibition in the cellars. Every second and last Sat Apr–Oct, you can see the eye-catching Fountain Show from 3pm to 6pm. For more details, call 00 33 1 64 14 41 90 from the UK or visit **vaux-le-vicomte.com**. Disney also offers an **evening excursion** to Vaux-le-Vicomte with an English-speaking driver, tour of the château and entrance to the carriage museum and gardens May–Sept. The bus departs at 7pm from the main bus station and returns at midnight (evening meal not included, but there are several restaurants to choose from). It costs £38 adults, £12 3–11s.

BRITTIP

A perfect complement to any visit to Vaux-le-Vicomte is dinner at the L'Ecureuil gourmet restaurant, which is open 11.30am–6pm (until 11pm on Festival of Light evenings).

The nearby city of **Melun** is also worth exploring. The ancient capital of the Capétiens kings offers some interesting walks, an artistic museum and the listed building of St Aspais Church – plus its speciality, the Brie de Melun, often regarded as the ancestor of all Brie cheeses. Just outside the city, the fortified **Château de Blandy-les-Tours** is a superb example of 16th-century military architecture and a little-known gem of the Ile de France.

Bohemian **Barbizon**, 'The Painters Village', is about 70km/44mls away to the south (down the N104, A5B, N105 to Melun, N372 and the N37). Here, against a backdrop that various landscape painters have made utterly timeless, you can discover the Auberge Ganne, a museum-home of the 19th century and a tribute to an era of artists who influenced the world's landscape and colourist painters. Call 00 33 1 60 66 22 27.

Beneath the Eiffel Tower

Fontainebleu

Take a slight detour to the south-east and you come to **Fontainebleau** and its 16th-century château, home to the kings of France from the Middle Ages. Another major architectural and artistic gem in the panoply of French monuments, its extensive gardens and Napoleonic Museum of Military Art and History offer a fascinating glimpse into another world (**musee-chateau-fontainebleau.fr**).

Travel still further (about another 10km/6mls south-east) and you come to **Moret-sur-Loing**, a medieval city between the Seine and Loing rivers. Wander the town and see why it was the inspiration for Impressionist painters like Monet, Renoir and, especially, Sisley.

Pompidou Centre

Further south still you come to **Souppes-sur-Loing** and the stunning **Château Landon**, perched on a rocky outcrop overlooking the verdant valleys of the Fusain. The medieval city boasts a host of memorable monuments, including the Nôtre Dame church, the St Severin abbey, St Thugal tower, St Andrew priory and the beautiful Parc de la Tabarderie.

Closer to home

Nearer to Marne-la-Vallée (just off the A4 at Ferrières-en-Brie), you have the **Château de Ferrières**, a sumptuous pastiche of Renaissance architecture, embellished with one of the most extraordinary English parks in France. The town of **Champs-sur-Marne** just to the west (on N34) boasts another stately home emblematic of the bourgeoisie in the Chateau de Champs-sur-Marne, the residence of Madame de Pompadour in 1757, with stately gardens, flower beds and ornamental lakes.

Then travel east for 20km/12mls on the N34 to **Coulommiers**, another medieval town whose commander's fortress-style residence was built by the Knights Templar in the 12th century. Visit the St-Anne Chapel, the round dovecote and the stunning

St Quirace, Provins

Capucins Park. You can also enjoy some picturesque river trips from Coulommiers on the Grand Morin.

A short drive to the north-east is another destination full of Middle Ages character, that of the Episcopal city of **Meaux**. The impressive St-Etienne Cathedral is well worth a visit, along with the Episcopal Palace (which now houses the Bossuet Museum) and the Jardin Bossuet. On certain weekends in Jun–Sept you can also enjoy the stunning Meaux Grand Spectacle Historique, an epic event featuring 500 actors, dancers and equestrians, re-enacting the saga of the city.

BRITTIP

Don't leave Meaux until you have tried the local culinary speciality – Brie and mustard.

In between Meaux and Coulommiers you will find the **Abbaye de Jouarre**, the region's most outstanding sacred site, with 12th-century crypts displaying some astonishing early Merovingian sarcophagi. Food lovers will be interested in the Musée Briard, which traces the history of Brie's cheese-making traditions.

Provins

The jewel in the region's crown, though, is the World Heritage Site and medieval city of **Provins**, some 60km/37mls down the D231 to the south-east. Pass the 12th-century ramparts and you are truly transported back to the Middle Ages, with narrow streets, half-timbered houses, monuments – and dungeons!

The bell tower, Provins

Bateau mouche in Paris

Here you can try various medieval crafts, such as calligraphy and stained glass making, design coats of arms and watch the free-flying birds of prey. Provins provides the perfect setting for various period events (**provins.net**) organised every summer and, if you happen to be in the area during the last week of Aug, definitely stop by to experience some of the week-long **Carnival**, which is one of the highlights of the Seine-et-Marne region. There are also 3 large-scale medieval shows, including a spectacular jousting competition.

The church at Auvers-sur-Oise

BRITTIP

Disney offers a day-trip to **Provins** with Regional Bus Line, including entry to many of the town's main attractions during Apr–Nov at £28 adult, £10 children. It departs at 10am most days and returns at 7pm.

Auvers-sur-Oise

Art lovers may well be lured away to the north-west to spend a half-day or so in the charming village of **Auvers-sur-Oise**, the burial place of painter Vincent Van Gogh. Although the great artist lived here for only 3 months before his untimely death, his stay produced some of his most startling work, and its inspiring influence is still present today (not surprisingly, as Cezanne, Pissarro, Daubigny and others also painted here). The village also hosts an annual International Musical Festival (late May–Jun), which attracts some high-quality performers.

Start by visiting the Office de Tourisme on Rue de la Sansonne to see the 15-minute audio-visual presentation on the village and Van Gogh, then wander out and drink in the wonderful scenery, quaint farms and cafés that inspired so many great painters. To reach Auvers-sur-Oise, take the A15 out of Paris to Exit 7 (Mery-sur-Oise), then pick up N184 alongside the River Oise into the village (**auvers-sur-oise.com**).

Now it's up to you!

And that, folks, is that. You now have the essential wherewithal to not only plan and prepare for your holiday in *Disneyland Paris*, but also to get the most out of it when you are there. As you can see from the last 2 chapters, there is a lot more to a holiday here than just theme park frolics (although, if you choose to do just that, you will still have a pretty good time!).

It is a world of almost infinite charm and substance, a combination of Imagineering pixie dust and ages-old culture and allure. The Walt Disney Company wasn't that crazy when it brought its major slice of Americana to Europe and, while it was not an instantly comfortable fit, the Franco-European influences now sit easily and enjoyably alongside the transatlantic ones.

Most of all, however, we hope you have taken on board how much artistry is involved in providing such obvious entertainment, whether it be the rides, shows, restaurants or hotels. The resort is the product of 50 years of imagination, perspiration and inspiration, with some pretty amazing architecture and engineering thrown in along the way (not to mention the vast backdrop of Paris and its environs).

After numerous visits to Disney theme parks (we lost count many years ago!), we still find them absorbing, fascinating and downright fun. There is so much involved, we would hate for anyone to pay their hard-earned money and then miss some of the essential 'Magic'.

So, we challenge you to keep this book with you at all times, read and inwardly digest the contents before you go and then get out there and have FUN!

Bonnes vacances…

Château de Versailles

Your Holiday Planner

Here is a way to help you decide what you can do given 3 or 4 days in *Disneyland Paris*. This planner is simply designed to give you an idea (from our own practical experience) of what a typical family might be able to achieve in the time allotted. Obviously, you are free to make up your own schedule (on the blank form at the end), but be aware of the different requirements of the theme parks and associated attractions. The 2 examples are designed around a visit in high season (the summer), and are for different modes of transport and different durations (reflecting 2 of the most popular packages that were booked in 2009). Have fun with your planning!

Example 1: 2-night/3-day trip with Eurostar

Day/time	Schedule	Notes
Day One		
9.53am	Depart London St Pancras	Check bags in with *Disney Express* at station
1.31pm	Arrive Marne-la-Vallée	
	Have lunch in *Disney Village*	Nice and quiet in Planet Hollywood!
2.45pm	Head to *Disneyland Park*	Closing time 11pm
	Visit Discoveryland	Get FastPass for Buzz Lightyear
4pm	Disney's Once Upon A Dream parade	
4.30pm	Return to Discoveryland; do Star Tours, Honey I Shrunk the Audience and Buzz Lightyear	
6.30pm	Stop for dinner	Have a bite and watch Cinema Mickey in Videopolis
7.15pm	Head into Fantasyland, catch Winnie the Pooh and Friends, Too	
9pm	Leave the park and walk back to *Disney's Hotel New York* to check in	Our bags are already here!
Day Two		
9am	Breakfast at Parkside Diner in hotel	Visit hotel concierge desk to book La Grange restaurant at Billy Bob's Country Western Saloon for dinner

Day/time	Schedule	Notes
10am	Off to *Walt Disney Studios Park*; do Studio Tram Tour, then head for Moteurs…Action! Stunt Show	Get FastPass for The Twilight Zone™ Tower of Terror
11.45am	CinéMagique showing, then Tower of Terror	
1pm	Stop for lunch at Disney's Blockbuster Café	Check out the cool *Pirates of the Caribbean* décor!
2pm	Take in Armageddon show, then head for Toon Studio	Stop for autographs and photos with characters in Toon Plaza
2.45pm	Catch the parade	
3.15–5pm	Complete Toon Studio	
5.15pm	Finish Studios with 2 goes on Rock 'n' Roller Coaster	Not much of a queue by this time
6pm	Dinner at La Grange restaurant upstairs at Billy Bob's Country Western Saloon	
7.30pm	Return to *Disneyland Park*; spend time in Frontierland and Adventureland	Phantom Manor extra spooky at night!
10.15pm	Find a spot to watch Disney's Fantillusion parade	Find a great spot in Town Square
10.45pm	Time to head back to the hotel – tired but happy!	
Day Three		
9.30am	Another slow start! Quick breakfast at Parkside Diner	Check bags in at hotel with *Disney Express* system. We'll see them later! Book late lunch at Blue Lagoon
10.30am	Back to *Disneyland Park* Start in Fantasyland and finish in Adventureland	Get FastPass for Peter Pan
1pm	Head to Frontierland, but then return to Adventureland for Pirates of the Caribbean	Get FastPass for Big Thunder Mountain
2pm	Lunch at Blue Lagoon, then return for Peter Pan FastPass ride	
4pm	Enjoy Adventure Isle and Big Thunder Mountain	Crowds lower during main parade
5pm	Final ride of the day – Space Mountain: Mission 2	Stop for photos in front of Castle on the way out!
6pm	Head back to the station	
7.25pm	Return on Eurostar to London	
9.13pm	Arrive at St Pancras	Still have to negotiate final journey home with tired kids!

Example 2: 4-night/5-day coach trip with Leger Holidays

Day/time	Schedule	Notes
Day One		
Noon	Pick-up from home bus station at midday	
1.30pm	Arrive Dover	
2.15pm	P&O ferry to Calais	Stock up with drinks and snacks on the ferry for the 4-hour coach journey to *Disneyland Resort Paris*
4.30pm	Arrive Calais; brief stop at hypermarket	Don't forget the 1-hour time difference!
Evening	Long, rather dull drive through northern France	
9.30pm	Arrive at *Disney's Hotel Santa Fe*	Check in and go to room
Day Two		
8am	Up for hotel breakfast	Book character lunch at Lucky Nugget Saloon at hotel front desk
9am	Off to the *Disneyland Park* for the day	Get FastPass for Peter Pan
Morning	*Disneyland Park*	
1pm	Stop for lunch at Lucky Nugget Saloon	Have fun with Chip 'n' Dale, Goofy and Pluto!
Afternoon	*Disneyland Park*	
4pm	Catch the afternoon parade	
5.15pm	Winnie the Pooh show	
6.30pm	Leave park and head for *Disney Village*	
7pm	Dinner at Planet Hollywood	Only 10-minute wait for table
8.30pm	Slow wander back to hotel via *Disney Village*	
Day Three		
9am	Slow start this morning!	Book character breakfast for tomorrow at Café Mickey in *Disney Village*
10am	Head for *Walt Disney Studios Park*	
11am	Queue up for Tower of Terror	
Noon	Meet Stitch outside the Stitch Live! attraction, then head to CinéMagique	Just missed midday CinéMagique? Go on to Art of Animation instead

Day/time	Schedule	Notes
1.30pm	Stop for lunch at Restaurant En Coulisse	
2pm	Stop at concierge desk in Disney Studio 1	Book dinner at Silver Spur Steakhouse
2.10pm	Queue for 20 minutes to get in to 2.30pm Moteurs…Action! Stunt Show	
3.30pm	Catch Armageddon attraction	
4pm	Stop for a drink at Studio Catering Co outside after show	
5pm	Take in the High School Musical Show	
5.30–6.30pm	Enjoy another hour at park	No queues for Magic Carpets ride and Rock 'n' Roller Coaster
7pm	Head next door and have dinner at Silver Spur Steakhouse	
8pm	Head back to Fantasyland for kids' favourite rides	
10pm	Bag a prime spot to watch evening Fantillusion parade on Main Street USA	Dad goes off to get drinks! Still long queues at most of the counter-service cafes
	Straight back to the hotel on the bus after parade	
Day Four		
8am	Manage to get everyone up and out in time for breakfast in *Disneyland Park*	
8.45am	Stop at City Hall to book evening meal at Blue Lagoon	
9am	Enjoy Fantasyland!	In the first hour, we do Peter Pan, Snow White, Pinocchio (twice!) and the Carousel before the crowds arrive
11am	Leave park for RER Station	
11.15am	Catch train to Val d'Europe	5-minute journey
11.30am	Visit Sea Life Centre	Spend 2 hours looking round all the exhibits, and children finish up in the soft-play area!
1.30pm	Have great lunch at pizza restaurant in Les Terrasses	
2.30pm	On to La Vallée outlet shopping village	Kids get to play in playground while parents enjoy a coffee!

Day/time	Schedule	Notes
4pm	Quick tour of Auchan hypermarket before catching RER train back to Disney	
5pm	Catch Animagique show at *Walt Disney Studios Park*	
5.30pm	Quick refreshment stop at Studio Catering Co	
5.45pm	One last Flying Carpets ride	
6pm	Time to leave for *Disneyland Park*	
8pm	Dinner at Blue Lagoon	
8.30pm	Just time for another trip to Fantasyland!	
9.30pm	Back to *Disney's Hotel Santa Fe* on shuttle bus	Pack cases for coach tomorrow
Day Five		
8am	Up early and straight off to breakfast	
10am	Coach departs for Calais hypermarket; then on to ferry	
3pm	Ferry leaves Calais	2pm UK time
4.30pm	Arrive back at home bus station	Mission accomplished!

Your holiday – have fun now!

Day/time	Schedule	Notes

Further reading

Disneyland Paris – From Sketch to Reality, by Alain Littaye and Didier Ghez (Nouveau Millenaire Editions $176.44, out of print and now collectable, on amazon.com). A truly sumptuous book, in full colour and with a wealth of brilliant photography, it charts the building of the *Disneyland Park, Disney Village* and the hotels. It also provides a magnificent insight into the creativity of the Imagineers.

Walt Disney Imagineering – A Behind the Dreams Look at Making the Magic Real by The Imagineers (Hyperion, £21.99). Another lavish 200-page volume providing a riveting look at how Disney's creative force thinks and works, with a fascinating series of original concept illustrations from their attractions worldwide.

Walt Disney Imagineering – A Behind the Dreams Look at Making More Magic Real (Hyperion, May 2010, price TBC). A second (hardback) volume, coming out in 2010 and offering more insight into the park's creators – and their creations – from 1998 to 2009.

Disney – The First 100 Years (David Smith and Steven B. Clark; Disney Publications, $50). For true fans of all things Disney, this 203-page epic charts the story of Walt and all his creations, from his humble beginnings to the 100th year after his birth, looking at the annual landmarks of the man and his company.

Acknowledgements

The authors wish to acknowledge the help of the following in the production of this book:

The Walt Disney Company, Eurostar, Leger Holidays, P&O Ferries, Port of Dover, Cityrama, Vienna International Hotels, La Vallée Outlet Shopping Village, Planet Hollywood, Sea Life Paris, Seaview.

In person: Sarah Hodson, Alix Vonk, Richard Leclerc, Karine Moral (Walt Disney Company), Richard Holligan (Eurostar), Anita Rogers (Leger Holidays), Michelle Ulyatt (P&O Ferries), Nick Stevens (LD Lines), Lisa Sabin (Norfolkline), Sara Whines (SeaFrance), Andy Brannan and Gualtiero Raimondi Cominesi (Planet Hollywood), Laurence Morel (Vienna International Dream Castle and Magic Circus hotels), Chantal Villeneuve (Sea Life), Bernard Kouao and Caroline Amphimaque (La Vallée).

Special thanks also go to Andy De Maertelaere, our principal research assistant, and to David Simpson (Seaview), plus all the hard-working people at our publisher Foulsham who do such a great job in bringing our work to life each year.

Photographic Acknowledgements

The authors would like to thank the following for providing additional photographs.

t = top of page   b = bottom of page

Disney 4, 6, 7, 8, 10, 11, 12, 14, 15, 16, 18, 19t, 21, 22, 23, 24aa, 25, 26, 27, 28, 29, 30t, 31, 32b, 33, 34, 35, 36, 37, 38, 42, 44, 45, 46, 61, 62b, 63, 64, 65, 67b, 68, 69, 70, 74, 75, 76, 78, 79, 80, 82, 83, 84, 85, 86, 87, 88, 89, 90, 91, 92, 93, 95, 103, 105, 111, 112, 113, 114, 115, 116b, 117, 118, 119t, 120, 121, 123, 124, 125, 128b, 129, 130t, 132, 133, 134b, 135, 138t, 139t, 140t, 141, 142, 144, 146t, 147, 148t, 149b, 150t, 151t, 152b, 153, 154t, 157, 158, 159, 160, 161, 162, 163, 168, 169t, 170, 171, 172, 173, 174,175, 176, 177, 178, 179, 180, 181, 182b, 183, 184, 185, 186, 187, 188, 189, 190, 191, 192, 193, 194, 195, 196, 197, 198, 199t, 200b, 201b, 202,, 203, 206, 207b, 208, 209, 210, 211

Brittany Ferries 52t; CDG 61b;a Euro Limousine Co. (parisairportshuttlez.com) 63; Eurostar 17, 41, 56, 57, 59, 60, 228t; Eurotunnel 54, 55, 62; Explorers Hotel 73, 96, 98, 99, 100; Formule I 108; Melissa Hobson 10b, 19b, 30b, 32t, 120b, 122b, 128t, 130, 131, 134t, 136b, 137t, 140b, 143, 145t, 148b, 149t, 151b, 152t, 154b, 155, 156, 166, 182t, 200t, 201t, 207t; Wendy Hobson 47, 219, 220, 221, 222, 223, 224t, 225b; Hotel du Moulin 97; Hotel l'Elysée 96; LD Lines 51; Leger Holidays 67t; Marriott's Vacation Club 107; Mercure 109; Norfolkline 48b, 50; Novotel 104; P&O 48t, 49, 53; Parc de Colline 106; Pamela Rhodes 226t; SeaLife Centre 20, 215, 216; Mark Squires 227; Sofitel 110; Simon and Susan Veness 5, 9, 58, 116t, 119b, 122t, 136t, 137b, 138b, 139b, 145b, 146b, 149t, 164, 165, 169b, 199b, 204, 205, 212, 213, 214, 217, 218, 226b; Vienna International Dream Castle Hotel 66, 101, 102

Index